ON
UNCLIPPED
WINGS

To Sandia
Romans 8:28

Ena X

(22/02/20)

ON
UNCLIPPED
WINGS

A true story

Eva Leaf

ISBN: 9781699377086
Imprint: Independently published

evaleaf.com
Cover photo by Tamara Bellis on Unsplash

This story is true. However, names and places have been changed, and some individuals are composites.

My deepest thanks to all who encouraged and helped in the making of this book.

Heal me, LORD, and I shall be healed;
save me and I shall be saved,
for you are the one I praise.
—Jeremiah 17:14

Introduction

There are some things that make a person sit up and take note. The description of psychological manipulation is one of those things, and I had to ponder it for quite a long time, just to take in the enormity of its implications. It also meant that I finally had a definition for which I was about to write.

Psychological manipulation occurs when people, societies, and organizations change the way we think and behave. It happens through lies, abuse, or destroying our self-esteem. It does it by removing from us any control over our environment and creating in us a powerlessness to act of our own accord. It also makes us think that anything we say, or do, or aspire to, is invalid. And, it is so devious that it is almost impossible to detect, for once we are subdued, we will give into every demand.

CHAPTER 1

I stood alone at the living room window that winter morning, taking one last look outside. The Texas sun felt warm. The irrigated fields across the road rippled in the breeze. My insides tingled with anticipation, and I glanced down at my watch. Only five more hours.

I shifted my gaze to our front yard. Desert sand. A few straggles of grass. Pa's beat-up old work van. The thick mud walls of our rented adobe house. I would never live here again, and for a moment I dared to smile.

But, suddenly, Pa shouted inside my head. "You will not leave! You WILL honor me."

I pushed him away, shuddering. I never meant for it to happen this way, him lashing out, him telling me I had to stop, because the Bible demanded children obey their parents. But I read the Bible too, and now I was getting the exact opposite. "Listen, daughter, and pay careful attention: Forget your people and your father's house."[a]

I had to leave. I had already given Pa my entire life, put aside my dreams for him, shown him incredible faithfulness. It was my turn now. His time had finally run out.

I took a deep breath and turned away from the window. Pa hadn't spoken with me in weeks. *"Please, dear God, help me. I have to ask Pa two questions. Maybe he will listen."*

I hurried toward laughter in the kitchen, where my siblings stood having breakfast, leaning against kitchen counters, bowls of cornflakes in hand. Their peaceful chatter jarred with my unease. "Where is Pa?" I asked. But no one had seen him that morning.

I dashed outside to hunt for him, out back where he kept his collection of vehicles, a backhoe, a broken-down crane, a small airplane with only one wing, and a half-dozen antique cars. I circled the cars, with tumbleweed caught in their wheel wells, small sand dunes piled up around them, rust eating away at their metal. Pa had told me to repair their bodywork, saying he would sell them as soon as he had painted them.

He assured me that with this money we would be able to flee from society. Evil was everywhere, and he had to save us, take us to the Amazon jungle, the safest place in the world. He had fled from evil once before, as a teenager in World War II, and we would do it again.

I believed my Pa and worked on those cars with all my heart. I sanded them, filled in holes, sanded them again. But Pa only ever painted one of them. The rest sat in the desert sun and wind, unfinished. Rust returned. New holes appeared, and we never did flee. Was I sad? Yes and no.

I sighed, circled the crane, the airplane, but I still couldn't find him. The only place left was his workshop. I hurried toward it. The side door was open a crack, the large silver padlock hanging on a nail. *"No!"* I groaned. *"God, he might be against my wedding, but couldn't he respect me just this once?"*

But then, maybe I should be more generous? Pa might have forgotten. I couldn't understand how. He had deemed my wedding a moral tragedy. "You won't get me inside that church," he had said. "You're breaking the Ten Commandments." "You traitor. Your responsibility is to keep your mother tongue alive. How can our people survive if children like you go off and marry detestable foreigners?"

How I wanted to tell him that I did care? It had been my desire as well. I had waited for years. I had prayed. I had trusted God for the right man to appear, but Pa had moved us over a thousand miles away from our people. How could I start a relationship when he had us flee from the influence of his own people as well?

I knocked on the workshop door. "Pa, may I come in?" I called out in our mother tongue.

There was no answer, just the clink of metal on metal coming from inside. I knocked again. "Pa?" Still no answer.

The hinges creaked as I pushed open the door and slid inside. The heavy smell of oil filled my nose. The flicker of the florescent bulb hanging from the rafters made me blink. Pa stood at the far end of his worktable rebuilding a car engine, his hands and overalls covered in black grease. He didn't look up.

I waited for him to acknowledge me, clasping and unclasping my hands, all the time reasoning in my heart. *"God, I have always put him first all my life. Please show him that he can do the same for me, just this once."* Finally, I found the strength to ask my questions, but I couldn't control the tremor in my voice. "Pa, maybe you forgot. I'm getting married at two o'clock."

Pa kept right on working. I swallowed hard to keep a lump from rising in my throat. Should I ask him my first question? I could already guess his answer. But I had to give him a final chance to change his mind. "Pa, please could you come to my wedding?"

Pa reached into a toolbox, hunted for a spanner, and chose one. "Pa, please," I begged, my voice rising in crescendo, my hands flying together as if in prayer.

Pa's big ethnic nose widened at the base. His eyes narrowed. He looked up. "You have shamed me."

I stared at him, my hands still in prayer. "How, Pa? What have I done wrong?"

"You have done nothing right, girl. You shame me by falling for that foreigner. You shame me by the way you act, thinking you're someone special, walking around with that idiotic grin. You shame me by going around asking for advice. And you tell me you have done nothing wrong?"

"Pa," I begged, "please don't say that. I love Michael, and it was you who told me to get advice. Don't you remember? You told me to ask Pastor John if I should get married. I can't help it if he told me the opposite of what you wanted to hear."

"Don't you tell me what I want, or don't want. I can't believe you could be so stupid. You really don't know anything." My head sank down as Pa hurled his words at me. My hands fell to my sides.

Pa laughed. "To think you want to get married. Foolish girl. No man could love you. If he knew who you really are, he would run a mile. What did you do to deceive that boyfriend of yours?" Pa laughed again. "He's going to wake up tomorrow morning to a terrible shock."

A tremor ran through my body. "Pa, please don't say that. Michael is a good man."

Pa dropped his spanner. It bounced on the wooden worktable. "Don't give me your opinion, girl."

"Pa, please! I'm thirty now. Not a little girl." I drew a deep breath. This was not going as I had hoped, but even now Pa could still find compassion in his heart. I had better ask my second question, before it was too late. "Pa, please walk me up the aisle?"

Pa slammed his fists on the worktable. Tools clinked around him. "Will you never stop shaming me? Do you think I want to walk YOU up the aisle? NEVER! All you have done is bring me disgrace and dishonor!"

I gasped. "Pa, I have honored you all my life!"

Pa looked at me with disdain. "Let me tell you this, girl. I am not your father. Don't you ever dare call me 'Pa.' Don't you ever come and see me. Don't you ever let me see your children. Over my dead body."

I could barely breathe, barely stand on my feet. "Pa," I whispered, "please listen. I have always done everything you told me. I have always been faith…"

Pa interrupted me. "No! You listen to me. I will not allow my family to go to your stupid shindig. I will not let them suffer shame because of your rebellion. Now, get out!"

I stumbled to the house, darkness swirling around me. Michael and I were to get married in the church school where I taught. My siblings were supposed to take part in it. Jana was to be my maid of honor. Karina, a bridesmaid. Mik and Filip, ushers. Peter, the ring bearer. There would be 250 guests. *"God, please not my family. How can I stand before all those people, alone? What kind of person will they think I am, that my family refuses to come?"*

Jana met me at the kitchen door, still in her blue and pink flowered pajamas, a cup of coffee in her hand. She drew me inside and closed the door. "What's wrong, Toma?"

I could barely speak. "Pa won't let the family come to the wedding."

Jana's mouth dropped open. She dumped her half-full coffee cup on the kitchen counter, some of it sloshing out. "What? Don't listen to him, Toma. I'm going to your wedding no matter what. Don't you worry."

"Thanks, Jana. But he's our Pa."

Jana threw her arms in the air. "He has no right to control you like that! Any other father would care about his daughter, want to get her married off. But not him. And then he has the nerve to say God only speaks to him and not to us."

I slumped against the counter, exhausted. "I know."

"Well, he's wrong, Toma. You know he purposely moves us away from any eligible young men, just so we can't get married. He wants us to be nuns. Sister Toma. Sister Jana, Sister Karina… Who does he think he would be, the priest in charge? Yuk!"

I couldn't help but smile. Jana had escaped home a year earlier, even though Pa had threatened her with God's wrath, with failure, and misery. I didn't know where she found the strength to make up her mind and leave.

Ma came in, a laundry basket under her arm. It was full of clothes off the washing line. "What's the matter, Toma?"

I told her Pa's ban, and she listened. She dumped the basket on the chipped kitchen table. "Where is he, Toma?"

"In the workshop."

Jana and I watched as Ma hastened from the kitchen. We heard the garage door creak open. "I wonder what she will say," Jana whispered.

I shrugged my shoulders. "Nothing she can say will change his mind."

We waited, and a few minutes later the car drove away, and Ma came back, her face pale. She looked at no one as she spoke. "We are all going to the wedding. Pa just gave us permission."

5

"Ma! Thanks!" I cried. "I thought my wedding was ruined." But sudden panic rose up inside me. "Ma! Pa took the car. How will we get to the church?"

"He doesn't have a tie. He went to buy one."

Pa was coming! The clothes store was just down the road. He would be back in half an hour, and everything would be alright. I laughed with delight and danced in circles around the kitchen. "Thank you, Ma!"

Ma grabbed the laundry basket and shoved it under her arm again. "Don't thank me, Toma. Why didn't you elope? It would have been easier on us all."

I stopped mid-twirl. "Ma! Please! You got married in a church. Why can't I?"

Ma didn't respond and walked down the hall. I watched her, my heart sinking yet again. "It isn't my fault," I whispered, uncertainty in my voice. "I'm not doing anything wrong."

Jana threw her arms around me. "You're doing the right thing, Toma. Pa is mad that you're finally escaping."

I drifted back to the living room window and stood there alone again, looking for Pa's car on the gravel driveway. He should have been back by now. Maybe if I dashed out to the road, I might see him coming.

But as I stood there, by the side of the road, watching cars and trucks drive by, their wind tugging at my t-shirt and jeans, the ache inside my heart grew. *"God, where is Pa? We need that car. I couldn't bear it if I never showed up and left Michael standing at the altar alone."*

I turned back to the house, and met Grandma in the hall, with pink curlers in her hair, a scarf wrapped around her head. She and Mik had flown in late the night before. She laughed and threw her arms around me. "Isn't this a wonderful day?" But then she held me out at arms' length and eyed my clothes. "Why aren't you getting ready, Toma? The wedding starts in four hours."

"I know, Grandma." But I couldn't. What if Pa never came back? What if we couldn't get to the wedding? What if I never got married?

I hurried to my bedroom at the back of the house. All of us girls shared it together. I pulled out an old suitcase from under my bed and packed some clothes for my honeymoon. Just in case. I looked at my watch again. Only three hours left.

I ran to the road and stood there again, but this time Grandma joined me as well. She dabbed her eyes with an old lace handkerchief. "Why is my son acting like this? I don't understand why he changed. He was loved so much."

"I don't know, Grandma."

We walked back to the house, side by side. Neither of us wanted to speak. I stared at the gravel as it crunched under my feet. *"God? I don't know what to do. Help me. Please help me."*

We stepped inside the house. Jana and Karina met us at the door, grinning, with merriment in their eyes. Jana held her make-up bag, and Karina my curling iron. Jana laughed. "There you are, Toma. We have been looking all over the house for you. Karina and I want to get you ready. You must look beautiful for Michael."

They led me through the dining room French doors and sat me down at the table. A half hour later Mik joined us, grinning his usual big grin. His mustache was trimmed, his face red from scrubbing. "You look real nice, Toma. Just like a bride should."

I forced a smile. "Thanks, Mik. But, Pa took the car. He hasn't come back. How will we get to the church?"

Mik held up a set of keys attached to an oily piece of white vinyl. He held them up high and jingled them. "Don't worry, sis. I'll get you there. Pa's work van is still here."

Hope surged, but then it crumbled. "Mik, Pa will get mad if you take his van. And, it's full of his tools."

Mik's eyes glinted with anger. "I don't care. I'm going to make sure you walk up that aisle. It's about time you got married. I don't want you to stay an old maid."

He stepped toward the open French doors and raised his voice. It carried throughout the house. "Hey, everyone! I need some help!"

I heard the patter of feet and Filip and Peter appeared. "What is it, Mik?"

"Let's empty the van, everyone. We have to get Toma to that

wedding."

They followed Mik out, and so did I. We gathered around Pa's beat-up white van. I grabbed Mik's arm. "Pa leaves his tools in there to keep them safe. They might get stolen if we put them in the workshop."

Mik flung open the back doors. "Toma, do you want to get married or not? Pa's tools will be safe in the house. We'll put them in the dining room." He grabbed a toolbox and slid it out. But, as I waited my turn to grab something from the van, Pa kept shouting inside my head, or was it my conscience? "You wicked, selfish girl. You will pay for this, YOU WILL PAY." But I grabbed a toolbox anyways and carried it into the house.

Suddenly, Grandma appeared. "What's going on?" she cried. "Why is a bride carrying a toolbox on her wedding day? This is all wrong."

"It's okay, Grandma," Mik called from behind. "We're almost done. I just need to sweep the van."

"The van?" Grandma's face grew pale, but she followed Mik outside. She looked inside as Mik tried to sweep. She shook her head. "Mik! This isn't fit for a bride! Look how oily the floor is. Toma needs a nice car."

Mik looked up from the floor to Grandma. He lifted his voice. "Does anyone know if Pa has some carpet?"

Filip raised his hand, a grin on his face. "I do!" he shouted. He turned and skipped with long leaps toward the workshop door, his untied sneaker laces trailing behind him.

Mik followed and together they carried out a brand-new white carpet. I stared in astonishment as they unrolled it in the van. It covered the bottom and went up the sides. Mik laughed. "I bet Pa didn't buy this for the wedding. It's perfect. Now we're ready."

"But, Mik," I said, "there are no seats. If I put on my wedding dress, it will get wrinkled. I will have to get changed in the church, but that means we have to leave right now. It takes forty-five minutes to get there, and the wedding starts in an hour-and-a-half."

Mik leaned against the van and grinned at me, his mustache stretching out. He patted me on the shoulder. "Okay, okay, Toma. We still have plenty of time." Then he lifted his voice again. "Everyone get your clothes. We're changing in the church. We're leaving in two minutes."

We dashed inside and grabbed what we needed, laid our clothes on the white carpet in the van, my wedding dress on top. But Ma and Grandma didn't show up. I ran to their rooms and knocked on their doors. They only came out ten minutes later, changed and combed. "Hurry," I cried.

I clambered into the back and sat down beside my dress. I shifted around, trying to find a comfortable place where the rivets from the van wall wouldn't poke into my back. Ma and Grandma sat up front with Mik. The rest of my siblings crowded in around me. Jana looked around and grimaced. Then she laughed. "You know, Toma, this is real style! How many brides get to go to their wedding in a beat-up old van?"

I smiled at her. "At least we will get there. That's the most important thing."

Jana squeezed my hand. "I'm so proud of you. You're actually getting married. I never thought you would."

I let out a shaky breath. "I couldn't have done this without Michael, without any of you. I'm not strong enough."

"But you are," Karina said. "And let me tell you, it gives us hope."

We all fell silent, staring at the dented walls in front of us. But with the sun warming up the van, it grew uncomfortable. I shifted and rested a clammy hand on my wedding dress. I studied its lace and pearls, its sequins. It didn't seem real. How could I be going to my own wedding with such misery in my heart? *"Please, God, I need to know if I am doing the right thing. Please give me a confirmation."*

"I already told you," Pa's voice interrupted inside my head. "You can't get married. You belong to me."

I looked out the back window at the pale blue sky. I felt the sway of the van, but I heard no comforting voice from heaven. I opened my small pocket Bible, but the words only blurred. *"God, is it true that I am selfish? Am I really that wicked? If Pa is right, I can't go on fighting."* A sudden, frightening determination filled my heart. I shuddered at its consequences. *"I need to find Pa right now and tell him I'm sorry. I can't fight him anymore."*

9

But, Mik would never have turned around, never have taken me back home. I looked at the van door. Maybe I could open it myself, jump out at the next red light, and somehow run the twenty miles back to the house. Maybe even hitchhike. But there was no handle on the inside of the door. I couldn't escape.

I pulled up my knees and grasped my legs. I hid my face in my lap. *"Help me, Jesus,"* I cried in my heart.

CHAPTER 2

We looked like any other family in our neighborhood. All our fathers worked from nine till five. We children played in the woods. Sometimes we'd have to show up late because of chores. Sometimes we swapped stories of how we got in trouble for lying or something just as terrible. Often, we dreamed of the school burning down. We were normal, inquisitive, happy.

In private my family lived a different life. On Sundays, we attended a church where only our mother tongue was spoken, where every adult there was a DP (displaced person) from World War I or II. We sang our national anthem. We ate our traditional foods. We children born in exile listened to miracle stories of escape. We were exhorted not to intermarry with the natives, and to keep our identity pure. We watched what happened when a young person chose to marry someone foreign, how the DP community felt betrayed and shamed. It instilled a holy fear inside us children, and we spoke our mother tongue with renewed zeal.

Into this mix, Ma received an unexpected inheritance, and she gave it all to Pa. He immediately left his job, bought three second-hand school buses, and got a contract with the local town council. Now he only had to work early mornings and late afternoons, taking children to and from school. He could do whatever he wanted the rest of the day.

He found a flight instructor and learned to fly. Then after buying a Stinson 108, a four-seater airplane, he built a runway in the field behind our farmhouse and an airplane shed in the burnt-out foundations of an old barn beside the house. He hung a huge canvas down the front of the shed as a door and kept his Stinson there. Two years later he decided to buy another airplane, a Bellanca, a four-seater with retractable wheels.

Pa landed that Bellanca on our runway one day. Jana and I raced down to look at it after school, still in our school dresses and thick tights. Mik sat in the cockpit, already in his play clothes. I could hear him asking Pa all sorts of questions and Pa answering, his voice earnest and quiet.

Jana and I walked around the Bellanca. We touched its tail, ran our fingers along its long sleek flaps. Its shiny white wings came up to our middles, the top of the airplane just above our heads. Pa looked up, a twinkle in his eye. "She's a beauty. Isn't she, girls? Made of mahogany, you know."

I nodded at Pa, my face dead serious. I had learned a bit about airplanes by then, even though I was only fourteen. Pa's Stinson 108 had been built with hollow aluminum rods and covered with painted cloth. The Bellanca sounded more like a proper airplane to me.

The next few days Pa checked the Bellanca and found only one simple problem; the landing gear warning light didn't work. He fixed that easily enough, and on Saturday morning we children gathered with Pa in the airplane shed. He wanted to take it up for a trip. Mik lifted the canvas that hung over the opening. Jana and I stood behind one wing, Pa behind another. We pushed the Bellanca out and onto the taxiway. "Stand back," Pa called. "I want to start the engine." We jumped back several yards.

I had expected Pa to ask us to first put blocks in front of the wheels. We did that for the Stinson 108, because to jumpstart the engine he had to pull at the propeller. Once Pa had tried to start it on his own, without blocks, and then run around and jump into the cockpit. I happened to be watching up from the house. The Stinson started moving all by itself. It trundled across the field, bouncing over ruts. Pa chased it, his arms outstretched, just like in a hilarious cartoon. He grabbed its tail and finally the door. He managed to jump in just in time, only yards before it collided with a stone wall!

This time Pa strode around to the Bellanca door and opened it. "It has a starter button," he said, laughter in his voice. "A lot easier on the pilot." He slid into the cockpit and a few minutes later the engine turned over; the propeller sprang to life.

The roar of the engine filled our ears; our clothes flattened against our bodies. I reached up to hold my hair down, smiling at the same time. I stood at an open door, observing Pa's freedom to come and go, looking at his joy. One day I would be able to do the same.

We waited for Pa to look up and grin. That was our signal that he was ready. We watched as he taxied down to the far end of the runway and turned the airplane around. He checked the flaps on the wings and tail, as every pilot did before they took off. He gunned the engine, and the airplane started moving. All our heads turned in unison as he gathered speed. Seconds later the Bellanca lifted off, and seconds after that the retractable wheels disappeared into the body of the plane.

Mik shielded his eyes as he gazed after it. "She's a beaut."

"Yup," I said, still looking up.

Pa circled around and zoomed high over our heads, dipping his wings in farewell. "Bye," we called, waving our arms.

We lingered there, not wanting to go back to the house, to the jobs Ma had lined up for us. Vacuum the living room. Wash the hallway stairs. Beat the throw rugs. Dust the furniture. Wash fingerprints off doorways. But finally, we turned and headed back. We had almost reached the house when we heard the drone of an airplane again.

We turned and searched the tree line behind us. The Bellanca reappeared a few seconds later. "Wasn't he supposed to be gone all day?" Mik asked. "I wonder if he forgot something."

We stood by the house as Pa circled the runway, positioning himself to land. He cut the engine and started to descend, but he hadn't lowered the landing gear. We took off running, waving our arms. "Pa! The wheels! Lower the wheels!"

"He can't hear us," Mik shouted. "Run faster! He might see us."

That didn't stop us yelling. "Pa! Pa!" we shouted, careering across the field. Then, suddenly, he gunned the engine, and we stopped to catch our breath. We laughed. Pa would be so pleased that we had warned him.

We watched him approached the runway again. What was wrong with him? Was he sick? He still hadn't lowered the Bellanca wheels! We took off once more, yelling at the top of our lungs. But Pa paid no attention. He adjusted his flaps and cut the Bellanca engine once again.

We ran. We yelled. But the airplane descended. Only a yard from the ground. One foot. Six inches. We stopped, our hands on our heads, willing the airplane to rise again.

It hit the runway. It lurched. It spun around sideways. It slid along the gravel, the sound of grating reaching our ears. It came to a sudden stop. Silence.

I shuddered, as if waking from a dream. "We have to get Pa out!" Jana screamed. "It might blow up!" But Mik must have already come to that same conclusion. He bolted past us, faster than I had ever seen him run.

I expected an explosion. Instead the airplane door flew open. Pa jumped out. He leapt a short distance away, then spun around. I expected him to fall to the ground, be sick or something. He beat the air with his fists instead. He jumped up and down, lifting both feet off the ground. "Idiot!" he shouted, his voice carrying over the field. "Nincompoop! Blooming idiot!"

I stared, not believing my eyes. A grown-up throwing a temper tantrum? That only happened in the cartoons on television. I had always thought that grownups were perfect, but Pa had just proved me wrong. He had always told us tempers were bad, and he had beat us when we strayed. Who was it then that disciplined adults? No one, as far as I knew.

Seconds later, we surrounded Pa. "Are you alright?" Mik cried.

Pa glanced at Mik, a dazed look on his face, his hands still clenched in fists. "I'm such a dipstick," he howled.

We stood beside him, as if at a tombstone. We stared at the Bellanca with grief. The propeller was bent, deep gouges ran down the sides, the mahogany wood had splintered. At least the wings hadn't torn off. But Pa suddenly laughed. "They say there are two kinds of pilots, those who have landed gear up, and those who will. I just joined the ranks."

My head snapped up, as if waking again. My mouth dropped open. Pa never laughed at our mistakes. He didn't show us compassion when we did wrong. But Mik disturbed my troubled teenage thoughts. "Pa,

14

didn't the landing gear light work? I thought you fixed it."

"It works just fine, Mik. I didn't go through the landing procedure. That's all. There is one for taking off, another for landing."

No one spoke. I couldn't take my eyes off Pa. All we had to do was spill our milk, and we got into big trouble. He had just crashed an airplane! Mik shuffled his feet. "But Pa, why didn't you?"

Pa laughed again. "I was in a rush. I forgot the map on the kitchen table."

Jana edged up close to me, standing behind me to hide from Pa. "If that had been us," she whispered, "Pa would have killed us."

I nodded, but this time Pa interrupted my thoughts. He clapped his hands. "I have an idea!" he called, energy in his voice. "Everyone, to the airplane shed. Mik, get the air compressor and put it in the back of the car. Girls. Find some inner tubes. The big tractor ones will do."

"Yes, sir!" we responded instinctively. No matter what Pa had done, he was our Pa; he was alive, and we would stick with him.

Together we jogged across the field and loaded up the car. Pa collected some tools, and we clambered in. Pa then shot out instructions as he drove us down. "Girls, I want you to flatten out the inner tubes and push them under the tips of each wing. Mik, you inflate those tubes."

"Yes, sir."

Pa brought the car alongside the Bellanca, and all four doors flew open at once. We leapt out and followed Pa's orders, him supervising every move. He watched us girls drop to our knees and pull back the gravel from the tip of a wing. We scraped with our hands, cut our fingers on sharp stones, but Pa didn't seem to notice the blood. Neither did we. We had an airplane to save.

Finally, we pushed an inner tube underneath, and Pa bent over to inspect, resting his hands on his knees. He looked over at Mik. "Fill it up."

Mik attached the compressor hose, and the inner tube grew big, lifting the wing up from the ground. Pa got down on his back to inspect. "Get another one, girls."

It didn't take long to lift the airplane, a foot, two feet, three feet, with inflated inner tubes under it on all sides. Pa walked around it a couple of times. "Mik, get into the airplane. You know which crank to turn. Let's see if we can get this lady to stand. Then we can push her back to the shed."

Mik clambered up onto the wing. He crawled to the open cockpit door. My eyes grew big. "Isn't it dangerous, Pa?"

Pa kept his eyes on Mik. "He'll be alright."

Mik slid into the cockpit. We could hear his grunts as he turned the lever. Sand grated inside the gears, but the wheels appeared unharmed. We heard the clicks as the wheels locked into place. "Well done," Pa called, and clapped his hands.

We clapped and cheered with Pa. We were witnessing a phenomenon. Who had ever seen an airplane suspended on inner tubes? No matter what Pa had done, no matter if he broke the rules, and had thrown a temper tantrum himself, he was always doing something new. We experienced things most children wouldn't believe, and that suited me just fine.

Pa grinned. "See what we can do when we work together. Now stand back, everyone. I want to see if the landing gear holds." He walked around the Bellanca and deflated several inner tubes. The airplane sank and finally touched down. The wheels held. This time we cheered even louder.

Pa inspected the damage. "It's pretty bad," he called out. "But not as bad as it could have been. Sliding on gravel must have protected it a lot. Let's get this lady back to the shed."

We spread out along both wings and pushed the Bellanca with all our might. "What will you do, Pa?" Mik asked, panting in between words.

"I got it for a deal. I'll sell it without fixing it. Someone will most likely want it."

Sure enough, someone bought it. But Pa didn't whistle like he normally did, when he sold something at a profit. One corner of his mouth turned up, the other turned down. I had never seen that expression before. "I took Ma flying the day before the crash," he confessed. "Maybe this was God's punishment. I only have a solo license. I shouldn't be taking anyone up. I had better start studying for my pilot's license."

I did a double take. I always knew God lived in heaven, but not that he paid attention to what was done on earth. I had no idea it was he who disciplined wayward grownups. Good thing I was still young. Pa's beatings as a father seemed somehow safer, predictable. But messing with God? Man, that was serious!

A few months passed by, and one Saturday morning as we sat in the living room having family devotions, a time of reading the Bible and prayer, Pa told us some news. He was finally convinced that he was a Christian! He said he had doubted it for years, but now, over the last few days, he had come to a life-changing realization. He could prove to himself he was God's child. His eyes shone.

I leaned forward, all ears. If Pa knew the secret, I wanted to know it as well. "I have such a desire to serve God," he said, "it makes my heart ache. Only God could have put it there. That kind of a feeling is supernatural. The heart usually wants to go away from God, but mine is drawn to him. This is how I know."

I studied Pa's earnest face, his serious smile. I didn't know God like that. I didn't have a burning fire inside me. In fact, I felt scared of a God who crashed airplanes just to get someone's attention. Yet, maybe I could.

But then I recalled a sermon in church. The minister had preached something different. He said that if a person wanted to become a Christian, he or she had to confess their evil deeds, pray for Jesus to wash away their sins, and ask him to come into their hearts.

I pondered Pa's way, the minister's way. I would do it my way. That afternoon, while Jana read a book in the living room, I hurried up to our bedroom. I knelt by the window on my side of the bed and rested my elbows on the windowsill. I gazed at the dull autumn sky. *"God,"* I prayed, *"please be my boss."* I couldn't think of anything else to say. My way didn't have much pizazz.

A couple of days later Ma stopped me in the kitchen. "What's happened to you, Toma? You've changed."

"Nothing."

"You seem happy."

I searched my mind. "Oh, that! I became a Christian two days ago."

17

Ma laughed and patted me on the arm. "That's wonderful! I fell in love with Jesus two years ago. He changed my life."

Come to think of it, she was right. She was more patient. She took us on long bicycle rides. She even bought me a box of pastels and paper, so I could draw. If God could change Ma, and he was changing me, without me even knowing it, I had better do something about it. I wrote to my cousin, asking for help.

Twice a week she wrote back, sharing with me what she had learned that week in her youth group at church. She was a good teacher, and it didn't take long for me to catch onto the basics. God was God and he deserved my best. He wanted to speak to me through the Bible. If I wanted to hear him, I had to read it every day. I also had to pray and tell others about him. But, most important of all, I had to do what he said.

I started underlining every verse that somehow felt special. My Bible filled up with markings, the margins with scribbled thoughts. My heart ached for God, just like Pa's. My love for Jesus stirred, just like Ma's.

A happy year and a half ticked by, and then the Watergate Scandal hit the news. Many of us high school students sat glued to a television set every spare moment we had. We watched as the events unfolded, burglars caught red-handed, telephones bugged, secret documents stolen, and the Nixon administration trying to cover it up.

We sat at lunchtime in empty classrooms, watching the midday news, eating our sandwiches without even tasting them. How could our government have become so corrupt? How could President Nixon have let Watergate happen?

We watched the trials as Chuck Colson, President Nixon's hatchet man, sat under oath, and almost everyone in that classroom had an opinion. "He's better off behind bars," declared one classmate, standing up as if making a speech.

"Sure thing," another cried, joining him. "We don't want politicians like that running our country."

"Yeah," still others said, nodding their heads.

I looked from one to the other, at their angry, contorted faces. "That isn't fair," I called out. "Can't you see? Chuck Colson is taking all the blame. The President is supposed to be in charge of his office."

My classmates gawked at me. The first one who spoke scrunched up the open end of his brown paper lunch bag. He blew into it and popped it. BANG! "Toma, you always see the good in everyone. You could even find something good in Hitler."

I grimaced and shrugged my shoulders. "Yeah, I suppose he loved his mother."

My classmates laughed, and we dashed off to classes, but at that moment a dreadful thought overwhelmed me. Chuck Colson was a hatchet man. So was I.

Pa had been having difficulties with some of the children on the school bus. He had asked me to sit at the back and take down names of everyone who misbehaved. But my heart sank. I didn't want to. Everyone hated a tattletale. "Please, no, Pa. Can't you see them yourself in the mirror?"

"I have to drive, and they know it's wrong. They need to get punished."

I sat in the back the following morning, but I couldn't make myself write down any names. Pa extended his hand, as I climbed off the bus. "Where is the list, Toma? I saw two kids fighting in the back."

"See, Pa. You saw them. I don't need to do it."

Pa's eyes flashed with anger, and I understood the warning. That afternoon two other children fought on the bus, and I wrote down their names. Pa telephoned their parents and kicked those children off. But everyone knew it was me who had tattled. They hated me as well.

But that wasn't all. Oh, the agony. I had done the same to my siblings, the ones I loved most in this world. Pa had instructed me that I was his eyes and ears, and if I didn't report the wrong doings they had done, and he found out, I would be the one who got punished. And I was, bearing the brunt of his rage. One instance was when a sibling lied, another when one of them sneaked out. But because of my silence, Pa beat me with his leather belt. Blow by blow, I bore their sins and mine. And I learned to comply.

Oh, the misery! I was a hatchet man! I slid into my classroom, sat at a desk, students milling around me. But I heard nothing, my mind whirling in confused circles. Pa told me that I had to obey him, no matter what, because God said so. He said it loud and clear, and dished out a lot of pain to enforce it. But I didn't see God like that. He sent Jesus, a guy who was incredibly kind. Yet he too demanded allegiance.

My friend, Helen, slid into a desk next to mine. "Hi, Toma."

"Hi," I said, not even able to look at her.

She leaned over. "Hey! Are you alright?"

"No! Of course not!" I wanted to cry out, suddenly feeling too tired to go on. I didn't have the capacity to please both God and Pa. And if I could, I would have chosen God and dumped Pa then and there. But I lived in Pa's house and ate his food. And, as far as I knew, God didn't have a place where I could stay.

So, whether I liked it or not, I had to choose Pa, and it was his house, his rules. It was his domain, his control. Somehow, I would have to figure out how to negotiate life in his harsh world. But what of God?

I needed some time without pressure from him. Pa's was enough. I would take a break, maybe for six months or so. God would understand my need for a home. He would understand when I stopped reading my Bible and praying. He wouldn't hold it against me.

But a little voice, deep down inside, tried to speak up. "Stop, Toma! You can't just go and dump God like that. He isn't a toy you can pick up and put down." But I didn't listen to that gentle voice.

I sat up straight and finally looked at Helen. "Yup! I'm fine." I dumped my God and replaced him with Pa.

CHAPTER 3

P a glanced over at Ma during supper one evening. He looked tired; his voice sounded tired. "Lila, the town meeting starts at seven o'clock, and I just found out Boyles is bidding for the school bus contract as well. Why does he have to? He has plenty of school runs already."

Not a muscle moved in Ma's face. She nodded her head just once. Then she turned to stare out the kitchen window.

Pa cleared his throat. "We should be alright. I put together a fair bid."

"Oh?"

Pa then told Ma that he had submitted three options to the town council. Ma looked back, a smile on her lips, but there was no twinkle in her eyes. "I trust you, Linard."

I studied Pa and Ma. Something was wrong. If Pa's bid was good, why were they so worried? I pondered about it all that evening. Suddenly Pa's voice rang throughout the house. "Children!"

Jana, Mik, Karina and I dashed to where Pa sat in his favorite chair by the living room window. We lined up, saluting him like soldiers. "Yes, Pa?"

Pa nodded. "That's the way I like it. It's early to bed tonight. I want lights out right now."

All of us let out our breath in unison. "But Pa, it's still early," Mik said.

"I don't want Ma to have to deal with any of you while I'm away. To bed right now!"

"Yes, Sir."

We knew better than to complain. But once in our bedroom Jana and I groaned. "I'm fifteen," Jana said. "Why does Pa still think he can order us around like babies?"

"I'm a year older, Jana. That makes it even worse. I'm going to finish my book. I found some new batteries for the flashlight."

We sat down on the double bed we shared, each on our own side. We didn't much like the idea of sleeping in one bed, but at least we had an imaginary line drawn down the middle. We threw off our clothes, leaving them on the floor, and slipped into the long flannel nightgowns Ma had sewn for us. Each of us grabbed a library book, and we hid together under the blanket. Jana even produced two apples.

Eventually the batteries ran low, and Jana dropped off to sleep. But I started to think about Pa. What if he didn't get the school bus contract? What if he never got another job? What if we lost our house because Pa couldn't pay the mortgage? What if we starved to death?

Jana rolled over, pulling the blanket with her. I tried to pull it back. "I hate this bed," I muttered, suddenly resentful. Pa had refused to buy Jana and me separate beds. He assured us Grandma's old one was good enough. He didn't buy us shoes. Jana and I had to mow lawns or babysit to buy the one pair we wore each year. He didn't buy us clothes. We lived off goodwill bags and what we could sew. But he could afford two airplanes for himself.

My mind then jumped back to a few weeks earlier. Uncle Bob had come for a visit one Sunday afternoon. He had sat in the kitchen with Pa and Ma. I sat in the living room reading a book. "Did you set aside the money for Toma's education?" I heard Uncle Bob say. I put my book down, intrigued.

There was a pause. "Why should Toma get money for university?" Pa said. "The other children didn't get a single penny. It isn't fair."

"But it was her grandmother's specific wish. Lila got her money. Toma was supposed to get hers."

"Toma is my child. I can do what I want with her money."

Uncle Bob's voice rose as he spoke. "Where is your respect for Toma? For her grandmother?"

"Where is your respect for me as her father?" Pa said, his voice even and firm.

I stood up and tiptoed upstairs, not wanting to get caught eavesdropping. I sat down on the top step, clutching my book to my chest, clutching at the dream I had to be a doctor. Ma had given me biographies to read. Albert Schweitzer, a doctor who started a hospital in Africa. Edith Cavell, a nurse who was executed for helping enemy soldiers. Florence Nightingale, a nurse who fought the establishment in order to care for soldiers. I wanted to be like them, to give my life helping others. That money would have made it possible.

The crunch of tires on our gravel driveway yanked me back to the present. I slid out of bed and looked out the window, pulling back lace curtains. It was Pa. I crept into the hallway, running my fingers along the pink flowered wallpaper. By the time I heard the car door slam shut, I was standing at the top of the green painted wooden stairs. I hesitated. Should I go down? I would probably catch most of what Pa and Ma said from up in my bedroom, my ears were that keen. But I didn't want to miss a word. I had every right to know what was happening. It would affect my life as well.

I drew in a deep breath and took a step down, putting one foot on the far right-hand side. It didn't creak there. I moved to the far left for the second step, and by the time I reached the bottom, the front door had opened.

I leaned against the wall in the hallway, hardly breathing, invisible in the shadows. I listened, hearing the rustle of Pa's coat as he came in, his footfall as he entered the living room. "Lila," he whispered, "I was underbid."

I pressed myself against the wall, willing my heart to stop pounding, waiting for Ma to answer. She didn't. I held my breath, waiting for Pa to say more. He didn't. Instead I heard a shuffle, and my heart flipped over. They might be going to bed and catch me red-handed. I flew up the stairs, bracing my hands against the wall and banister to take most of the weight off my feet. I slid into bed and covered myself. For a minute I listened, expecting Pa's footsteps on the stairs. But I didn't hear them, and I sighed with relief.

Pa and Ma eventually turned off the lights, and I reached over, pulling back the curtain to look up at the stars. Even though I had pushed God out, I wanted to tell him this emergency news. It was time to reestablish contact. *"God?"* I whispered. *"Pa lost his job."*

I waited for that same feeling of closeness to kick in, now that I was talking with him again. Nothing. *"God, we'll probably starve."* Still nothing in my heart. Where was he? It had only been a few months. How could he disappear like that? How I wished I had never gone downstairs.

The next morning Pa woke us at 5:30am, as usual. We changed into shorts and ran downstairs. We did our Air Force Exercises with Pa, and our chores. We sat down for breakfast as usual, eating porridge in silence, stirring in lumps of salted butter. But then Ma showed up, dressed, and I stared at her in surprise. Normally she came in at the end of the meal, still in her red flannel night gown, bobby pins in her hair.

Pa looked up at her, and Ma nodded as she slid into her seat. "Children," Pa said, "we are in a time of great testing. I didn't get the school bus contract."

He paused and looked at us each in turn, letting the enormity of his words sink in. He sighed. "Small companies like mine don't have a chance anymore. Why couldn't Boyles stay out of the bid? They're a huge company. They don't need another school run. Why did the town council allow it?"

He clenched his fists. "It's all about money. This world is falling apart. Everything is going from bad to worse. For the last three years God has been warning me that we must flee. I haven't been listening. It's time for us to go."

This was no news to me. The Cuban Missile Crisis had put the fear of war in Pa once again. The Communists might invade, just like they had when he was a child growing up overseas. He had told us many times how his family fled for their lives on bicycles, how they left everything behind. He told of a bomb exploding in their back garden, mowing all the cabbages down, and of living in a Displaced Person's camp. Pa was determined to be ready this time.

He reached over and put his hand on Ma's shoulder. "I won't be looking for another job, Lila. I need to put all my energy into moving."

"That's fine, Linard. You do what you think is right."

Pa smiled, his eyes moist. "My wonderful bride."

He finished the school bus contract for that academic year, and to pay the bills he sold one of the buses. After that he sat in his chair, silent, in the corner of the living room. He sat there all summer from morning till evening. He sat there as the next school year began. He sat there all that autumn. But he was busy the whole time, reading. He kept his Bible next to him on the coffee table, an airplane magazine on his lap, a pencil behind his ear. Every so often he removed that pencil and underlined a verse or circled an airplane ad. "We need to flee to the mountains," he kept saying, a strange glint flickering in his eyes. "I have to find a bigger airplane, so we can get there quickly. Evil is coming."

Pa's intensity instilled a nervousness in us children. We began preparing as well, buying matches and candles with the pennies we earned from doing jobs for neighbors. We packed our rucksacks in case we had to flee. We had nightmares, of bombs dropping on our house, of losing family members in dark places, of hiding behind Pa's rusted tractor as our house burned to the ground.

But we still had to live, go to school, and I worked hard to graduate from high school, as close to an "A+" as possible. Maybe I could win a scholarship. If evil was coming, I wanted to study to become a doctor to take care of my family. Someone had to watch over them.

Then just before the Christmas vacation, the principal called me into his office. He smiled as I entered, and he pushed his big black glasses to the top of his head. "Toma! I'm proud to tell you that all the science teachers have chosen you for the science award this year. You have been an outstanding student."

He handed me an envelope. "These are the forms you need to fill in. I want you to apply early. I am certain you will get it, with coming from a large family and doing excellently in school."

I looked at him, confused. "Get what, sir?"

He laughed. "A four-year scholarship! All I ask is that you don't tell your friends until it is announced at the end of the school year."

I grinned, and my heart fluttered as I left his office. My dream could finally come true. I didn't need grandmother's money after all. I would be able to take care of my family anyway. "This is amazing!" I whispered to myself. I could have laughed out loud and skipped down the crowded hallway, but I had promised to keep it a secret.

I hurried home after school. "Pa! Ma!" I called, even before I had closed the yellow front door. "I got the top science award in school. I can get a four-year scholarship."

Pa looked at me and flexed his fingers, his once oil stained hands now clean. "Oh!" he said, his voice suddenly mocking. "A science award for dummies. Didn't they have anyone else to choose?"

I gasped. Pa had never spoken to me like that. I fled to my room and sat down at my grey metal desk. I sat there a long time staring out the window, deliberating back and forth. Should I open the envelope and fill it in, or should I not? "Pa didn't mean what he said," I finally announced to myself. "He's just feeling grumpy today."

I pulled out the envelope from my purse, turned it around and opened it up. I read the first page and filled it in. Name: Toma Alexa Rose. Age: Seventeen. Female. Date of birth... Address...

I turned the page. Now they wanted to know my SAT scores, my results for the university entrance exams. But with Pa saying we had to move, I hadn't known what to do. I turned the next page. They wanted to know how much Pa earned, how much tax he paid. Well, this was a lost cause. No SAT's. And there was no way Pa would give me his tax information.

I covered my face with my hands. What should I do? I had to become a doctor. I didn't want my family dying in some remote corner of the world. The only thing to do was to take this one step at a time. Set a date for the SAT, and maybe by then Pa would have gotten over whatever was wrong.

Christmas vacation came and went. On the evening before we went back to school Pa stopped me as I hurried past. "Toma, I'm taking you out of school. I need help getting ready for the move."

I stopped dead in front of him, and he smirked. I could only imagine I looked ridiculous, with my face in shock, my eyes popping out, and my mouth wide open in astonishment. My voice wobbled as I spoke, as I grappled to find words. "Pa! I only have one more semester till I graduate. Please let me finish. I don't want to drop out."

"I don't care what you want. God told us to move. Go to school tomorrow and notify the principal." He then picked up his magazine, his pencil, and poised it on the page.

I stood there, numb, watching Pa read down a column. Maybe he could somehow look up and change his mind. He didn't. I waited some more, and finally turned away. I stumbled upstairs, and it felt as if a red-hot hand had just slipped inside my ribcage, squeezing life from my heart. I pressed my chest hard, trying to dislodge it, trying to ease the pain. It did no good.

I slumped onto my side of the bed, my feet dangling, my head hanging down to my knees. Jana jumped on as well, and the bed swayed underneath us, squeaking in all its loose joints. She crept to the middle. "Can I cross the line?"

I nodded, and she sat down beside me. "What's the matter, Toma?"

I looked up. "Pa wants me to drop out of school. He wants me to help with the move."

"What? Has he lost his marbles? All he wants is free labor."

At that moment, we heard slow footsteps come up the stairs and Ma entered the room, still wearing a stained flowery apron. Jana jumped to her feet, and Ma took her place. But Ma only stared at her folded hands. I stared at them too.

They were chapped from hard work and her veins popped out. Her wedding ring looked like it had shrunk around her finger. She finally spoke, her voice strained. "Worse things could happen, girl. You have no idea what suffering is. Pull yourself together." She never once looked at me. Then she stood up and walked out of the room.

I stared after her, blinking back tears. Weren't mothers supposed to protect their children, help them succeed in life? What had happened to her? Why had she turned against me? But Jana sat down beside me and interrupted my troubled thoughts. "I can't believe it," she whispered. "Don't do it, Toma!"

"What choice do I have?"

"You can do what is right, for one thing. Dropping out of school is wrong."

"It isn't breaking the Ten Commandments. I'm so mixed up, Jana. Maybe God wants me to quit. Maybe the end is coming, and we have to get away quick."

Jana snorted with anger and shook her head, her short hair obscuring her face for a moment. "It isn't God. It's Pa. He wants someone to do his jobs so he can sit in his chair and read his airplane magazines. I hate those magazines. I hate what's happening to this family."

Jana looked me straight in the face. "Don't let me down, Toma. Do what's right. You're the one who's supposed to break the ground, being the eldest. If you don't, who will?"

"I can't, Jana."

The next day I made an appointment with the guidance counselor in school. That afternoon I told her what Pa had said, but the pain in my chest almost choked me. The counselor handed me a box of tissues. "You have to stand up for your rights, Toma. You have the right to do what you want. Don't let anyone push you around."

I couldn't comprehend her logic. Of course, everyone got pushed around. Grownups had to go to work whether they felt like it or not. They had to drive the speed limit whether they liked it or not. Children had to go to school. Now Pa had ordered me to drop out, whether I wanted to or not.

The counselor leaned forward on her desk, her fingers pressed together. "So! What will you do?"

"I don't know. I'm so confused."

"Toma, all you have to do is tell your father how you feel. He will listen to you. Respect is a fundamental part of human nature. We have evolved from animals into considerate beings."

I cringed inside. In my opinion, evolution wasn't all it was trumped up to be. Why did everyone think it changed things for the better? All one had to do was look at Pa. And, I sure wasn't going to stand up against him. That was sheer lunacy.

I drew a deep breath and hastened from the counselor's office. Maybe God was punishing me for going behind Pa's back. I rolled up my skirts in school to make them look shorter. I unbraided my waist-long hair so I could look pretty. At lunchtime, I joined my friends behind the school where they secretly smoked their cigarettes. But none of these things warranted Pa's demand, and I hadn't done anything intrinsically wrong.

That afternoon Pa said nothing. The next morning, I got ready for school as usual. Again, Pa said nothing. That afternoon he didn't even look at me, and I figured he had forgotten. But after breakfast the next morning Pa called me to himself, looking at me through narrowed eyes. "Toma, why are you getting ready for school? I told you I need you at home."

I had to cover up my tracks, try to sound like I had taken him seriously. "I haven't talked with the principal yet." Then the counselor's advice came to mind. Pa would respect me if I told him how I felt. I would give Pa the benefit of the doubt. Maybe I had judged him unfairly. "Pa," I said, trying to sound confident, "I don't want to quit."

"What?"

"I asked the guidance counselor..." I never finished the sentence.

Pa rose from his chair. "You did what? You talked to someone about this? You just shamed me and yourself. I knew I made the right decision to pull you out."

I cowered under his towering height. "I didn't mean to. Sorry, Pa!" I cried.

But Pa grabbed my elbow. He squeezed it hard. "Get into the car. I see I can't rely on you for anything. I will talk to the principal myself."

I didn't dare pull away, and Pa yanked me across the room, out the front door and down the steps. He pushed me toward the car. "Get in, girl."

Twenty minutes later, we strode through the glass front doors of the high school, into the office at the side. A secretary sat at the far end of the room. Pa didn't even wait for her to look up. "I want to speak to the principal."

She got to her feet. "He's in a meeting."

"I'm taking my daughter out of school. I want to see him right now."

The secretary strode up to the counter. "What do you mean?"

"My daughter isn't coming anymore."

The secretary looked at me. "You're Toma Rose."

"Yes, Ma'am."

"I just printed your report card from last semester. We will be handing them out today. You got straight A's again, and congratulations for winning the science award. Why do you want to quit?"

Pa interrupted. "I told you I want to speak to the principal."

My knees felt weak. I had to sit down. There was a straight-backed, wooden chair leaning against the far wall. I slumped into it and watched as the secretary entered a side room. She reappeared a few seconds later, the principal with her.

The principal strode over to the counter. He ripped his glasses off his nose. "Toma is one of our top students," he almost shouted at Pa. "If you pull her out, she loses everything."

Pa shrugged. "She's just turned seventeen. She can legally leave."

The principal and Pa glared at each other. But the secretary approached, apologizing. She whispered something into the principal's ear, slipped him a piece of paper. He turned to me. "Toma," he said, his voice suddenly gentle, "all you lack is one credit in P.E. to complete the basic requirements. I will waver that. Don't worry. You will not leave this school a drop out."

He signed the papers and threw them across the counter. He didn't even look at Pa. "Sign these," he said, his voice husky. Then he turned his back on Pa and disappeared into the side room again.

Pa signed the papers, alone at the counter. His eyes gleamed with satisfaction, but no one saw it, except me. I shuddered. Now Pa could do anything, and no one would ever know. I followed him out of the office, trembling, and went to empty my locker.

"Someone, please help me," I cried in my heart. *"God, where are you?"* I listened inside my heart. There was no stirring inside me. Nothing. Didn't God care for me? Sure, I had dumped him, but he was supposed to be patient and kind.

We left the school and drove down the highway, but I didn't take in the snow-ladened woods. I never saw the snow-covered fields or frozen ponds. Only one thing thundered inside my head. "I hate you,

Pa. I hate you."

We drove up the driveway of our house, and Pa turned off the ignition. I threw open the door to escape. "I'll be in the airplane shed," he called. "You've wasted enough of my time. I want you down in five minutes."

"Yes, sir."

I crept into the house, and Ma didn't acknowledge me. I changed into long johns and jeans, pulled a couple of torn sweatshirts over my shirt. A few minutes later I waded through the snow and pulled back the canvas that hung down the front of the airplane shed. I slid between two layers to get inside, and as I emerged, I looked around. Pa stood at his work bench, holding an engine part, his normally clean hands dirty now.

A space heater hummed in the center of the shed, not far from Pa's airplane. But it spewed out more smell than heat and the whole place reeked of kerosene. I coughed as it caught at the back of my throat. I blinked back tears. I was supposed to be in school, not in this smelly shed. "Pa! I'm here."

Pa didn't respond, and I stood there waiting. He finally pointed to a pile of bulldozer engine parts laying on a pallet. "Wash those in diesel fuel."

Jana was right. This had nothing to do with fleeing from evil. That bulldozer had been sitting in pieces for at least seven years. Pa just needed a servant, a hatchet man, someone to do his dirty work, and I was easy game. "When I'm eighteen, I'm leaving," I whispered to myself. But then I groaned. I still had another eleven months.

CHAPTER 4

In my last semester at high school, we talked about a new phenomenon called the "Stockholm Syndrome." A robbery had occurred some months before in Sweden, in August 1973, where hostages had been taken captive. The strange thing was that the hostages bonded with the robbers during their six days of captivity. Our sociology teacher sat on his desk as he spoke. "It's surprising that people can do that. It shows how little we understand about the human mind."

I raised my hand. "But how can that be? What person would ever consider liking his captors, especially if they want to destroy him?"

The teacher shrugged his shoulders. "Toma, it baffles the whole world."

But a month after Pa had forced me to quit school and work for him, forced me into isolation, not allowing me to see my friends, the same thing happened to me. I had been working in the airplane shed all alone, like I did every day, and Pa came in to check on me. My eyes lit up. My heart filled with friendliness toward him. To see another human being felt like water in a desert. "Hi, Pa! May I go to the bathroom?"

Pa nodded and I reveled in his generosity. I smiled. "Have you found an airplane?"

"Not yet."

I thrilled inside. He had just talked with me like a human being, sharing his inner thoughts. But as I tramped up to the house, it hit me. "This is all wrong," I whispered out loud. "I'm seventeen! I shouldn't have to ask permission to use the bathroom!"

But my psychology teacher never thought to tell us what to do if we ever got caught in a similar predicament. He never even gave a hint. At least those Stockholm hostages had all of Sweden, the whole world, focused on their problems. No one knew mine. Who was going to negotiate with my captor? Who was going to rescue me?

The only way forward, I figured, was to bury my desires. I succeeded for most of every day, except for a short time each morning and afternoon. Pa let me chauffeur Jana and Mik to high school and back. But as I watched Jana climb out of the car, her petite body unfolding from the back seat, her wearing pretty clothes, I woke up, as if from a stupor. I looked at my blackened, scratched hands, my oil stained canvas work clothes, and I wanted to throw back my head and howl.

Jana always waved good-bye to me and smiled. But she didn't have a clue what went on in my heart. Then one day she spotted a friend and called out to her. They walked side by side up the sidewalk, laughing and chatting. I stared after them and the ache inside me almost exploded.

"God, help me," I cried out in the car, hitting the steering wheel with my palms. *"Why can't I see my friends? Why do I have to work for Pa? Why am I singled out for torture?"* But there was no stirring in my heart. Where was God? Couldn't he just gloss over my neglect of him and pretend it never happened?

I wiped my tears with the back of my hand and pulled away from the high school. But the pain in my heart was already growing dull. I couldn't let it happen this time. I would concentrate on it all the way home and tell Ma.

I found Ma in the kitchen washing dishes. "Ma," I begged, "it isn't fair! Why does Jana get to go to school and I don't? Why is Pa treating me like this?"

"We did it for your sake."

"We? What do you mean, 'we'?"

"I was in on it too. We noticed a change in your attitude. Pa had to take you out."

"Why didn't you tell me? You know I always listen to you."

"That isn't how Pa and I operate. Now, don't get upset."

I ran from the house and down to the airplane shed. "They didn't even give me a chance," I sobbed. "Why do they always have to use force?" I cried until my tears ran out. I wiped my nose on my sleeve and got back to work.

I had already filled in all the rusted-out holes on an old station wagon. I had sanded the body filler as well. Now all I had to do was cover the chrome with masking tape, to protect it when Pa resprayed it. I picked up the tape, tore off a strip and started working on a door handle. "I suppose that's the way it is," I whispered out loud, a harsh resignation settling in my heart. "No use trying to fight. I always lose."

That evening Jana and I sat in our bedroom reading. We heard Ma's footsteps on the stairs. We looked at each other and raised our eyebrows. It could only mean something was not right. Ma never came upstairs anymore.

She stopped at our bedroom door, and stood there, already in her flannel nightgown. She looked around at our bedroom as if inspecting it, and her eyes settled on Jana. "Jana, Pa and I have noticed your attitude. You're getting proud and need humbling. I want you to wear braids to school every day."

I looked from Ma to Jana, my eyes growing big. I couldn't see any pride. But now I felt torn in two. On one side, laughter bubbled up inside me. Now Jana would finally understand how I felt. She could sympathize with me. On the other, I stifled a scream. Ma had taken my complaint and turned it into a punishment. All I had done was cry out for mercy. Why had I ever spoken to her?

Jana shrank back from Ma. "How am I proud?"

"Just by asking that question you prove it."

Jana's face went white. Her lips trembled, but she didn't reply. She didn't cry either. That was one thing we had learned growing up; we never cried, or things got worse.

Ma left us, and when we were sure she couldn't hear us anymore, Jana spoke, but her voice wobbled. "What's the matter with Pa and Ma? They did what they wanted at our age. Remember Ma telling us how Grandmother didn't want her to cut her hair and how she did it anyway? Why can't she let us do what we want?"

I didn't know what to say. If Pa and Ma were hard on Jana, I wasn't going to step in and save her. That would cost me my skin, and just maybe, if they spent some of their harshness on Jana, there would be less to throw at me. That was what I called survival, pure, selfish, cruel survival.

The next morning Jana tried to braid her hair, but it was too short. She tried pinning it, but it kept slipping out. I could see her suppress a smile when she told Ma how she couldn't do it.

Ma turned to me. "Toma, you do it."

Deep inside something bothered me, but I didn't stop to listen. I grabbed a comb and started parting Jana's short silky hair. I tried to braid it.

In the end Jana looked just like a little girl, with two puny knots sticking out from her head. She would certainly get teased in school, especially as a sixteen-year-old. Tears streamed down her face.

I didn't know what to say. "Jana, don't cry."

She fled.

That morning as I dropped her off at high school, she slammed the car door extra hard. I jumped in shock, and it jerked me awake. What had I done? I had hurt my own sister.

I stared after her, at her little braids. I gasped. I had made them myself! "What did I do?" I wailed. "Why did I listen to Pa and Ma?"

I drove home keeping that feeling alive, not wanting to forget it this time. I found Ma in the kitchen again. "Couldn't you choose a different punishment for Jana? Not something that makes her friends laugh at her?"

"What are you talking about, Toma? If you hadn't brought Jana to our attention, we would never have noticed. It's your fault."

"But I didn't say she was proud," I cried. "I didn't say anything bad about her."

I fled to the airplane shed and pushed my way through the canvas. I ran over to the airplane and kicked its wheel. I kicked it again and again. That was the closest I could get to punishing Pa and Ma. They had twisted my words to suit their whims, and I, their handy hatchet man, could conveniently get blamed.

35

How I needed someone to talk to. Forget Pa and Ma. Jana was out of the question. The only one left was God. I picked up my Bible, a year-and-a-half after I had closed it. I hadn't meant for it to be so long. I read the underlined verses where once my heart had stirred. I listened inside. Nothing.

But I kept on flipping pages and found another verse, this time about Jesus. "Son though he was, he learned obedience from what he suffered."[b] I shuddered. *"God? Is this what you have been doing, trying to get my attention. I'm back. I'm finally listening. I'm sorry for dumping you."* But there was still no stirring in my heart. *"God? Could it be that a simple 'sorry' isn't enough? You want me to prove it with my life."*

Around that time Pa heard of a house for sale in some remote mountains to the west, about 1500 miles away. He drove out and a week later he rang home. Ma answered, and when she put the telephone down, she smiled. "Pa just bought us a place. It needs a bit of work on the inside and out. He says he got it for a good deal."

I ran to the airplane shed and burst into tears. I reasoned with myself for the next three days. Why did we have to move to those miserable mountains? How could I ever become a doctor out in the middle of nowhere? All my avenues of hope would be gone. But were they? With Pa not home, I could finally think clearly. I could still take those SATs. Maybe I could apply for another scholarship.

As soon as Pa returned, I asked him. He scoffed. "If you want to waste your time, go ahead. You're not even good at being a mechanic."

I signed up anyway and showed up for the test. But as I waited in line, I overheard those standing around me. They had studied for the SAT and were confident they would do well. I didn't even know I should have studied. What was I doing? I was just a fraud.

I started to tremble, and when I sat down in the examining hall, I couldn't even take in the spoken instructions. I barely understood the words on the page. My hands shook. And when the test scores came back, Pa was proved right. I scored in the bottom five-to-fifteen percentiles. What had I been thinking, that I could have dreams? I was a nothing, with no brain.

Then our house suddenly sold, and we only had two months to

pack. I looked at all of Pa's stuff, his two buses, a dump truck, a car, another airplane he had bought, a Cessna 150, all his spare parts and tools. "Pa? What will you do with all your junk?"

Pa nodded. "Take it with us. I want you to unscrew the seats in both buses and stack them up. That will give us plenty of room to take everything."

"And the Cessna and dump truck?"

"I'll hook the Cessna to the back of one of the buses, and I'll come back for the dump truck."

"But Pa, the Cessna can't go down the highway with its wings sticking out. No one would get past."

Pa chuckled. "We'll take the wings off and hang them from the ceiling in one of the buses." I chuckled with him, relieved that at least I could still hold an intelligent conversation.

After that, I worked ten, twelve hours a day, sorting, cleaning, and packing Pa's things. I didn't have time to think. But on the day before we moved, while Pa was still in the airplane shed, I sneaked into the house to ring my high school friend, Helen. I hadn't been able to telephone her for a month. "Helen," I whispered, "we're leaving tomorrow."

I tried to hold myself together but failed. I burst into tears before she had time to answer. "Why don't you run away?" she said.

"I can't. Pa needs me."

"You'll be eighteen in a month. Just leave. Come, stay with me. My parents won't mind."

"Thanks, Helen. I just wanted to say, 'Goodbye.'"

The next day, Mr. Bradley, Pa's friend from church, also came over to say goodbye and help. He shook Pa's hand and got straight to business. "Linard, I see you have four vehicles. How do you plan to take them with you?"

Pa shoved his hands in his pockets. "Well, the dump truck I plan to leave here until I can come back and get it. I had hoped Lila could drive a bus, but when she tried to sit behind the wheel yesterday, she couldn't squeeze in." Pa laughed, as if it was a joke. Ma was expecting a baby in only three weeks' time.

A look of disbelief passed over Mr. Bradley's face. "I should hope not, Linard. How about parking the dump truck and bus behind my barn? You can leave them there as long as you need."

Pa thumped Mr. Bradley on the back. "Thank you, my friend."

Then Mr. Bradley stayed on to help Pa with packing the heavy things. They worked all through the night, and only finished at dawn. We waved goodbye to Mr. Bradley as he headed off to work, and a few hours later we left as well.

All the children climbed into the bus. Pa started the bus engine and pulled out of the driveway, the Cessna 150 trundling behind. I followed him in the car, Ma beside me. We drove down the road we had lived on for eleven years. But not a single neighbor stood outside to wave. "How odd," I thought. I couldn't imagine what had happened, that they couldn't even say goodbye.

Three days later we reached the mountains and followed a highway that ran along a valley, bending around each ridge. The deeper we drove in, the less houses there were, and these looked tiny and homemade. Then Pa slowed down and signaled 'left'. I slowed the car down and looked left.

A logging trail rose straight up into the trees. I gasped as Pa turned toward it. "What in the world?" I cried out. "That isn't a road. He won't make it."

Pa tried anyway, but the bus stalled, with half of the Cessna still straddling the highway. Cars slowed down to go around it. Then Pa put on the flashing school bus lights and backed down again. The traffic stopped in both directions, and cars got out of the way.

I suddenly laughed. "I bet those people have never seen anything like this before." But Ma didn't answer. She looked straight ahead and held her stomach with both hands.

Pa continued backing down the middle of the highway. He stopped a minute later and revved the engine. He raced up the highway and up that first incline. The Cessna bounced like a toy behind him, but he made it and kept on going.

I tried to keep up with the car, dodging potholes and roots, staying away from the cliff edge on one side. I wove back and forth. But ahead, Pa drove with his head hanging out of the school bus window, looking at the edge of the cliff only a yard from the school bus wheels. I shuddered. "This is crazy." Again, Ma didn't answer.

The trees ended as if someone had drawn a line, and we drove out onto level fields. Hundreds of cattle grazed on either side of the road, and a stillness settled over me like peace after a storm. I looked up at the horizon. A mountain rose about a mile in front of us. It shimmered in the setting sun.

A few minutes later, just as the road started climbing again, Pa stopped. I pulled up behind him. The school bus door opened and Mik sprang out to open the gate. I looked at him, as if seeing him for the first time. How long had I been asleep? He had grown up without me noticing, a tall, slim lad, brown-eyed like Ma. I vaguely recalled he had a chemistry set and liked blowing things up.

Karina tumbled out next and dashed through the gate. She looked dirty and disheveled. Her short braids flapped around her shoulders. Finally, Jana stepped out. She stood thin and hunched over, carrying Filip, asleep on her shoulder. He was only three, and it had been her job to keep him happy during the trip. I could never have done that.

Pa and I pulled the vehicles up near the house and I climbed out to look around. A mist had gathered in the field in front of the house and the woods behind were already dark with night. I lifted my eyes to the mountains surrounding us in all directions and it took my breath away. We had fled there to escape from evil and I had expected it to look awful. "It's beautiful," I whispered.

I headed toward the house, a long, low structure shadowed by trees, tucked in at the base of the mountain. The ground literally started rising fifteen feet from the back door, and the house was unfinished, just as Pa had said. Half of the cinderblocks still lay exposed. The other half was covered in fieldstones and cedar cladding. To the far side lay a large manmade pond.

While Pa and Mik hunted for the house key, I found Jana and walked with her around the house. She didn't drive me away. We looked in through the windows, but we couldn't see anything inside, even when we pressed our noses against them. "I hope it's nice in there," Jana said.

"Me, too. I want a bath. I feel so yucky."

At that moment we heard Mik's voice. "Come on, everyone. Pa found the key."

We gathered around a glass sliding door at the back of the house and watched Pa turn the key. But when he tried to slide it open, it refused to budge. "How long has this house been empty?" I asked.

"About two years," Pa said, and then he turned to Mik. "Get the WD40 from the bus. It's in the glove compartment."

Mik darted off and, seconds later he handed Pa the spray can. Pa doused the runners, top and bottom. The door squealed as he pulled it open. Then he reached inside and found the light switch. Nothing. Again, we waited as Pa hunted for the electricity box. I heard the click as Pa flicked the switch, and a lightbulb inside the house flashed on. We stepped inside and huddled together.

I tried to take it in as I looked around. Polished cement floors. Not the nice pine ones we had in our old house. A huge unfinished fireplace. Only three bedrooms. We used to have five. No interior doors. No toilet. Wires hanging from ceilings where lights should have been. No kitchen. No water. Even the ceiling sagged all over the place. The only civilized thing in the whole house was the electricity and a tub, but even the tub hadn't been attached. To top it off it looked like a lumber yard. Boards leaned against walls. Sawhorses. Rusted saws.

Ma nodded. "This is good, Linard. At least we have a roof over our heads."

I gawked at her, mouth open. How could she be so positive? Was she equating this with her DP days, when she had nowhere to live? But Pa smiled and put his arm around her. "I'm glad you like it, Lila. We can fix it up just like we want."

Ma smiled back. "It will take a while, but we can do it."

I stiffened. Ma could stay here if she wanted, but not me. Only one more month, and I would leave. I wasn't going to choose to live in hardship. I had experienced enough of it already

.

CHAPTER 5

I stirred in my sleeping bag the next morning, the sun waking me up as it streamed in through dirty curtainless windows. My sisters were still asleep, still in their everyday clothes, on the uncovered mattresses we had carried in the night before. I looked around at our bedroom. Cobwebs shimmered in the morning sun, clinging to the cement block walls. Planks of wood stood propped up in one corner. Bags of cement in another. Maybe it was all a horrible dream.

"Time to get up," Pa called, his voice sounding cheery throughout the house.

My sisters groaned; I groaned, and we wriggled out of our sleeping bags, placing our feet on the floor. Small puffs of dust rose up, making us cough. We yawned and dragged ourselves to the living room, our clothes wrinkled and dirty, sleep in our eyes. Pa greeted us, a big grin on his face. "Boy, did I sleep well last night."

We didn't answer and squeezed onto the hearth with him, the only place to sit in the house. But when Ma appeared, Jana and Mik sat on the floor, making room for her beside Pa. She didn't sit down. "We need food and water, Linard. I need the bathroom, now."

Pa looked over at Mik. "Go dig a hole behind the house. And everyone else, clean up this place. I'll get supplies." He looked up at Ma. "Lila, I'll take you into town and find you a bathroom."

Pa and Ma drove away. The rest of us stood in the house alone, but then we headed outside to the bus to unpack all the household things. Mik found a shovel. He headed up the mountain. We found brooms.

The vacuum cleaner. We emptied the house of boards, cement, and abandoned tools. We stacked them in the garage. Then we swept and wiped and vacuumed. We carried furniture in. But Mik finished before us and raced back down. "Want a grand tour, anyone?" he called. "I made it look real nice."

All of us children followed him up, around some trees, and behind a bush that only came up to my chest. The hole was two feet deep, and he had stamped the soil around it to make it hard. He had even hung a roll of toilet paper on the bush.

Mik grinned. "Isn't it great?"

Jana wrinkled her nose. "Great, if you're camping."

"This is better than camping. This is permanent."

Jana groaned. "I hope not."

I looked at her miserable face and Mik's excited one. I probably looked as miserable as Jana, but I couldn't help smirking. "What's so funny?" Jana said, eyeing me sideways.

"Nothing really." But that got me thinking. Maybe if I took things the way Mik did, more like an adventure, it might help the next two months pass more quickly. It was certainly worth a try.

Not long after Pa and Ma came back laden with food, and news that they had found a spring at the bottom of the mountain. "Mik," Pa said, "come with me. We need to figure out how to get that water up here."

Mik laughed and jumped into the car with Pa. We girls continued with the furniture. Jana and Karina screwed together beds, and the giant dining room picnic table Pa had built. I hung old bed sheets over bedroom doorways. Then we set up a makeshift work table in the kitchen area with two sawhorses and a huge piece of plywood.

Two hours later Pa and Mik lumbered back with two brand-new aluminum barrels in the car, two-thirds full of water. Mik whooped as he climbed out. "What a swimming hole down there," he said, his eyes sparkling. "There is even a rope hanging from a tree. This place is fantastic."

Pa overheard him and grinned. "Children, God is good. We haven't even been here twenty-four hours and already we have food and water." Pa's voice rose and fell with excitement.

Maybe he was right. The evidence was right there in front of me. Food. Water. But... I had thought goodness meant a lot more than just physical needs, like kindness and freedom, respect and justice. Maybe I was wrong.

Four days later Pa called us together. He sat at the end of one of the couches we had set at right-angles to the fireplace. He held a cup of coffee in his hand. "It's Sunday. Let's go to church. I saw one down the highway."

I looked at Pa in surprise. He had stopped us going to our last church, just months after he pulled me out of school. He had told me it was a bad influence on young people. He even assured me it was a dating agency. Had he changed his mind? I wasn't going to complain. Getting out was better than staying in that house.

We piled into the car, Pa and Ma in front and the rest of us stacked up in back. We could fit us older ones side by side and have a younger one on our laps. I always had Karina, as I was the eldest. Pa drove fast the first mile along the dirt road, even though the car sagged with all our weight. But as soon as we reached the slope Pa slowed down to a crawl. We wove from side to side to miss the ruts. But a few minutes later he stopped in front of an especially big one. "I can't go on. I'll damage the car. You big kids will have to get out. I'll meet you at the bottom."

Mik hooted and leapt from the car. He sprinted down the road before even Jana and I could get out. It didn't seem to matter to him that he had clean clothes on, that he would reach the bottom hot and sweaty. The two of us girls slid out and stepped to the side to let Pa drive by. We smoothed down our skirts and set off jogging.

"This isn't fair!" Jana called between breaths. "Why couldn't Pa get out and run? He weighs as much as the two of us?"

I grimaced, but we kept on jogging and finally skidded down the last steep slope. Pa was leaning against the car, his arms folded across his chest. He scowled, as we came to a stop in front of him. "Did you enjoy your walk, ladies? Mik got here ten minutes ago. Now we will be late for church. It started at ten o'clock."

We stood before him, pulling our damp shirts away from our

chests. "Sorry, Pa," we chorused and climbed into the car. But I caught Pa staring at me in the rearview mirror, scowling yet again. I looked away, overcome with guilt. Maybe if I had sprinted down, not jogged, he might still be smiling.

Then Karina slid onto my lap, her body pressed against mine. Sweat trickled down my back and front. Forget about looking nice for church. I should have sprinted down and kept the peace.

Pa finally stopped in front of a tiny church building with an old billboard out front. He read the faded lettering out loud. "Mountain Fellowship. Sunday service - 10:30am."

Pa laughed, tilting his head back. "Amazing! We're on time after all! God is in control of everything. It's obvious he wanted us to come."

We drove into an almost empty parking lot, and I turned to study the church. It sat tucked between a hill and the highway, a wooden building raised on cement blocks, weeds growing around the foundations. Behind it I noticed an outhouse. I sighed. Our new house fit right in with the area, and I had better get used to it.

Everyone climbed out, but I hid behind the car door, wanting to smooth the wrinkles from my clothes. They looked worse than before I had ironed them. I glanced over at Pa. His shirt still looked freshly starched. He looked cool and rested.

Jana slinked around the car and stood beside me, trying to tidy her clothes. "I want to go home," she whispered.

I nodded. "Me too. But I'd like to know what people look like around here. I hear they're called hillbillies. Maybe they're different somehow?" But Jana shrugged her shoulders as if she didn't care.

A pickup pulled in, and an older couple climbed out. I studied them from behind the car door, taking in their details. The lady wore a hat with a feather on top, and her drab brown skirt hung uneven below her knees. The lining sagged in one place. The man wore a brown pinstriped suit too big for his frame, and black polished shoes. They looked twenty, thirty years out of date, but that comforted me. I would fit right in.

Jana and I hastened to join Pa and Ma, and as we climbed the stairs to the church, a stooped, white-haired lady appeared at the door. She handed us each a hymnal, and smiled, revealing a partial set of brown teeth. She said something, only a few words, but I couldn't understand a single thing. I nodded and smiled, as if I did.

We filed inside behind Pa and Ma and walked up the aisle. I glanced around. There were no children, no young people, just older ones, mostly with grey hair. We slid into two rows of straight-backed wooden chairs up at the front, and I figured we took up a quarter of the seats.

People kept coming in, and the building soon filled. The pastor stood up exactly on time, a kind looking man with broad, stooped shoulders. He spoke, and his voice was deep. It rose and fell in some strange lilt, but at least I could catch a word now and then. He told everyone to pick up their hymnals, but I couldn't figure out which number he said.

Someone tapped me on the shoulder, startling me. "It's page thirty-eight," a woman's voice whispered.

I turned to thank her and blinked instead. The lady wore a super blond wig, like the ones women wore at parties and bars. It framed her smiling face. Didn't she know she shouldn't wear it in church? Didn't she know the difference between parties and religion? I managed a slight smile and turned back quickly.

The wig lady whispered other instructions in my ear, and I did appreciate it. She must have known what it felt like to be a stranger in that church. I determined to thank her after the service, but Pa stood up as soon as it ended, and we all stood up with him. That was the Rose family protocol; we always followed his lead.

Pa headed for the door, and we followed him out. The pastor shook our hands one by one, and I expected Pa to lead us to the car. But Pa stopped at the bottom of the steps, and the congregation flowed out around us. They welcomed Pa and Ma, congratulating them for their large family. Then someone asked Pa why he had moved us to the mountains.

Pa nodded his head in all seriousness. "God told us to leave our home and come here. We want to raise our children away from evil."

That got everyone's attention. They stared wide-eyed at Pa, and I could tell what they thought behind their sudden shy smiles. Only people of faith could move a large family to such a desolate place. Only people with integrity would follow God.

I looked around at their upturned faces. Why did they believe him? I tried to look at Pa through their eyes. First, he was tall and handsome, with a big straight nose. His sky-blue eyes and melodious voice gave the effect of kindness and goodness. Add to that Filip resting in his arms and Pa looked like a veritable saint.

Then there was Ma, sparkling like a jewel, standing close to his side. She smiled, her teeth perfect and white, and she directed her gaze toward Pa. I could see she was so very proud of him. Not only that, she looked the epitome of vulnerability and strength, with one arm tucked in Pa's, the other resting on her huge belly.

And we children, we surrounded them quiet and respectful, like saplings around two oaks. Oh! We really did look like the best of the best. What a picture we made!

Then the wig lady approached me, but she had removed her wig. Her real hair was brown and flattened down. She shook my hand and smiled. She treated me like an equal, and that caught me off guard. Did she want some information? Did she suspect that something must be wrong, that our family just seemed too good for real life?

I looked down at the ground to avoid her eyes and noticed part of her wig hanging from her purse. She followed my gaze and laughed. "Oh, that!" she said, "In church, most of the ladies wear hats, but my husband isn't a Christian and won't let me come to church with one on. A wig is like a hat. It covers my head, and my husband likes this one best. I don't come to church all the time either. Sometimes my husband wants me to stay home. Some people don't like it, but I don't listen to them. The Bible says, 'Wives, submit to your own husbands.'[c] That's more important."

I looked up at her with sudden new eyes. How I wished I could be like her and stand up for what I believed. "Enough about me," she said. "What about you? Have you finished high school yet?"

My gaze dropped again, and I crossed my arms. No one had asked me about my life for almost a year. I looked up at her, but I couldn't tell her the truth: that Pa had forced me out of school and made me work like a slave; that he didn't work himself and sat in his chair all day; that to the outside world he looked pretty perfect, but at home he raged and hurt me if I disobeyed even the smallest command. But I didn't want to be disrespectful toward Pa and Ma. "I'm hoping to start university in January," I said, "and study to be a doctor." The words just popped out, but they sounded so good, I didn't even bother to correct myself.

"Wonderful!" the wig lady exclaimed, and she turned to a woman beside her sharing the excellent news.

I cringed as the lie spread from person to person, and I pulled away, escaping to the car. "You weasel." my conscience shouted. "You just lied to that lady. You made her lie." I groaned. Why was I so afraid of the truth?

I sat on the car bumper and stared at the cars on the highway. They all knew where they were going, but I had no idea. In fact, all I had were stupid lies. I wasn't going to anywhere soon, especially to a university in January.

Jana joined me a few minutes later. "What's the matter, Toma?"

"Nothing."

Eventually we drove off, and Pa chuckled. "That was great! We must go to that church again."

I agreed, not really thinking of what I said. My mind was on that lady with the wig. She believed in God like no one else around me. God was real to her. I could see it in her eyes. She stood up for her beliefs no matter what others thought of her. People tried to push her around, but she and God found a way forward. I stared out the car window as we drove. Maybe one day I could be like her.

Pa stopped at the bottom of the mountain so we big ones could get out. He waved as he drove off. "See you at the top!"

The three of us stood there, watching our car head up the mountain. I sighed as we started the steep climb up. It would take us at least an hour to get back to the house. I looked up at the sky, the trees, the huge boulders, and cliffs. A faint shadow of joy seeped into a corner of my heart. I had felt it before. *"Hi, God,"* I whispered.

The next morning Pa woke us up at 5:30am, as usual. We hurried through exercises, chores and breakfast. At 7:30am the school bus lumbered up the road. I dashed to the kitchen and handed out the sandwiches I had made early that morning. I watched my brother and sisters sprint to the road, waving their arms for the bus to stop. A few moments later I was alone. Again.

I reluctantly turned toward the house. What was I supposed to do? There was no airplane shed, no greasy engine parts to wash. Pa set me to work straight away. All morning I attached light sockets to all the wires hanging down from the ceiling. All afternoon I took care of Filip while Ma rested. Pa sat in his chair.

At 3pm I heard the roar of the school bus. I grabbed Filip's hand and we dashed outside. Maybe my siblings would have news from the outside world. They were my only contact with reality.

Mik tore up the driveway, his face alight with excitement. "I found out something really weird," he called. "I have to tell Pa and Ma."

We followed Mik in, and when he spotted Pa and Ma's heads poking above the top of a couch, he dashed around to them. "Pa! Ma! At school a boy told me that a wild hermit lives in the valley." Mik pointed out the door. "He said the hermit hates people and shoots anyone who comes near his place. Then he eats them."

I shuddered. "Mik! You must have heard it wrong!"

"I didn't. I asked some other kids at school, and they told me the same thing. They said he's crazy, and no one goes there. He used to live in a lunatic asylum but escaped."

Pa scoffed. "They're only trying to trick you, so they can have a good laugh. That's what happened to me when I first came to America. I couldn't speak English, so some boys took me under their wing. They taught me swear words but told me they were good ones. One day I swore at a teacher, and thought I was being polite. The boys just laughed and ran away. Mik, those children are pulling your leg. It's just a pack of lies." Pa stood up. "Time for me to get to work."

But Mik stared after Pa and then back at us. "I don't think they were lying."

The rest of us shrugged our shoulders. How could we tell what was true or not? "Just be careful, Mik," Ma said. "There are people out there who will try to take advantage of you."

The next weekend, on Saturday morning, two gunshots echoed across the mountains. It startled me at first, but then I thrilled. Finally, something exciting was happening. Maybe someone had been shot and needed rescuing. Maybe there was a feud between mountain folk. I had read about such things in "Lorna Doone."[1] "I'm going out to investigate," I called. "Anyone want to come?"

Jana joined me, and we headed down the road, jogging, our sneakers sending up small clouds of dust. We searched the woods on either side. Nothing. Suddenly, Mik flew past us, running full pelt. "I'll check further ahead," he called.

Jana and I slowed down to a walk, and Mik reappeared a half hour later. He puffed hard, and perspiration ran down his face. "I didn't find a thing," he panted. "Did you?"

Jana and I shook our heads and stopped to let Mik rest. But then we heard branches snapping in the woods, and saw a boy running toward us, in baggy jeans and a floppy blue sweatshirt. "That was the boy who told me about the hermit," Mik whispered. He then waved his arm and called out, "Hello." The boy stopped before us, gulping in deep breaths of air, and looking over his shoulder at the same time. His hands trembled as he rested them on his knees, his voice came out in gasps. "I went to spy on Old Reggie. He shot at me."

Mik's eyes grew big. "The hermit? Why did you do that?"

The boy suddenly grinned and shrugged his shoulders. "I made a bet with some kids in school. I guess Old Reggie got mad when I threw rocks at his shack." With that he straightened up and disappeared into the woods.

I looked after him. "I don't think he's lying or acting. He looked scared."

Mik nodded. "He's telling the truth. I want to go and see for myself."

"Don't, Mik."

Mik grinned. "I'll be okay."

We talked about it at lunch time and Ma shook her head. "It can't be. There is no such thing as a hermit these days, especially in civilized America."

At that moment, a man appeared at the kitchen door. He waved and Pa strode over and opened it. "How may I help?" Pa said.

The man extended his hand. "Joel McKay from down the road. I

---

[1] Richard Doddridge Blackmore, United Kingdom, 1869.

just dropped by to see how y'all are doing?"

Pa shook his hand. "Thanks for asking. I'm Linard Rose. Please, come in."

Joel McKay pulled off his cap as he entered the kitchen, and I couldn't help but stare. This was a hillbilly, and he had just stepped into our house! I took in the details. Blue denim overalls. A wrinkled white long-sleeved shirt. Lace-up boots that looked as old as him. He had white curly hair that hung around his ears. His pale-blue eyes looked unusually bright, especially against his deep tanned face. He spotted Ma. "Good day, Ma'am. You have a real nice place."

Pa waved his hand toward a couch. "Have a seat, Mr. McKay. Can you tell us a bit about this house? Why did Mr. Smith never finish it?"

Joel McKay sat down. His eyes twinkled as he looked around at us children. Then he redirected his gaze toward Pa and Ma. "Old Smith and me were friends. He was a good builder, too. He chose a good place for this house. He knew these mountains like the back of his hand. You see, we get tornados up here, lots of them. On this here bench…"

"Bench?" Pa said, sitting forwards, his elbows on his knees.

"Yep, it's like a step in the side of the mountain. Ours is a big one, about 300 acres, and this bench here is smack in the middle of a tornado path. But because your house is at the edge of the bench, right where the mountain starts to climb, you'll always be safe." I gasped in disbelief, relief and panic, all at the same time.

Joel McKay paused. "Old Smith built this house for his sweetheart. It didn't work out though, and he just didn't have the heart to finish it." He then pointed outside. "See yonder pond? It's shaped like a heart. Old Smith had it specially dug. Yep. He took it real hard."

Jana gave Joel McKay a cup of coffee. He took a sip and looked in his cup. "I think it was all for the best though. People said she dabbled." He raised his eyebrows knowingly.

I studied our neighbor's face. Dabbled? I knew just what he meant. I had heard people use it for occultic things. Help! This was too scary, and I turned to Jana. A strange kind of grimace twitched at her lips as well. She, too, had come to the same conclusion.

But Joel McKay didn't notice, and he raised his cup, holding it up toward Pa. "You have water? I didn't know old Smith dug a well."

Pa grinned. "We got it from the spring at the bottom of the mountain."

Joel McKay laughed. "Ah yes! People say it has healing power. They come from all over to drink it. I think they should try prayin' instead."

"Are you a Christian?" asked Pa.

Our neighbor laughed again. "Yes, sir! Bought by the precious blood of the Lamb. Me and my wife go to church regular-like." We all laughed.

With that Joel McKay drained his cup and rose to his feet. "I must get back. I said I'd only be gone a few minutes." He extended his hand to Pa and Ma. "Pleased to meet you, Mr. and Mrs. Rose. Good to have believing folks up here. This mountain needs it."

But, as soon as he drove away, Pa called all of us children together again. "Listen to me, children. I don't want you to believe what Mr. McKay said. He's just having some fun with us. It's what the locals do for a laugh."

Jana elbowed me in the side. "Toma, let's go check out the pond. If it's shaped like a heart, he's telling the truth." We dashed outside.

The pond did look like one: a proper valentine heart. We stared at each other. All those stories of tornadoes and witches must be true. "Oh no!" Jana whispered, a tremble in her voice. "What if that lady cursed this place, just to get even with Mr. Smith?"

My mouth went dry. "I hope you're wrong."

CHAPTER 6

I hugged my blanket close to my chin that night. Images of that rejected lady filled my mind. I could almost see her standing outside the locked house, her face twisted in pain. I could almost hear her muttering angry words. I hardly dared to breathe. Had she sent see-through people to flit around the house? Did they hide in dark corners during the day and only come out at night?

Somewhere in the night I snapped awake. Somehow the ceiling light in our bedroom had been turned on, and I shielded my eyes from its brightness. I remembered turning it off the evening before. "Jana! Karina!" I whispered, thinking they might have done it. But all I heard was the faint intake of breath from under their blankets.

Maybe someone else had turned it on. I strained my ears, listening for movement in the house. I heard nothing. Maybe I had forgotten to turn it off after all. But as I climbed out of bed to flick the switch, I remembered that for several mornings now the light had been on when I woke up, shining dimly in the morning dawn. Something odd was happening.

At breakfast that morning I looked around the table, looking for possible culprits. "Who turned our light on last night? Is someone playing a joke on us girls?"

I studied Mik's face, Pa's face. They shook their heads, with not a twitch of a grin on their lips. But at midnight it was shining again.

I climbed out of bed and found a sheet of paper. I scribbled an "x" on it, just to prove to myself I wasn't making it up. But I didn't bother mentioning it to anyone else.

Three nights later the light woke me again. I pulled the covers off to get out of bed. What was going on? Someone was doing this on purpose. But as I set my feet on the floor, I heard heavy footsteps. Thump. Thump. Thump. It sounded like Pa, and he was blazing mad, maybe because I was wasting electricity. "Carelessness is a sin!" I could already hear him chide.

I flicked the light switch off and dived into bed. There was no way I wanted to face his wrath. I would pretend to be asleep. But, those thuds? Where were they coming from? Not in the house. They were above my head! Someone was walking in the attic!

But no one could walk in the attic; one had to jump from rafter to rafter and at the same time scramble over diagonal ones. It was impossible to stomp up there. Petrified, I crept to Pa and Ma's doorway. I knocked on the two-by-four plank that made up their door. But as I stood there, the stomping moved to above my head. Could it be Pa up there working in the night? "Pa!" I cried.

As soon as I spoke the stomping stopped. Instead I heard a shuffle in Pa and Ma's bedroom. A few seconds later the sheet that hung over the doorway was pulled aside. Pa appeared; his eyes half closed. "What's the matter with you, Toma?"

My mind began to race. Pa had come to his door far too quickly. Maybe it hadn't been him in the attic. But if it wasn't, who else could it be? My voice shook as I spoke. "Pa! I heard footsteps in the attic!"

Pa listened, tilting his head, with his ear pointed toward the ceiling. "I don't hear a thing."

"It just stopped."

"Go to bed and don't bother me with your dreams."

"I wasn't dreaming, Pa. I heard it."

"I won't repeat myself, Toma. Go to bed."

I fled to my room and hid under the blankets. What if Pa had a secret hatch in his room that led up to the attic? He had dismissed me far too quickly. Was he hiding a secret up there? A demented relative, a crazy first wife we had never heard of? I had read of such things in "Jane Eyre."[2] I reached out into the dark and felt the floor by my bed, searching for the piece of paper with the "X" on it. I shuddered, expecting something to grab my hand and pull me under. I found it and scribbled an "O", this one for footsteps.

The next morning, I determined to inspect Pa and Ma's room, to find out if Pa had a secret. The moment they sat down for coffee, I slinked into their room. I scoured the walls for hidden doors, for sliding hatches. I couldn't find a thing. But that night I heard those same footsteps again. This time my bedroom light was off. I lay in the dark, unable to move.

I heard Filip whimper from the boy's room. He, too, had heard it, and I waited for Pa or Ma to wake up. They didn't.

Filip finally bawled out, and Pa and Ma's bed creaked in the darkness. "What is it, Filip?" I heard Pa call out.

The stomping ceased the instant Pa spoke. It started again a few seconds later, even louder. It now moved from one end of the attic to the other, filling the house with booms. The ceiling should have been shaking and feet poking through the sheet rock, but nothing happened, only the noise. I stifled a cry. It was a ghost! That dabbling lady had put it there.

A light flicked on in the living room and the stomping instantly stopped. Help! Where had the ghost gone? Where was it hiding? It could pounce out on me at any unsuspecting moment. Then I heard Pa and Ma whispering and the swish of Ma's night gown and slippers gave away their location. They were in the boy's bedroom. I rested my head back onto my pillow. They would know what to do.

They came to our room a few minutes later. I squinted at them through a slit in one eye, watching their silhouetted forms in the doorway. They bowed their heads and held hands. "Dear God," Pa whispered, "if anything evil has happened in this room, please take it away. Cleanse it and don't let that spirit ever come back again. Protect Toma, Jana and Karina. In Jesus' name. Amen."

They stood there a few moments, looking at us three girls, and for the first time in years I felt Pa loved me. I couldn't keep still for sheer joy and stirred under the blanket. "We must go, Lila," Pa whispered, his voice soft and gentle. "We don't want to disturb the girls."

[2] Charlotte Bronte, United Kingdom, 1847.

I had never heard Pa speak like that. Maybe I had misunderstood him. He still cared for me; he just didn't know how to show it. My insides filled with warmth, and I fell asleep smiling.

The next two nights I woke at midnight expecting the ghost to cause more havoc, but nothing happened. Pa and Ma's prayers must have driven it away. But how could a few simple words get rid of evil? How did Pa and Ma know what to say? And why did God answer their prayers, and not mine?

I didn't claim to understand how God worked. After all, I had abandoned him and let him down. Maybe one day I would know how to pray, just like Pa and Ma. Maybe one day I could be close to God. I was trying hard, reading my Bible every day, underlining verses. But it was different now. There was no tingle of excitement as I read. Just quiet sadness.

A few nights later I was jerked from deep sleep again. This time Pa stood over me, dressed, his hand on my shoulder. I cried out and pulled away from him. He was the ghost, and he didn't know it. He was sleepwalking, and unconsciously tormenting us. "Pa!" I whispered, hoping he would wake up.

"Toma, I'm taking Ma to the hospital. The baby is coming. Get up right now. I'm leaving you in charge." Then he hastened from the room.

I let out a sigh of relief! Pa was okay. A few seconds later I heard the kitchen door open, and when I looked out the window the car was already halfway across the bench. The headlights cut into the night, bobbing up and down in jerky movements.

Now I was alone. In charge. Responsible for the welfare of my brothers and sisters. I had better check the back door to make sure Pa had locked it. I ran barefoot across the cold cement floor and found it was still slightly ajar. I slammed it shut, turning the key. Maybe the ghost hadn't noticed and was still outside.

I started pacing the living room floor, constantly glancing up at the blackness in the windows around me. Why hadn't I put any curtains up yet? If that ghost decided to stare in at me, with its grotesque and leering face, I didn't know what I would do.

The wind started blowing. Trees creaked around the house. I

shuddered and paced even harder. I had to do something. Maybe praying out loud would do the trick. *"Please, God, please,"* I whispered as loud as I dared, just in case that ghost was listening outside the window, *"keep us safe."*

An hour passed and still I paced. I wanted to stay awake. Pa had told me he needed me, and no matter how inviting the couch looked, how my eyes felt like closing, Pa had trusted me. I wasn't going to let him down. Maybe God had kept me home for this moment, to take care of my brothers and sisters. There was no one else. *"God, now that I have helped, please tell Pa I can go to university now. There might be someplace that accepts me just on my grades."*

I sighed with relief. I had been faithful to the end. In a few short weeks I would finally turn eighteen. God would honor me for my sacrifice and let me go.

A huge weight landed on top of me. I started in confusion, finding myself on the couch, with Filip sitting on top of me.

"Why are you sleeping here?" Filip said. "Where is Ma? Where is Pa?"

Everything flooded back, except lying down on the couch. I stretched and yawned. "Ma is having a baby. I don't know when they'll be back."

Filip slid on to the floor. "Where is the baby?"

"Inside Ma's stomach."

"How did it get there?"

I sat up and rubbed my eyes. "God put it there." Actually, I had no idea how babies were made. Sometimes I did try to figure it out, with Ma giving birth every few years. Did it happen when couples held hands? Or when they kissed? Or could it be an airborne germ, and one caught it like a cold? I hoped not.

Filip patted my face with his hands. "Toma? Why isn't anyone going to school?"

"It's Saturday."

"When is the baby coming home?"

"I don't know."

We waited all morning for a telephone call, and I kept glancing over to the front door where the telephone hung on the wall. Something awful must have happened. What if Pa and Ma never made it back? What if the baby had died? What if Ma died? I would have to become a bread winner. What a progression in my life, from top science student, to high school dropout, to becoming a single parent to a bunch of children, all before I had turned eighteen.

I shuddered. I had better get on with life. There was no use sitting around. I checked the chart Pa had set up the week before, to find out who should start the fire. Pa had welded a pot belly stove and put it smack-bang in the middle of the house. "Karina," I called, "it's your turn to light the fire."

Karina hurried out of the girl's bedroom, still reading a book. She put on rubber boots and headed out the door. "Can't a person ever rest in this house?" she called back. But a few seconds later she rushed back in. "Look!" she shouted, pointing out the window. "Pa!"

I ran to the window, expecting to see the car. Instead, Pa was walking up the road. I cried out; my worst fears confirmed. Ma had died in childbirth.

I watched Pa climb the barbed wire fence and cut across the field. I blinked back tears, as Mik, Karina, and Filip shot out to meet him. They gathered around him and Pa tussled Mik's hair. He gave Karina and Filip a hug.

They missed Pa. I didn't blame them. No one could ever take his place. I sure couldn't.

When Pa reached the house, I ran out to meet him on the front porch. "Where is Ma?"

Pa smiled. "She's okay. Guess what? You have a baby brother. Peter." My insides uncoiled like a wound-up spring, and tears came to my eyes. But this time I laughed.

Pa clapped his hands. "Come on, everyone. I want to tell you what happened. It's quite a story."

We gathered around him, and Filip clambered onto his lap. Pa put his arm around him. "When we left last night, I was afraid Ma would have the baby right there in the car. Each time Ma has one, the baby

57

comes faster. But halfway to the hospital, on the highway, the engine started jerking, and then it quit."

"No!" we cried.

Pa paused for effect. His eyes sparkled as he looked around at us. I could tell he liked our response. "I must have gone too fast down the mountain and knocked a hole in the gas tank. I didn't know it though, because the fuel gauge is still broken. I thought I had fixed it."

We stared at him wide-eyed, mouths open, hanging on every word. Pa continued. "We glided to a stop, and I realized what had happened. But Ma was moaning as if the baby was about to come. I had to do something, and quick. I looked down the highway and saw headlights coming. I ran onto the highway and waved it down.

"It turned out to be a van full of workmen, and the driver tried to pass me." Pa chuckled. "I wouldn't let them. They would have had to run me over."

"My wife is having a baby," I shouted. "I've run out of gas. Take us to the hospital."

"The driver looked at me like I was crazy. 'Flag down the next car,' he said. 'We've been working on the roads. Everyone is filthy. This is no place for a lady.'"

"It's nighttime, man," I said. "There won't be another car." I pulled the van door open and pushed the man closest to me. I told him to move over."

"That man didn't say a word. He just pushed over. Actually, they all changed seats to make room for Ma. I ran back to the car and half carried Ma to the van. The men took their hats off and nodded at her, but I don't think she even saw them. The van driver started driving, but really slowly. Ma started moaning again. "Faster, man!" I shouted. "Faster! The baby is coming!"

"They took us to the emergency entrance at the hospital, and I carried your Ma in. Your baby brother arrived four minutes later. Talk about close."

I laughed. We all laughed. But Mik suddenly turned serious. "Where is the car?" he asked.

"On the side of the highway where I left it. Come on all of you.

Let's take the bus down and tow it home. Toma, you will need to steer it."

Once we got home, Mik helped Pa all afternoon. They removed the fuel tank, patched it up, and put it back on. The next morning Pa brought Ma home, and she sat straight down on the couch where she usually sat beside Pa. We gathered around her and she untucked a white blanket, showing us a little sleeping face.

Pa bent over as well. "We must celebrate with a special cake," he said. "I'll go buy the ingredients." But then he straightened up and grinned. "I'll have to buy an oven too." We all laughed.

Pa left a few minutes later, and us girls crowded around on either side of Ma. It was comforting to sit next to her, and I wanted to rest my head on her shoulder, but Ma wasn't the hugging type. I made sure our knees touched instead.

Ma straightened the blanket around Peter. "The doctor said I would die if I had any more children. But God moved the world so Pa and I could marry, and each of you children is our special creation." Ma sighed. "How I wanted to keep on creating."

I studied Ma's face as she spoke her thoughts. It didn't make sense. Did God really move the world so Ma and Pa could meet? Maybe. Ma had been born into a wealthy family. Pa had not. Instead he had watched his father go off to war, as a lieutenant in the army. Pa and Ma would never have met if it hadn't been for that war, driving them from their homes, from their country, to the same DP camp overseas. Even there they didn't meet, not until they settled in the same city in America.

I stood up suddenly and hurried to my room. This needed more thinking through. God wouldn't have orchestrated World War II, where millions died, just to bring Pa and Ma together. God didn't do things like that. That was against who he was. Also, Ma said the only reason we were born was because we were her and Pa's creation. If that was true, logically, it explained why they treated me the way they did. They thought I was their property, so they could treat me how they wanted. But that was wrong. The American Civil War was fought over this very thing, the right for each individual to live free.

59

Suddenly, Pa's voice rang throughout the house. "I need some help," he called.

I hurried from my room and found him struggling in through the kitchen door, an electric oven in both hands. On top was balanced a paper bag with cake mix, canned peaches and whipping cream. "Toma, Jana," called Pa. "Bake us a cake."

Jana and I leapt to it, and an hour later Pa took over the next stage of the cake. All of us children gathered to watch. Pa hadn't decorated one in years, and he was a master at decorating. We watched him add icing sugar to the whipping cream and beat it until it was stiff. We watched him drain the peaches and cut them into paper thin slices. He sliced the cake into layers and placed the first layer on a plate. He arranged the peaches on top, not letting the tiniest bit of cake show through. He spread half an inch of cream on top of the peaches, and then placed another layer of cake on top of that. Cream oozed out on all sides. Pa repeated the process again and again.

In the end the cake stood four inches high and sagged slightly to one side. Pa straightened it with his hands and scooped the rest of the cream on top. Then he spread it down the sides. With the five slices of peach he had set aside, he shaped a "P" for Peter on top. He stood back to admire his work. "There it is! Toma, get us some plates."

CHAPTER 7

One day Pa ran a series of tests on me. He did it on occasion without telling me, trying to access the depths of my heart. I hated it, as Pa always seemed to use it against me. In his opinion, these tests exposed great evil in me. Ungratefulness. Rebellion. Selfishness.

Now he sat on the couch in the living room, watching me vacuum the hallway. He sat there a while eyeing me, as I pulled the big red industrial vacuum cleaner behind me. Then I heard him whisper through the roar, "Toma!"

I turned off the vacuum cleaner and hurried over to him. I always hurried now. I had to hurry. Pa had finally drummed into me the pecking order of life. He told me often enough, "You will obey me as if you're obeying God. You will work, as if working for God, and even when I'm not looking, God still is. Nothing escapes his notice."

And to highlight it, only a few months earlier he had revealed his strategy for me. "Toma, I will always say no to anything you ask. If you want something bad enough, you will have to fight me. But remember, I always win." I knew my place, but it didn't mean I had to like it.

I stood before Pa with a nervous fear. Would he ask me to do yet another thing? But I smiled to mask my heart. "Yes, sir. You called?"

He looked up at me and shook his head. "Nothing," he said.

I went back to vacuuming, yet I was certain he had called. It was the way he looked at me that proved it. What was he doing? Playing with me? Making me think I was crazy? Later that day I heard him call again; this time he was in the garage. I heard him from my bedroom at the other end of the house and with the sliding door closed between us. I ran outside. "Yes, Pa. You called?"

Again, he looked at me, but this time with a peculiar expression in his eyes. "Nothing, Toma. I just wanted to see how good your ears are."

I relaxed and laughed. "They're pretty good, Pa,"

"I can see that. I had better be careful what I say."

I couldn't understand what Pa meant. What could he possibly say that he didn't want me to hear? But that evening I overheard him in the living room, as I read a book in my bed. "Lila," he said, his voice low, "have you noticed Toma? She seems happy. I tested her to see if it is real. I called her twice and she came smiling. We did the right thing taking her out of school."

"I agree, Linard. We saved her in the nick of time."

Saved me from what? From finishing high school? From university? From having friends? I stifled a scream. My choosing to be happy had backfired on me. It had justified their actions. I stared at the cement blocks in front of me. *"God,"* I finally whispered, *"I can't bear it anymore. Everything I do gets twisted. Only one more week till I turn eighteen. I can't wait to leave."*

But Pa must have had good ears as well. He set about to thwart my prayers. The next morning, he called me to himself. "Toma, we're heading back east the day after your birthday. I want to get the bus and dump truck. I've talked with Mr. Bradley, and he's expecting us. He says we can stay with him."

"We?"

"You and me. You will drive the school bus back."

I just about stopped breathing from shock. "Pa! I can't drive a bus. I've never driven anything with that gear-shifting thing. I don't even have a license to drive one either."

"It's called a shift stick, Toma, and don't you worry. In this State you don't need to take a test to get a trucker's license. You just show up and pay for it."

"But, Pa, I don't want to!"

"I have no option," said Pa. "It's both of us together, or me making two trips. It's easier this way."

"Pa, please! Don't make me." I could already envision a horrible accident, me mangled on the roadside somewhere, and no matter how tough it was at home, I didn't want to die. Not yet, at least.

But Pa refused to listen to my plea for mercy, and he kicked his plan into action. He bought a car with a shift stick for the trip. We built an outhouse and I painted it. Pa chain-sawed piles of wood for the pot belly stove, enough for a month at least. I stacked it under the eaves of the house. But all this preparation didn't make sense. By my calculations it would take two days to get there, one day to turn around, and three days to get back. We would only be gone a week.

The days flew by, and on my birthday, I woke up early. I stared out the window at the fading stars. *"Hi God, I'm eighteen today. That makes me an adult. I can finally do what I want."*

I strolled into the living room, trying to put on that adult feel, but I couldn't muster up a sense of importance. I tried squaring my shoulders, holding my head up, but at that moment Pa strode in. "Let's go, Toma. The driver's license office opens early." So much for airs, I was still a subordinate to Pa.

It took us an hour to get to the office, and a half hour to buy the license. I looked at the laminated card as we walked out and laughed at the absurdity of it all. I could drive anything on the road, even a military tank. What a badge to get as I entered adulthood! But Pa interrupted my thoughts. "It's time for you to learn how to drive with a shift stick. Get into the driver's seat."

I followed Pa's orders, his subordinate, and, in the parking lot next door, he taught me how to use the shift stick, how to work the clutch and gas. Or, let's say, he tried to teach me. I stalled the car dozens of times, and it lurched forward like a drunken man. After about a half an hour, Pa threw up his hands. "Now I know why they invented the automatic. It was for people like you!"

That rebuke got my attention. I had to stop fighting Pa and accept that I was going on this road trip. I had to set aside my hopes of wanting to live a long life, and humbly accept that I might never come back. I would rather die physically, than live with Pa's anger for the rest of my life. That was a damnation I couldn't bear.

I pulled myself together, and in the end, Pa said I had grasped it enough to drive him home. With trembling hands, I put the car into gear, and inched it out onto the highway. If I could make it home, I just might have a chance of surviving this trip.

An hour later I stopped the car outside our house. My siblings swarmed around and greeted us, but no one wished me a happy birthday. I entered the house and Ma said nothing as well. I didn't know what to do. In my opinion, turning eighteen was an important day. I would only become an adult once in my life.

I pretended that I needed to use the outhouse and hurried outside. But I hid behind it instead. I stood well away from the wall and looked up into the dull grey sky. *"What should I do, dear God?"* I asked. I didn't need to remind God of the history. On my sixteenth birthday, Ma had erupted. Grandpa and Grandma had bought me a special sixteen layered cake and given me sixteen presents as well. Ma had told them that they had wasted money on me, and that they should treat all her children equally. As a result, no one did anything about my seventeenth birthday.

Then an idea popped into my head. I would do it myself. I would make my own cake and do my own party. Turning eighteen was important! But I had never made a cake from scratch, only ever from a cake-mix box. I ran back to the house. It was high time I learned. I was an adult now.

I found a recipe book stashed in a box, and, in the end, the cake even looked like a cake. After covering it with icing, shaping an "18" on top with raisins, I set it in the middle of the table. "Who wants a piece of cake?" I called.

The family gathered, even Ma. Pa laughed. "This is the way it should be. Birthdays should be a time to serve." He pitched a note, and everyone joined in, singing me, "Happy birthday." I looked down into my lap most of the time, afraid of Ma's reaction. The one time I did peek, she was smiling at Pa.

Everyone thanked me, ate, and left. I got no presents, no congratulations, but I didn't mind. There had been peace, and that was the best present of all. But late that evening Mik appeared at my bedroom door. "Toma!" he whispered and handed me a small crumpled paper bag. "Happy Birthday!"

I took the bag, taken aback, and pulled out a spray can of deodorant. I held it up, turned it around, took off the lid, and pressed the knob a little into my hand. I smelled it. I hadn't owned a deodorant can in years. "I don't know what to say, Mik. Thanks!"

Mik grinned, an impish grin. "You need it. Actually, it's for the trip."

I covered my mouth to suppress a laugh. "Thanks for the hint," I whispered.

Jana and Karina appeared as well. They both held something behind their backs. Jana produced a brand-new blue and white toothbrush, Karina, a bar of perfumed soap. I could have crumbled to the floor with joy. They had spent their life's savings on me. "Thanks, Jana. Thanks, Karina. I don't know what to say."

Jana smiled. "Don't say anything. Just come back. And don't forget to say 'hi' to everyone back home. I wish I was going too."

That night I lay in bed, my heart feeling like it would burst with joy. *"Dear God, thank you for my sisters and brother. Thank you that they love me. It is so nice to be treated as special. I love them so much."*

The next morning, I packed a few clothes and my presents into a blue backpack Mik had lent me. I walked out to the car with the family. Pa was already there, spreading a sleeping bag on the back seat. "What are you doing, Pa?" I asked.

"We will be driving straight through. One will sleep. The other will drive. It should take us thirty-six hours."

My eyes grew big, but I didn't say a word. What kind of a superhero did Pa think I was? But then, maybe that's what adults did, superhero things. I climbed into the car and rolled down the window. "See you in a…" I called.

But Ma interrupted me. "Linard, sweetheart! Come back quickly." She blew him a kiss and he smiled at her.

I looked up at Ma as we drove toward the gate. Again, my heart felt like bursting. I loved my Ma, and I couldn't believe how much I loved her. Maybe going away showed what was really in the heart. And, Jana too. And my siblings. I would miss them so much. But then I looked over at Pa.

I sucked in a deep breath. Had Pa added up the ingredients of this crazy trip? Fifteen-hundred miles. A sixty-seat school bus, with airplane wings hanging from the ceiling. A scared eighteen-year-old who had never driven a bus. Pa had his head in the clouds. It was as if Pa was telling me to jump over a cliff, and I was obediently hurtling full speed ahead, like a lemming headed for the brink. I had already jumped high in the air. I might as well whoop out a, "WHEEEEE!!" as I plummeted to my death.

The next thirty-six hours passed in almost total silence, and when we reached Mr. Bradley's farm, Mr. Bradley thumped Pa on the shoulder. "Good to see you, Linard."

"You too, my friend," Pa said, and I could tell Pa meant it.

We strolled behind the huge red barn to inspect the bus and dump truck. Mr. Bradley stopped. "Linard, how are you going to get both vehicles back?"

Pa smiled. "Toma has a trucker's license now. She will drive the bus and I the dump truck."

Mr. Bradley looked from Pa to me. He shook his head. "That's an awfully big responsibility, Linard. She isn't experienced."

I glanced at Pa, hoping he could listen to sense, but he just laughed. "Oh, she'll do fine. I will keep an eye on her."

We rose early the next morning and I expected Pa to check the tires and say, "Good-bye," to the Bradley's. But I followed him into the bus instead, and he pointed to a wooden box full of car parts. "Toma, today I want you to clean those with diesel fuel. There is a place in the barn where you can work."

I gawked at Pa. "I thought we were heading straight back."

"Do as you're told."

Pa lifted the box and carried it into the barn. I followed him in, and Pa placed it on a table. He walked out again without another word. I watched him climb into the car and drive away. Where was he going? To a friend's house? To buy some more parts?

I dashed to the barn door and slid it almost closed, enough to let in light, enough to keep out the wind. I rubbed my hands together and blew on them. My breath came out in billows. Then I looked at the table in front of me. A can of diesel fuel and a brush sat there, ready for me to use. I reached out a hand to get to work, but then I hesitated. Should I do what Pa wanted or walk away and never come back?

I had better be good. It wouldn't do to make a scene at the Bradley's house. That would only embarrass Pa and taint my reputation. I had lost everything else. Why should I lose that as well?

I grabbed the brush and washed each tiny part, my fingers numbing with cold. But I finished two hours later, and Pa still hadn't returned. I ambled to the house. "Mrs. Bradley, may I use your telephone."

She smiled and pointed to one at the front door. I picked it up and dialed Helen's number. I knew it by heart. How I hoped she would answer, but the telephone rang and rang.

I was just about to hang up when I heard a click. "Hello?"

My heart jumped into my throat. "Helen," I almost shouted, "I'm back."

"Toma," she shrieked, "When can I see you?"

"Pa won't let me use the car. I'm sure of that. Can you come out here, to the Bradley's'?"

"I can't. Dad is on a business trip and took our car. At least we can talk on the telephone." I slumped to the floor. We were only seven miles apart, but it could have been a thousand. I listened in a daze. "But Toma, you're eighteen now. You don't have to do what your father says. Leave him. Come stay with me."

I rested my forehead on my knees. "I can't, Helen. Pa still needs me. He's depending on me to drive the bus."

"What?"

At that moment I heard a car on the gravel driveway. I jumped to my feet and looked out the kitchen window. Pa had just climbed out of the car and was headed toward the barn. I trembled. He would explode if he didn't find me working hard. "Bye, Helen," I whispered. "I need to go."

I hung up and dashed to the barn, but Pa was already inside. He turned and looked at me, irritation in his eyes. "I told you to work!"

"I finished everything you told me to do." Then I looked down at his hands. They were empty. No shopping bags. No new engine parts.

67

"Pa, where did you go?"

"None of your business." But it was my business, even though I didn't dare say. Whatever he was up to, it delayed us from going back. It delayed me from leaving home for good.

Day after day, Pa gave me jobs. Day after day, I shivered alone in the barn, stamping my feet, warming my hands in my armpits. Day after day, he left me there alone to work. Did Pa regret moving to the mountains? Did he have a special friend somewhere, and we would never get back to Ma and the children? Or was he just having a breakdown in the woods somewhere? I didn't know, and I didn't dare ask.

Pa decided to telephone Ma one evening, after we had been there a week. I could guess from the conversation that Ma wanted to know when we would be heading back, but Pa refused to give her a date. He telephoned the second week, and the third. He telephoned three days after that. "Hi, Lila... Yes, we're still here... I don't know when we will be back... I can't give you a date... Don't cry, Lila... Yes, I still love you... Can't you wait a few more weeks... Don't say that... I love you... Alright... Alright."

Pa hung up and found me in the bedroom, hiding in my sleeping bag. I looked up as he came into the room and his face was gray and lined. "Toma, Ma isn't coping. She wants us home right now. I can finish the rest of the jobs there." He said it as if it was an enormous sacrifice.

I stared at him. I could have told him that at the beginning of our stay. What wife wanted to be left alone for a month, especially with a two-week-old baby and a bunch of kids? I could have saved him the agony, but he would never have listened.

The next day we almost threw things back into the bus, and I sidled up to Pa that evening. "Pa, you still haven't shown me how to drive the school bus. We'll have to leave it behind."

"No! You can still drive it. It isn't hard. I'll take you around the block tomorrow morning. And, by the way, you will be towing the car."

"Pa!" But he didn't seem to notice the panic in my voice. He yawned.

That evening he chatted with Mr. Bradley in the living room, and their laughter filled the house. I sat in the kitchen alone, staring at the wall. Pa had enjoyed his friends for three weeks, talking and joking his time away. I had only seen Helen once and for no more than an hour. *"God,"* I prayed, *"I know Pa doesn't like me having friends, but if it's right to talk with Helen, please may she be in."*

I picked up the telephone and dialed her number. Amazingly, she was the one who answered. "Helen," I said, my voice breaking as I spoke, "we're leaving tomorrow, and I hardly got to see you." I got no further and started sobbing. I had to hang up the telephone.

Mrs. Bradley heard me and bustled from her bedroom, her dressing gown tied snug around her waist. She put her arms around me and stroked my hair. "It will be alright, Toma. It will be alright."

At 6am the next morning, Pa led me to the school bus. The car was already attached. He pointed to the driver's seat. "Toma, get in! It's just like driving the car."

"But I can't," I said, my voice shaking. "I don't know how to reverse with mirrors."

"We will be driving on major highways and going straight ahead. If there is any reversing to be done, I will do it."

I doubted Pa would be there at the instant I needed him. He would be driving the dump truck ahead of me. But I turned the ignition anyways, forgetting to press in the clutch. The bus jerked forward and stalled.

"Don't rush," Pa said, resting his hand on my shoulder. "Just take it nice and slow."

I tried again and succeeded this time, but my hand shook as I reached for the shift stick. It shook as I tried to put it into first gear. Finally, the bus began to move. Pa chuckled and patted my shoulder. "See! You can do it!"

He stood beside me as I edged the school bus onto the road. He watched as I put it into second gear. "That's my girl."

I managed a two-mile circuit, down deserted country roads. But the entire way was covered in potholes. I only got as high as third gear. "Pa, I can't do it," I said. "I don't know how to get it into the higher gears."

"It's just like the car, Toma. Just follow the instructions on the shift

69

stick." He pointed to the knob on top, at a diagram.

Back at the Bradley's, I stopped the bus, but when I let go of the steering wheel my hands shook violently. Pa grinned and thumped me on the back. "It will be easy, Toma. You wait and see."

Pa jumped out, but I stayed sitting in the driver's seat. A quote from Queen Esther came to mind. She had thought she would die, and I took her words as mine. *"If I perish, I perish,"* I whispered.

The Bradleys' came out to wave goodbye to us. I waved back and put the bus into gear. I released the clutch, but it only stalled. I restarted the bus, but it stalled again. I tried five times and my heart leapt for joy. Maybe the bus had broken down.

Pa backed up and jumped out of the dump truck. He almost ran to the bus. "What's the matter?" he said, his voice sounding civil. But with his back toward the Bradley's, they couldn't see his livid face, his clenched fists.

"I don't know. This stupid bus won't go."

Pa reached over and released the emergency brake. "That is the first thing you do. And watch your attitude. You're walking on thin ice." A tremor ran through my body, but at that moment it never occurred to me that I could act like an adult. I could refuse to drive, stand up, and walk away.

Pa leapt from the bus and chuckled heartily. "Lady Drivers!" he called out to Mr. Bradley. "They can't be trusted. Can't even remember to release the emergency brake!" But Mr. Bradley didn't smile. I knew he was against me driving that bus. He had already told Pa several times.

A strange kind of peace settled over me. I started the bus and put it into gear. *"God? I wonder where Pa and Ma will bury me."* And lemming-like I leapt high in the air. WHEEEEE!

CHAPTER 8

A snowstorm hit us only sixty miles into the trip. The windshield wipers groaned as they swished back and forth. The visibility was poor, and I could barely see Pa up ahead. Cars had emptied from the highway. "This is dangerous, Pa," I wailed.

Pa must have heard me. He signaled to tell me he was pulling over, and I followed him to the edge of the highway. But as we did, a snow plough passed us, and Pa swung the dump truck into the cleared path behind it. I did the same and we crept behind it at twenty miles an hour. Soon we were the only three vehicles on the highway. "This is how I like it, nice and slow," I said out loud.

We passed through the storm and kept on driving. Twelve hours in total, and I could barely keep my eyes open. I started chanting to control my blinks. "Eyes open. One. Two. Blink. Eyes open. One. Two. Blink..." But the blinks grew longer, and my head kept jerking up.

Without any warning Pa signaled and pulled over to the side of the highway. I hit the brakes, coming to a stop behind him. He hastened over. "What's wrong, Toma? You're weaving all over the road."

"Am I?"

"We'll stop at the next truck stop. It's only ten miles from here. You can make it."

I nodded, and when we pulled into the truck stop, I rested my head on the steering wheel, the engine still running. Pa dashed over, turned the ignition off and put the emergency brake on. "You will sleep in the car, Toma. That can be locked. I'll sleep in the bus to guard the things."

I looked up at him with unfocused eyes. A vague sense that he actually cared about my safety flicked across my mind. I mustered my strength to ask him a question. "It's below freezing outside, Pa. Can I have the heater on in the car? I'll leave the window open a sliver."

"No."

I didn't even bother questioning him. Pa might be saving me from asphyxiation, but now I could freeze to death! Either way I wouldn't feel a thing. It would just happen.

I climbed from the warmth of the bus and strode to the car. It still had four inches of snow on top, and when I opened the back door, some fell onto the sleeping bag. I brushed it off and climbed in. My plan was to leave my black, steel toed boots on, to keep my feet warm. But the boots cut into my ankles, so I took them off.

I noticed my socks, damp with sweat. I needed to change them, but my clothes were in the trunk of the car, and Pa had the key in his pocket. I groaned, too tired to put my boots back on and disturb Pa for a pair of measly socks. My socks would dry in the warmth of the sleeping bag. "It will be alright," I muttered out loud, and wriggled in again, with my coat, hat, and gloves on. I curled up into a ball.

The sound of someone pounding on the car window woke me from deep sleep. "Time to get up," came Pa's muffled voice. "We're late."

"Yes, Pa," I called, and looked at my watch. It was 5am.

I could hear the bus and dump truck engines already running, but I couldn't see a thing. The car windows had frosted over on the inside. I scrapped a little ice off to peek through the hole. It had snowed in the night. Then I noticed my feet; they felt heavy and somehow cold. I drew them out of the sleeping bag and gasped in alarm. The ends of my socks had frozen stiff!

I tore off the socks and touched my toes. The outside half of each big toe, and the tips of all the rest, had turned pure white. They felt cold and clammy to my touch. I tried to warm them in my hands, to blow warm breath on them, but nothing helped. "So much for saying it would be okay," I chided myself, and images of my toes turning black and falling off flooded my mind.

Pa knocked on the window again. "Hurry up. What's taking you so long?"

I pulled myself together. "Can I have the key, Pa?" I called, calming the panic in my voice. "My clothes are in the trunk."

I opened the car door expecting him to give me the key, but a few seconds later he threw the backpack in and it hit me square on my chest. Like a floodgate, my emotions unraveled. *Is there no shred of respect in him? Even if I died, he would get angry with me.* But then that same strange peace washed over me. I hadn't died. I had survived against all odds. *"I must be really special to you, God,"* I whispered. *"You must really want me to live."*

I put on clean socks and laced up my boots. I climbed out of the car and tried to stand in the snow. Instead I fell forward onto my knees. What was going on? I grabbed the car door handle and pulled myself up. I still couldn't find my balance and steadied myself on the car. It took a minute, but with each step the walking grew easier. I balanced myself as I knocked on the bus door. At least I would still be able to walk.

Pa was sitting in the driver's seat and opened the school bus door. A wave of heat hit me. I looked up and saw ice sliding down the windshield in huge melting chunks. Pa must have had the engine running for a couple of hours at least! He must have been cold. Why didn't he think of me?

I stumbled up the steps and swapped places with Pa. I reached for the key and turned it, forgetting the bus was already running. The starter motor screeched, and I yanked my hand away. Pa swung around, his eyes blazing. "Watch it, girl!"

I shuddered. "Sorry, Pa. I didn't mean to."

"Sorry doesn't repair a starter motor!"

"I'm sorry, Pa. I really am."

Pa turned to leave, and I reached for the ignition key once more. I almost turned it, again. *"God! What's wrong with me? Please wake me up."*

God answered my prayer, but only an hour later. I had placed my boots up against the heater to thaw my toes, and now they throbbed, as if caught in a vice. To pass the time I studied the pain... Somehow it felt familiar. I tried to figure it out. Was it like when I walked in front of a swing and got kicked in the head? Or when my brother shot me with

73

an arrow? Or when I smashed my fingers in a door? None of them fit.

Then I noticed my aching heart. I pulled in a deep breath. Frost bite and a wounded heart both felt the same. "I have finally arrived," I announced out loud. "Pain on the inside, pain on the outside. I'm a well-balanced individual now."

I looked at the dump truck in front of me and nodded. "Thanks, Pa."

Again, we drove all day and into the night, Pa's red taillights guiding me. "I could do with stopping," I called out to Pa. But suddenly a truck's headlights flashed me from behind. It wanted me to pull over and stop!

"No way, Jose!" I called out to that truck. Did he think I was crazy enough to pull over in the dark? I drove on as fast as I could.

The trucker kept on flashing and pulled up beside me. Then he hooted his horn. We raced side by side and I finally looked over. I expected a goofy grin, as if he was having fun, but his face looked dead serious in the reflection of the lights. He was shouting at me, waving with one arm, pointing at the back of the bus. I looked in the mirror and noticed showers of sparks flying up. Why hadn't I seen them? I nodded and waved, signaled to Pa and pulled over. The trucker pulled over as well.

I had no flashlight, but I decided to inspect the damage anyway. I leapt into blackness and something hit me hard in the chest. I staggered back, winded, and gasped out in pain. What had just happened? Was this a trap? Had someone just hit me? But, how could anyone have known where I would stop? Then my fingers encircled something cold.

At that moment the trucker approached, holding a flashlight high. I was clinging to a shiny metal post that reached up to my chest. It could have smashed up my face, but at that moment I didn't care. I looked at the tall, burly trucker, advancing with rapid strides, his face lit up in grotesque shapes, as every passing headlight shed moving light on him.

I gasped for air, as if being strangled to death. What if that man had no morals or respect? What if he wanted to do me harm? He was a grown man, and I a skinny teenager. I couldn't fight him. I couldn't run away into the dark. And, no one would see me to rescue me.

I spotted Pa, running, his winter coat flapping around him. "What's going on?" he yelled. "Why did you stop?"

The trucker looked back at Pa, his fists doubling up. "Do you know her?"

"She's my daughter."

The trucker relaxed. "She's had a blowout. That tire could have caught on fire. I have seen trucks burning on the sides of roads because the driver hadn't noticed."

Pa ran right past the truck driver. "Everything's under control."

The truck driver stared after Pa. "I can see that," he scoffed. He waited until he saw my reaction to Pa, and then he headed back to his truck.

Pa stopped in front of me. "Didn't you hear an explosion, girl?"

I looked up at Pa, searching my brain. "Yes… but I thought it was outside somewhere. Maybe a stupid hunter too close to the highway. Maybe some mining. I saw signs for mines a little way back."

"Watch your attitude," Pa snarled at me, and he strode off to the back of the bus.

"What attitude?" I thought. The one where I worked hard, or put my life at risk? The one where I did what he said no matter what?

I sat down on the school bus steps, too tired to move, leaning my head against the folding door. I cradled my body, trying to keep warm, and thought of the man who had just saved my life. "Whoever you are, thanks."

"Toma," Pa called a minute later, "the next truck stop is thirty miles from here. We will take it slowly. Thankfully the other wheel is still sound and can support the weight."

I looked back in his direction. "What other wheel?"

Pa pointed his flashlight at the back of the bus, and I could just make it out in the shadows. "I never knew there were four wheels back there."

Pa swung his flashlight into my face. "I can't believe it, girl! What planet are you on?"

I squinted at him, and at that moment I didn't care. I was doing my best. I wasn't a seasoned warrior like him.

We drove into the truck stop with emergency lights flashing. But as soon as we stopped, I limped to the rest rooms, locking myself into a cubicle. Had my toes already gone black? Had they fallen off?

I sat down on the toilet seat and tore off my boots and socks. My toes were still white, but when I touched them, I couldn't feel a thing. I pressed harder and still felt nothing, even though a fire burned mercilessly inside them. I stared at them. Maybe they would fall off eventually and I would have to accept my inevitable fate. No more running barefoot. No more wearing flip flops. No more cutting toenails with ancient nail clippers that kept falling apart.

I laced up my boot and made my way back to the bus. I wouldn't tell Pa about my toes. What would he do anyways? Find a hospital? I doubted it. That would only cost more money.

We set off at 5am, as usual, and four hours later we left the interstate highway. "Pa," I cried out, "you said we would only drive on highways. What are we doing cutting cross country?"

I tried to keep up with him as he zigzagged down narrow roads. I sat bolt upright in the driver's seat, clutching the steering wheel, hardly daring to breathe. A half hour later a river loomed into view. It looked about a half mile wide, and the bridge across it was narrow, with no sidewalks on either side, just white metal girders railings about a yard high.

Three trailer trucks and five cars were headed in my direction. I gripped the steering wheel hard, my knuckles turning white. *"Help me, God. There isn't enough room for me and them,"* I cried, my voice cracking, my throat dry. *"I won't make it!"*

I imagined the bus disappearing into the murky cold water, trucks and cars piled on top of it. I imagined me floating away, pressed up against the windshield.

I guided the school bus onto the bridge, trying not to hit the side. The first trailer truck raced toward me. I could hardly breathe. This was it. My time had come. But I couldn't bear to see myself die. I squeezed my eyes shut and kept them shut.

Seconds passed. More seconds, and still I felt no crunch of metal, no wave of cold water. I opened my eyes. I was still on the bridge, but at the far end of it! I looked in the side view mirror. The trucks and cars had safely crossed over. What had just happened?

I kept on driving, my hands clammy with sweat, my body quaking. But suddenly I dared a small, shaky laugh. *"God, you did it again. You must really care. I must be special. I can hardly believe you want me to live!"*

I took a deep breath, strength seeping into my heart. How many times had God spared my life? Not freezing to death. Getting over the bridge. And, oh yes! I had forgotten. That morning the brake line had broken as I started the bus. If that had happened while I was driving on those windy roads, on the highway, I could have crashed and died again. God had spared me three times at least!

But with all my rejoicing, I lost sight of Pa. I drove faster, hoping to find him around the next bend. Nothing. I drove even faster. Nothing.

I cried out in fear. I had no idea where I was, no money, and no map. I didn't even know the telephone number or address of our new house. Had Pa abandoned me on purpose? I couldn't imagine so. The wings of his Cessna hung in this bus. I knew at least those were important to him.

I approached a huge intersection with warning bumps on the road, a green light ahead of me. I looked left and right hoping I might see Pa's truck. Instead I noticed a car racing toward me, as if they hadn't seen their red light.

I hit the brakes. Tried to shift to a lower gear. Tried to beep the horn. I smashed into that car instead.

The impact threw me forwards, and something flicked inside my head, like a switch. I felt nothing. I heard nothing. But I could still see. The car I had hit started clicking in front of me. It moved around the front of the bus in slow, jerky movements, just like an old-fashioned slide show. The driver inside the car moved in those same strange jerks, hitting the steering wheel with his chest.

The school bus stopped, but the car kept going. It clicked out of sight. But for some reason I glanced into my rear-view mirror. The car I had just hit careered toward the car I was towing! It rammed into it and lurched to a stop.

I stared in frozen horror, and only one word came to mind. Revenge. That driver was going to make me pay for having hit him. But I didn't know that the impact of the crash had spun him around, and the driver never thought to take his foot off the gas. He never meant to smash into that towed car.

I sat there staring in the rearview mirror. Was that man dead? Had I killed him when I smashed into his car? Had he killed himself when he smashed into mine? A movement caught my eye. I turned. A dozen people came running toward me from all directions. Someone pounded on the school bus door.

I pulled the handle and the door unfolded. A police officer sprang in, panic on his face. "Where are the children?" he bellowed.

I stared at him in confusion. I moved my jaw and a sound finally came out. "What... what children?" I stammered.

"We just notified all the schools in the area to see if this bus is one of theirs." But I only looked at him, at all the ambulances, police cars and wrecker trucks arriving. It didn't make sense.

An ambulance man dashed inside as well. He rested his hand on my shoulder. "Are you alright?" he asked.

I nodded. "Why are there so many ambulances?" I asked.

The ambulance driver looked down at me, a strange expression on his face. Maybe I wasn't alright, after all. "For all the children we thought were on the bus."

I nodded again, as things clicked into place. It was 3pm. The end of school. Children would be going home by bus. Then more movement caught my attention in the rearview mirror, and I turned my gaze back to the smashed-up car. Ambulance drivers had gathered around it.

I couldn't breathe as I watched them open the door. Was that man dead or crippled for the rest of his life? How could I ever live with myself?

The man moved his arms and head. He climbed out of the car! He talked with the ambulance men. My breath caught. I started breathing again. I had been spared, and so had he.

I finally climbed out, and people milled about. Pa had abandoned me, and all I had left was a smashed-up bus. I looked down the highway searching for him. Maybe one day he would change his mind and come back to find me.

A few minutes later his dump truck appeared. Pa jumped out and ran toward me. My heart leapt within me. Pa still cared. I ran toward him, my arms outstretched, tears running down my cheeks. "Pa!"

I expected Pa to hug me, to comfort me, but he grabbed my shoulders instead. He squeezed so hard, it hurt. "What did you do?" he hissed.

I choked back my tears, trying to pull away. "Pa! It wasn't my fault."

He squeezed even harder. "Don't lie to me."

A police officer strode over, and Pa let go. He and the officer started talking. I stood by and listened. But they didn't seem to need me; so I wandered back to the bus. I sat on the bottom step, watching Pa and the officer inspect the damage. I heard Pa say that the bus could still be driven, but the car was now a total write-off.

Pa finished the paperwork. The intersection was cleared off, and finally everyone left. Only then did Pa turn to me, as we stood at the side of the highway. "What is wrong with you?" he yelled. "Can't you do anything right?"

"It wasn't my fault. Please believe me, Pa!"

Pa's eyes nearly popped out of his head. "You've had a rotten attitude this entire trip. All I've heard is, 'Stupid this' and 'Stupid that'. Actually, it's stupid you. I don't think you should drive anymore. We're only fifty miles from home. I'll get Ma to do it."

I nodded, trembling, but too thankful to speak. I didn't want to drive that school bus anymore. I couldn't.

Pa parked the bus in a parking lot and telephoned Ma. I climbed into the dump truck and waited for him. He returned, his face haggard and white. "What am I going to do?" he cried. "It's all your fault. Now the police know we have no insurance on the vehicles. If it wasn't for that rotten attitude of yours, none of this would have happened. I should have beaten it out of you back at the Bradley's house."

I stared at him in horror. Would he start beating me again? I was an adult now. But in my head, I could already hear the swish of his leather belt as he pulled it off.

Yet, now at least it made sense. Pa could get into serious trouble, and it would be all my fault. Oh, how I didn't want that to happen.

Pa drove us back, and I sat hunched up against the dump truck door. I kept glancing over at him, hoping he would reach over and show me a little kindness. But no. I would have to wait till we got home. At least Ma would show she understood, push back my hair, and say it was alright.

We drove through the gate and I jumped from the dump truck. I ran to Ma with my arms outstretched. But she pushed me aside. She didn't even look at me. She hastened toward Pa, tears running down her cheeks. She hugged and kissed him again and again. "You're home, my darling! You're home!" she sobbed.

I stood there watching them. Didn't I matter? But at that moment arms slipped around my waist. I twisted to look, and Jana laughed as I did. "You've lost weight, Toma. You're really skinny now. Or maybe, I just haven't hugged you enough."

I smiled and hugged her back. At least she was happy to see me, the person I had hurt most in my life. My brothers and sisters joined her as well, one big mass of arms and laughs. I laughed as well, overcome with joy.

But then Pa called over to us. "I'm taking Ma to get the bus. Toma, you're in charge, even though you don't deserve it."

"Yes, Pa."

The next day an insurance company rang Pa, and he recounted the conversation to us immediately, a broad grin on his face. "The insurance company says the other party is guilty. They say the man should have seen the school bus, and, whichever way they looked at it, he was at fault. And actually, it didn't matter what the school bus was carrying. As a result, they will overlook our lack of insurance and send us $600 for the car. All we have to do is make sure we get insurance as soon as possible." Pa laughed. "God is so good to us."

"We prayed for $600," Ma exclaimed. "Now we can celebrate Christmas and buy what we need. I am tired of cabbage soup." Pa hugged and kissed Ma, and Ma turned pink.

But Pa refused to talk with me, except for curt instructions now and then. He even left the room when I came in, and after a week of this kind of rejection, I couldn't take it anymore. I had to make peace. I had to apologize. Wasn't it correct that peace was more important than truth? Being accepted more important than justice? I would tell Pa I had done wrong, even though I knew I hadn't.

I hurried to the living room, where Pa and Ma sat having coffee. Both were chuckling over some private joke, but when Pa looked up, he scowled. That didn't put me off.

I took a deep breath. "Pa, you were right. You should have beaten me. The accident was my fault. If it wasn't for my rotten attitude, it wouldn't have happened. I'm sorry I was so selfish."

Pa nodded, his face clearing. "I'm surprised you finally agree. I didn't think you had it in you. You have been very difficult this past month, and you gave me quite a fright with that accident. Thankfully, God turned it to good." Then he looked at Ma and raised his eyebrows, in that, "You see! I told you so," kind of way.

I stumbled from the room, suddenly feeling sick. What had I done? I had just sold myself to Pa for nothing. I, with my own words, had stripped myself of worth, of respect, of autonomy. I had just set Pa free of any guilt. And I did it to keep a false peace.

I had to get away. But where? I stumbled up into the woods and hid behind a tree. I slumped down into the rotting leaves, grasping my toes with their searing pain. I bowed my head, but no words came out. I prayed with tears instead. I was a slave, and now I knew it.

CHAPTER 9

Joel McKay, our neighbor visited again, bringing his wife this time. She didn't look anything like her husband. He was tall; she was short. He was thin; she was not. His eyes reflected peace, hers, impishness. She smiled, and dimples pulled in at her cheeks.

"This is Sally," Joel McKay said, and his eyes lingered on her. I could tell he loved her.

Ma smiled and drew her in. They sat on one sofa, Pa and Mr. McKay on the other. We girls sat with Ma. Mik and Filip with Pa. A little while later Pa called over to Ma. "Lila, Mr. McKay says our pasture is the best on the bench and that we should buy some cattle. He says there is a cattle auction in town every Saturday. I think I should go."

We all turned to look at him. This was something no one in the family had thought of before. Ma stared at Pa and her eyes grew big, but she nodded. "Sounds good, Linard."

The next Saturday morning Pa left early for the cattle auction. That afternoon he drove up the road, a cattle truck following behind. Karina opened the gate, and the driver and Pa drove straight into the middle of our field. They lowered the ramp on the back of the truck.

I expected the cattle to step off quietly, but they shot out like bullets, bucking like crazy. They charged across the field, their tails in the air. "That's twenty critters," the driver said. "I hope your fences are in good shape."

We watched the brown and white cows disappear, but Pa didn't show any concern. "Everything is fine."

The man nodded and drove off. Only afterwards did Pa turn to us, a grimace on his face. "Find some hammers and nails. Check those fences right now. I should have thought of that before."

Karina and I followed the fence in one direction, Mik and Jana in the other. Ten minutes later Karina and I found a place where the barbed wire hung down to the ground. Wads of cattle hair hung from the barbs. We nailed it up and found Mik and Jana. "The fences are fine," Mik said, "but we only found five cows up in the woods."

Karina gasped. "We didn't find any! We need to tell Pa."

We dashed back to the house, and as we opened the sliding door, the bitter smell of coffee filled our noses. Pa was sitting on the couch, just taking a sip. But we didn't question why he wasn't out searching. We lined up before him like soldiers on duty. Mik gave him the report.

Pa listened, holding his cup in both hands. "Right. That makes fifteen cows missing. We still have three hours till dusk. Follow the tracks through the woods, and see if you can find them. I'll take the car and hunt down the road." He gulped down his coffee and strode out.

"Figures," Jana said, as soon as he had left. "He sits in the car. We do all the running." But none of us answered her. That was the way it was.

We headed outside, back to where we had nailed up the barbed wire. On the other side of the fence we found plenty of cow tracks, but they had split in two directions. Mik and Jana followed the ones that headed down toward a ravine, and Karina and I followed the ones that went straight up the mountain.

Karina and I followed them onto a trail cut into the side of the mountain. Now it was easy to see which way they went, and Karina set off jogging, following their tracks. I tried to keep up, but the pain in my toes held me back. I trotted instead, in a crooked kind of way, hoping that Karina would eventually slow down.

A mile later I finally caught up. Karina was standing at the edge of a field, looking at a man up ahead. He was gazing across the field at a large herd of cattle. We strode toward him. "Hello!" I called.

The man turned around. He had a toothpick between his teeth. He looked like a hillbilly, but he didn't dress like one. He had normal everyday work clothes on. "Lose ya critters?" he drawled.

I nodded. "Yes, sir! But we didn't get a good look at them. I know they're brown and white. They bolted from the truck as soon as we let them out."

"You buy them at auction?"

Karina and I nodded.

"Happens. They jump your fence?"

Again, we nodded.

He broke into a smile, and every crease in his face grew deep. "Happens. It always amazes me how them critters can jump."

Karina raised her hand, as if talking to a teacher. "They did lose a lot of hair on the barbed wire fence."

The man chuckled. "They always do and never learn... Are you them new folks that's just moved into Old Smith's house?" Again, we nodded.

The man pulled his toothpick from his mouth and beckoned for us to follow. He led us into the field, but then he stretched out his hand, with the toothpick still pressed between his fingers, and motioned for us to stop. He continued by himself. "Sook, Sook," he called as he walked in among the herd. The cattle twitched their ears and looked at him. They moved one way or the other when he touched them.

Karina and I watched mesmerized. "How does he do that?" whispered Karina.

"I don't know, but he sure is a professional."

A few minutes later the man headed in our direction with seven cattle in front of him. He grinned, the toothpick back in his mouth. "They all be yours. Head down yonder, the way you come. Turn left at the road and you'll be home."

We took his place behind our cattle and the man watched us, his eyes eagle sharp. We waved our arms and got them to move. "Sook, Sook," we called, just like he had. But the man shook his head. "They haven't an idea," I heard him say.

The cattle finally trotted in the direction we wanted, and it helped that old barbed wire fences ran along both sides of the track. At least it kept the cattle together. But at the road, Karina and I made a great discovery. Cattle can't tell the difference between right and left. Or, they're so smart they turn the wrong way on purpose.

Karina and I didn't know what to do. No matter how much we yelled, waved sticks in the air, or tried to get in front of them, they simply refused to listen. If it hadn't been for a car coming down the road, we would have lost those cattle again. The driver rolled down his window. "Need any help?" he called. "I'll drive behind them and get them to your gate."

It seemed like everyone knew who we were! I waved my arm in thanks. "We have to open it first," I called.

The driver waved back. "I'll drive real slow."

We cut through the woods and opened our gate. We positioned ourselves in the middle of the road on the opposite side, ready to guide our cattle in. But three of them charged past us, almost knocking us to the ground.

The car stopped again, this time by our gate. The man leaned his head out. "Go get them. I can wait."

We sprinted across the field to get ahead of the cattle. Halfway across something grabbed my ankle. It wouldn't let go. I saw white light and fell headlong into the thigh-high grass. Was there something evil lurking down there, pulling me into the earth? I shuddered, but I had to find out. I crawled to the place where I had fallen and pulled the grass apart. It was a mole hole.

I didn't even bother to look at my ankle. Karina still needed help. I pulled myself up and climbed over the fence, waving my arms with Karina. The man climbed out. He called out, "Sook," and he guided them into our field.

Karina and I called out our thanks, and as we closed the gate Karina turned to me, a strange look on her face. "What happened to you, Toma? One second you were there, the next you weren't. It was spooky. I thought that devil stuff had made you disappear."

I pulled up my jean leg to look at my ankle. I gasped. It had already swollen double and turned purple and blue. I showed it to Karina. "It was a mole hole. There are mounds everywhere."

Karina took my arm. We walked side by side back to the house, and she slid the back door open for me. Pa greeted us, another cup of coffee raised to his lips. "Hi girls! Did you find any cows?"

Karina stayed behind to tell him the news, but I hobbled back to my room. I sat on the bed, pulled a box of scrap material from underneath, and tore an old pink sheet into strips. I wrapped the strips around my ankle, wincing with pain. When I finished, I inspected my frost-bitten toes. They too throbbed with constant pain. I almost laughed at the absurdity. Pain in my ankle. Pain in my toes. Pain in my heart. What did that make me? More than balanced. I was three-dimensional now.

Mik and Jana got home an hour later, and they sank onto the opposite couch, wiping sweat from their faces. "There was nothing," Mik said. "And when we found a field, we had no idea if any of the cattle were ours."

"Well, children, that's eight still missing. What a lot of money down the drain. I'll ask the neighbors what to do."

The next day Joel McKay dropped by and Pa told him the news. "It happens all the time," Mr. McKay replied. "I'll pass the word around."

A week later a cattle truck stopped at our gate and honked. Mik sprinted over to open it. I hobbled after him, from the new vegetable garden Pa had ploughed. "Got some critters in the back," the man called down. "Are you them folks that lost some?"

"Yes, sir," Mik said, and the man drove in. But the man didn't climb out when he stopped the truck. He just sat there, looking around.

Mik ran to get Pa, and when Pa finally arrived, the man opened his door and slowly eased himself out. He put his hands on his back and straightened up. Only then did he shake Pa's hand. "Howdy, there. Old Joel tells me you lost eight critters. When I first seen them in my field, with no identifying markings, I says to the wife, 'Wife, about time the Lord did us good. Ain't often he thinks of us.' Then old Joel comes and tells us the news. Tarnation. I thought it too good to be true." The man paused and grinned at Pa.

Pa pulled out his wallet. "I appreciate this. Let me pay you for the gas. That's the least I can do."

The man raised both hands, palms forward. "No, thanks! We be neighbors, even though we be seven miles apart." Pa smiled, and they lowered the ramp.

I expected a bullet of hooves and horns shooting from the trailer, instead the cattle ambled out. They sniffed at the grass and pulled at it with their lips. Pa joined me where I stood as the man drove off. "Toma, I'm putting you in charge of these cattle. When I was ten or eleven, I spent the whole summer looking after a farmer's cattle. I even gave them names."

I recoiled from Pa. Did he think I was still a child? Maybe he hoped I was. I pulled myself together. It was time to regain the dignity I had lost. "Pa, actually I want to get a job. I'm eighteen now. If it's alright with you, I would like to stay at home until I save up. I still want to be a doctor."

Pa smirked. "You foolish girl. What good do you think you would do as a doctor? No one would come to you. No. We fled from the world and I won't let you mix with it again. It is a wicked place out there, and bad things happen in hospitals. I'll take you to the feed store. They have books on how to care for cattle. I'll buy you what you need. If you want to study, learn about them." Pa then smiled at me friendly-like, patted me on the back, and turned back to the house.

I stared after him, speechless. I put my hands on my head and looked over at the mountains on the other side of the valley. *"What's wrong with me, God? Why can't I fight for myself?"*

The answer hit me like a punch in the gut. I had a character flaw, a strange one. I was always too nice and tolerant, to the point of ridiculousness. This was a vice, not a virtue. I always took anything that was slung at me and smiled a beautiful, "Thanks," in return.

I stared at cattle in front of me. I hated myself. I hated Pa. "I hate you too," I cried at them.

But Pa had bigger plans for me. A couple of weeks later he bought a milk cow. I learned to milk and how to make butter from the cream. A few months later Pa announced that we needed even more cattle. But this time I didn't grimace, and it suddenly dawned on me - I liked those critters. They had become my friends.

Pa went to another auction and I couldn't wait to see what these new cattle looked like. I stood by the truck as they bolted out, all crazy-like. I inspected them one by one. "Look, Pa!" I said, pointing to a black one with huge white udders. "She might make a good milker."

Pa smiled. "See what you can do."

So, I gave the cow that afternoon to settle, and when she looked calm, I tiptoed up behind her with a rope. She sensed me and backed away, kicking her heels in the air. She ran to the other end of the field, her huge udders swaying wildly from side to side. I tried again, this time bribing her with feed. "Come on, Blackie," I cooed. But the cow shook her head and bolted again.

Mik sat watching me from the porch, whittling a piece of wood. He stood up and cupped his hands around his mouth. "Hey! Toma! She's full of energy. Chase her around the field and get her tired. Then you can catch her."

"Good idea!" I called back. "How about helping me?" Mik closed his pocketknife and dashed across the field, leaping and whooping as he came.

I handed him the rope. "You chase her first. I'll get Jana. We can take turns."

Mik charged after Blackie and she pranced away, head held high, eyes half closed, as if she was the one in control. Ten minutes later Mik flopped down, red-faced and puffing, his crew cut matted down with sweat. But Blackie ambled off to eat some grass.

I took over, and then Jana. Each of us did a ten-minute stint and then we collapsed. "Mik, your turn again," I panted.

But as Mik hauled himself up, I noticed Pa standing at the living room window. He sauntered outside. "Stay where you are," he called. "I have an idea."

A minute later we heard the roar of his motorcycle, and he sped around the corner of the house. "Clever Pa," said Mik, and he sat down to rest. But Blackie took one look at Pa speeding toward her, and her eyes grew big, her tail rose into the air. She fled to the other end of the field.

Pa shot past us, a wild grin on his face. He chased Blackie several times around the field, tooting his horn every time he passed us. But suddenly, with no warning at all, his bike flipped over. He somersaulted through the air and landed in a heap. Jana screamed. I stared. Was this more devil stuff, wanting to get rid of our Pa?

We rushed over and gathered around as he lay face down in the grass. He groaned and rolled over, his face white. He lifted his hand. His index finger pointed out sideways at right angle to his hand. "I think it's dislocated," he moaned.

My stomach churned. "What are we going to do?" I cried. "Where is the hospital?" But then I stopped. What was I thinking, wanting to be a doctor? I couldn't even cope with a dislocated finger. Pa was right. I really did have delusions of grandeur.

Pa grabbed his finger with his other hand. "I can do it myself," he panted. He gritted his teeth. He pulled at his finger, his arm muscles bulging. He cried out in pain as it popped into place, and his body trembled from the shock.

I, too, had trembled plenty of times in front of Pa, and he had always acted as if it was amusing. But now that I stood at the other end, it wasn't funny at all. I stared at Pa, sensing his pain, and a thought popped into my mind... If Pa could get hurt, that meant he was mortal. If he was mortal, he wouldn't live forever. If he wouldn't live forever, he wasn't a god, even though he acted like one. I shuddered at this unexpected revelation, but I didn't know what to do with it.

Mik and Jana picked up the motorcycle. The front wheel and fork had buckled in half. Pa must have driven into an especially big mole hole. "I'll be alright," Pa said. "Don't give up on that cow."

Mik and Jana put down the bike, but they hesitated. "Go on!" Pa said.

They took off sprinting and I joined them. I had to get away. Pa was wrong to demand utter allegiance. I was equally wrong to give it. But once I had given it, how could I retract it? *"Help me, God,"* I cried.

Only a few minutes later, Blackie finally limped to a stop. I crept up behind her and slipped the rope around her neck. She shook her head in protest but remained still. Everyone cheered and headed back to the house, pushing the motorcycle with them. But I stayed with Blackie and stroked her ears. "Looks like we're both in the same boat, old girl. We've both been caught, and don't know how to escape."

CHAPTER 10

An expensive red and white pickup pulled up to our gate. Mr. Redfern owned a farm about three miles from our house. I dropped my hoe in the potato patch and sprinted to the gate. "Hello, Mr. Redfern," I called as I unlatched it.

He looked down at me and smiled, a grey-haired man, with dark eyes and thin lips. "Is your Pa home?" I nodded, and Mr. Redfern drove up to the house. I went back to hoeing.

An hour later Pa and Mr. Redfern strolled out to the garden. "Toma," Pa called, "Mr. Redfern is going on vacation. He wants you to look after his cow. You can walk down on Tuesday morning."

I nodded, pleased to have a good reputation, and I didn't mind milking three cows for a week. But it did seem odd to me. He had a neighbor next door. Why was he asking me?

Tuesday came, and I walked across to his farm. Everyone knew that if you transported a lactating cow, she could very well lose her milk. The best way to get her from one place to another was to lead her there by foot.

I approached the old wooden farm house and saw a brown Jersey cow tethered to the front porch. I patted her head and stroked her sides, and, like an old pro, I examined her udders. She was practically dry. Her udders were tiny and shriveled up, just like an old, dried-out apple. Why did Mr. Redfern want me to milk her? "Well, old lady," I said, shaking my head, "I wonder how much milk you will produce."

Mr. Redfern came out at the sound of my voice, smiled, and

introduced me to his cow. "This is Dorothy. Thanks for helping me out." He seemed pleased, and I could only assume he couldn't wait to go. Farmers hardly ever got a chance to rest. He untied the tether and handed it to me. "I'm sure you'll get along just fine."

I smiled and took hold of the rope. "We will, Mr. Redfern. Have a nice vacation."

Two hours later I let Dorothy loose in our field, and that evening I strolled out to get her for milking. I looked out across the bench as I crossed the field and noticed a strange car drive up the road. I wondered who it was. A man, was all I knew. But at that instance something surged through my body, something I had never felt before, a tingling sensation, a hunger, a drive. I suddenly wanted to be with that man, more than anything in the world. I wanted him to hold me. The suddenness and intensity almost knocked me off my feet.

I stopped in the middle of the field, watching the car pass by. My hands hung limp by my side. *"What just happened to me, God?"*

I looked around me, uncertain if it was real. But my pounding heart told me otherwise. *"God, this isn't love. This is lust, passion, all mixed up. I hate it. Take it away."* But nothing happened, and my heart still pounded.

I led Dorothy up to the milking shed, grabbed my milking stool, sat down, and leaned my head against her side. After washing her udders, I tried to coax out some milk, but all I could get was a few short squirts. I looked at the dribble in the bottom of the bucket. It was lumpy, a sick yellow color, and I wanted to throw up. This just didn't make any sense. Dorothy could have stayed at her home.

I let her loose, walked up into the woods, and poured out the milk behind a tree. It oozed through the leaves and disappeared, leaving yellow flecks on top. But as I stood there, I vaguely remembered reading something in my Bible that morning. I had even underlined it.

I ran to my room and read it. It said, "Satan rose up against Israel and incited..."[d] It had sparked a thought that morning that Satan was still busy, and he stood up against believers to incite them to self-destruction. And, if he could break them and get them to sin, he had won another battle against God.

I reeled at the verse. I had been warned in advance. The devil was trying to destroy me, make me impure, do things that were wrong. He wanted to ruin my life. But how did one fight the devil? How did one fight against lust? I didn't know.

Suddenly, another wave of emotion hit me, this time even stronger. I wanted to collapse, but I was already kneeling on the floor by my bed. Then I remembered how Pa and Ma had booted the ghost from our attic. Maybe I could do the same. I bowed my head and stared at my hands. *"Dear God, please take that evil spirit away. I ask it in Jesus' name."*

I waited, but nothing happened. I waited some more, but my heart still pounded, just as strong. *"Alright, God. Maybe you want me to do something about it. I'll pray more each day. I'll read the Bible more. I'll think about you even more. I'll fill my mind, so there is no room for evil."*

Two days passed, and nothing changed, even though I had done everything I promised. The car drove by again, and the passion inside me grew stronger. I didn't think it was humanly possible. I had to find help.

Could Pa and Ma? They might not react so well, especially with me falling in love with a stranger, a native. Maybe Jana? She would think me crazy… Grandpa and Grandma? I would never be able to get to the phone… There was no one else.

Every day I fought those feelings. But by Saturday morning I had no more strength, no hope, just darkness. *"God, I can't hold out anymore,"* I cried. *"I'm really scared. Help me, please."*

I ran out into the field, just as the first rays of sun touched the mountains. Maybe if I ran fast enough, I could outrun the devil. That's what the cows did to escape pesky flies, and the devil sure was a pesky one. But I stopped mid-field, panting for breath. It hadn't work, and neither had I expected it to.

I held out my arms like a drowning girl, reaching out toward the rising sun. I whispered my parting words. *"JESUS!"*

Suddenly, like an on/off switch, the passion vaporized. It was totally gone! I stood there, my arms still in the air, and my heart still. I looked around me, stunned. *"God! What just happened?"*

I drew a deep breath and ran over to Dorothy. I guided her up to the milking shed. How could something so strong suddenly go? How could passion turn off like that? And where did that evil ever come from? Would I ever find out?

The following Tuesday, Mr. Redfern arrived for the cow, but he came with his cattle truck! Something fishy was going on, and he proved it even further by not asking me how it went. He didn't care about Dorothy's milk. He chatted with Pa and Ma instead.

I turned away and headed out to the field, to bring Dorothy back to his truck. Suddenly I heard Mr. Redfern call my name. I turned and waited for him to catch up. He smiled, a strange brightness in his eyes, and he asked me only one question. "Did something special happen to you this week?"

I stared at him. How did he know? I hadn't told anyone about my struggle. Suddenly I understood. He wanted me to get married. He had compassion on me and saw that I was a prisoner in my father's house. His hex would have made me fall in love with the first stranger I saw. But I didn't want that kind of help. I wanted my first love to be real.

I pulled away and pretended I didn't understand. "Dorothy is a nice cow. Not much milk though." The gleam in Mr. Redfern's eyes disappeared. He turned and walked away without another word.

Now, I had to get away, and I hurried to the bottom of the field. I hid behind a pile of earth, making myself as small as possible. Then I remembered a book I had read. It had said evil spirits could travel in cows and cats. Dorothy must have been sent carrying a love hex.

I could barely breathe at the horror of that truth. But then a different scenario played out in my mind… What if that evil had jumped onto one of my siblings? How would they have coped? I almost didn't, and my heart suddenly filled with gratitude. *"God, thank you that it was me, not them."*

I stood up, finally calm, and hurried over to Dorothy. I led her to the truck and tethered her there. I stroked her soft brown ears and whispered in her ear. "Good bye, old girl. It wasn't your fault."

I watched as Mr. Redfern pulled Dorothy up into his truck. He drove away without acknowledging me. But then he looked back as he turned out of the drive, confusion and wonder on his face. I knew just what was going on inside his head. "How could that girl resist my magic? Where did she find the strength?"

But it often seems that the result of trauma is a clarity of mind. Now, I could see that I had to get away with more urgency than ever before. Not only was my home life destroying me, the pain in my chest increasing with every month, but the mountain was dangerous as well. I had to escape before it was too late. Yet if I went to Grandma and Grandpa's, Pa would certainly find me there. Helen was the only safe place. She wouldn't give in and reveal where I was.

I wrote to her, asking if I could stay, and early the next morning before anyone awoke, I took a stamp and envelope from Pa's desk. I waited for the mailman to come up the mountain. When I saw him, I ran to the gate and put the letter in his hand. Every day after that I ran to the mailbox, making sure I was the first one there. There was no way I wanted Pa or Ma to discover my plan.

Two weeks later I received a reply, and I tore the letter open on the spot. "Come right now," Helen wrote. I grasped the letter to my chest. Now I could plan my escape.

Ma had the only suitcase in the family, and I didn't want to ask her if I could have it. There was no doubt she would ask me questions. Instead, I hid a small cardboard box under my bed. I would use it for travelling, carry it under my arm.

Every day I took something different from the house, a towel, a washcloth, a bar of soap… But there was one thing I didn't know how to solve, find the money for the bus ticket. *"God, please!"* I prayed. *"Please can you do a miracle."*

A few days later another letter arrived. Grandma had written to me. I stood by the mailbox and tore it open, hoping to find $20 inside. She sent a recipe instead, with delicate red flowers printed on the side. I turned toward the house, wanting to cry. But then another idea popped into my head. I was going about it all the wrong way. I had to find the money myself!

Mik had once found $20 in a ditch. Maybe the same could happen to me. I searched the road for miles every evening, but after a week I only found a penny. What good was a penny for the trip? *"Why aren't you helping me, God? Can't you see I have to leave? Can't you see how I am dying here?"*

I ran inside. What was I going to do now? Another idea came to mind. Maybe God himself could show me exactly what to do. At lunch break the next day I sat on the porch. I rested my Bible on my knees. I listened to the emptiness around me. The quiet breeze in the trees.

Birds diving in silence as they chased after insects. Billowy clouds moving north without a noise… A question presented itself to me. I didn't like it. I pushed it away, but it kept coming back.

"Toma," it said, "why are you miserable? You keep blaming Pa and Ma for everything sad in your life. But the pain they inflict doesn't add up to the pain in your heart. The pain inside you is much bigger. And Pa and Ma aren't actually that horrid. They give you food and drink. They give you a clean bed and clothes. They don't lock you up in a dark cupboard. Why are you so miserable?"

I didn't know the answer. Maybe the Bible could tell me. I opened to the last place I had been reading. My eyes fell on the next verse. "You are not restrained by us, but you are restrained in your own affections."[c]

I stopped and stared at the verse. I read it again, and again. Was this implying that I had imprisoned myself, that I was the one holding myself back? My affections in life, what I wanted out of life, those had become my prison?

I slammed the Bible shut and jumped to my feet. I looked up at the sky. *"God, are you saying it isn't Pa or Ma after all? It's me! This is pretty hard to take."*

I went through my affections one by one, of wanting to see my friends from high school, of still wanting to be a doctor and having a proper boyfriend, of wanting to be safe, and escaping from Pa and Ma. That verse was right. These things really did hold me captive.

"God, I have been blaming the wrong people the whole time. I had thought Pa and Ma should make me happy. I thought it was them who should set me free. I'm sorry for getting it wrong. I want to be free to follow you."

That evening I took the first step. I gathered together everything that reminded me of my affections, photos of friends, gifts, my bronze trophy for being the top science student in high school. I pushed them into my pockets and meandered outside. I had to bury them somewhere, like a corpse.

I found an old hole that Pa had dug to try and build a well. "Goodbye," I whispered, and threw my affections in. They landed at the bottom, about six feet down. *"God, there goes everything that was precious to me,"* I prayed. I quickly covered them with clumps of earth, before I could change my mind.

The next morning, out of the blue, Pa decided to fill in the hole with his backhoe. I watched him bury my affections under six feet of soil. It was just like a proper grave. There was no turning back.

That evening I wrote to Helen again, and told her I had changed my mind. I told her about the verse and how I had put God first. But this time my heart filled with dread. What if Helen didn't want to write to me anymore? What if she didn't want to be friends with a religious freak? After all, I was the one who had done all the changing.

I checked the mailbox every day after that. But the weeks wore on, and my fears increased. I figured I would never hear from her again. Why did being a Christian have to cost so much? Why couldn't some parts be easy?

A full month later I received a letter, and my hands trembled as I tore it open. Helen sounded happy for me. But I slumped down on the grass by the side of the road all the same. I bowed my head, pressing the letter to my chest. I could trust my friend. Could I trust God? I loved him, but I was also perishing. If God was going to be my boss again, I had to know that he had my back. There was no doubt he would probably let me experience other near-death situations, as he already had, but would he get me through EVERY time? I didn't know.

I sat there for quite a while, staring down the deserted road. Not a car or truck could be heard anywhere. I picked up a stone and threw it. It bounced along and landed at the side of the road. I threw another one and watched it roll to a stop. I sighed. I would just have to take that leap into the unknown, jump over the cliff, my arms outstretched. I would be a lemming for God. If this was real, God would catch me with his parachute, land me safe at the bottom. *Well, God… I'm yours… For better or for worse.*

CHAPTER 11

One Saturday afternoon, Mik found me by the pond, filling two five-gallon buckets for the garden. "Hey, Toma. I saw Reggie today. You know, that hermit down in the valley."

"You what?" I said, turning to look at him, spilling some of the water. "Are you crazy? He shoots people."

Mik grabbed one of the buckets and helped me carry it to the garden. "Reggie's a really nice guy," he said. "People don't like him because he's different."

"Mik! Different doesn't mean safe."

"I know, Toma. But can you come with me tomorrow and play the guitar for him? He said he would like a church service on Sunday. I think he's a Christian and I know you're serious about God."

I set down my bucket and looked at him, taken aback. "How do you know that? I haven't told anyone anything."

"You read the Bible and pray. And you've changed a lot. You're happy."

If that was the case, I had become a good actress. Trusting God wasn't an easy business. But I was glad my sadness didn't show. Who liked living with a miserable toad? "Alright, Mik. But if there is a stitch of trouble, I'm out."

Mik grinned. "He used to go to church, but he hasn't been off his property in forty years. I don't think people understand him. He only shoots his gun in the air to scare off the kids who tease him."

The picture of Reggie shooting his gun like that didn't comfort me. What if he tripped? But what concerned me most was the forty years. How could he not leave his property in all those years? Reggie was a prisoner, if ever there was one. Compared to him I had nothing to complain about!

That next afternoon I packed my guitar and three hymn books, and Mik and I set off down the road. "How did you find him, Mik?"

"Have you noticed that strange car drive up the mountain and leave two hours later?"

I nodded and gulped. We knew everyone who lived on our mountain, and strangers hardly ever ventured up. "Well, I followed him, to see where he was going. He parked his car down the road and took some groceries from the trunk. He put them into a backpack and headed down the hill. I didn't follow him because he might have spotted me. But when he left, I hunted around, trying to find a marker or something. The man had to know where to stop. Finally, I spotted it about two yards up, a notch in a tree. I waited about two hours, until he came back. Then I hiked down myself."

"The grocery man wasn't carrying a gun, was he?"

"No. But the notches were pretty hard to find. It took me a long time to get down. Then I noticed smoke and saw a shack. I could hear someone talking. I thought two people might live there. But this old man came around the corner, talking to himself."

Mik stopped speaking and pointed to a tree on the side of the road. I looked up at a notch, then followed him down a path I could barely make out. We wove between the rocks and trees in single file, and Mik told me the rest of the story, calling back to me as we walked along. "I saw Reggie's gun leaning against the house and decided it was now or never. I knew he couldn't run to get it. I walked out into the open and said, 'Hello!'"

"You didn't!" I cried, interrupting him.

"Yup. Reggie almost jumped out of his skin. I told him I lived up on the mountain, and if he didn't mind, I would like to visit with him. He said, 'Does the whole world have to turn up on one day?' I took that to be a 'yes.'"

I laughed. "Imagine two people turning up on one day and that being a crowd. I wonder what he will say when I show up."

Mik grinned. "A multitude, probably. Anyway, Reggie wanted you to come."

"What? Have you been talking about me?"

"No. He asked if I had a sister, that's all. He hasn't seen a proper girl in forty years. He said his sister came down about fifteen years ago, but she doesn't count."

"Thanks for not sharing that bit of information, Mik. I wouldn't have come if I had known."

"I thought you might say that. Don't worry. You won't regret it."

We kept on clambering down the mountainside, scrambling over fallen trees. But I kept a look out for poisonous snakes, and I never lifted my eyes from where I put my feet. It was a habit that came out of knowledge. One of our neighbors lost some fingers from a snake bite, another had a big hole in his leg. Everyone took snakes seriously.

An hour later we stepped into a meadow. Bright yellow daffodils grew in the middle, in a straight row. That could only mean that there once had been a homestead, and those flowers had been planted there on purpose. I hastened over to look for foundations and spent a few minutes searching. But there was nothing left, not even a chimney stack.

I stood by the daffodils and listened to the silence. I could almost hear the laughter of children, the sighs and tears of their parents as they tried to survive in that valley. Later I discovered that eleven children had been born there, and, for all their efforts, the only thing left was their flower bed.

"Come on, Toma," Mik called. "We're almost there. No talking now. I don't want to spook old Reggie."

I nodded and followed Mik into stillness. A few minutes later, I noticed the scent of smoke. A minute later I spied a wooden shack between trees, perched on two-foot-high posts. On the other side of the shack ran a brook and whoever had built it knew the brook must flood. The shack itself looked like it hadn't been painted in decades, yet, it still had bits of white paint caught in the cracks.

Mik stopped, and I almost bumped into him. "Hello, Reggie!" he called. "Mik, here. I brought my sister."

I heard a grunt and a shuffling sound. A few seconds later a man's head appeared around the corner of the shack, but only four feet from the ground. His white hair looked like it had been hacked off with dull scissors and stood in every direction. When the rest of him appeared, I gasped. Reggie was bent over double at the waist, like an upside-down capital letter "L." He shuffled toward us in a wrinkled flannel shirt and jeans that hung around him like a sack. He held his arms straight back to keep himself balanced.

Mik approached him one slow step at a time, his hand outstretched, as if Reggie might fly away like a wild bird. I followed in Mik's shadow, only a foot behind him. "Good to see you," Mik called. "Remember, I promised to bring my sister. Well, here she is. Her name is Toma."

If Mik could feel safe with that hermit, maybe I could too. I stepped out from hiding, and Reggie reached up a filthy, wrinkled hand, with long broken nails that looked like claws. At the same time the other hand moved even further back, to keep him balanced. I shook his hand, and his grip was firm. I had expected it to be weak. There was more to this man than met the eye.

"Pleased to meet you," Reggie rasped, and he lifted his head sideways to look up at me.

I stared into his face and almost took a step back. Only one eye looked up at me; the other one stared at the ground. He looked like a nightmare. Now I understood why people feared him and spread all kinds of rumors around. "Good to meet you too," I rasped.

Mik bent down and looked Reggie full in the face, as if they were good friends. "We've come to sing some songs, Reggie. Would you like that?"

Reggie grunted and motioned with his arm for us to follow him. He moved to the shade of a persimmon tree, and as we passed his open front door, I glanced in. Against one wall stood a rusted metal bed with quilts so old they had shredded, in the opposite corner a dented black woodstove, beside it a wooden chair. But there was something odd about the walls. They seemed to shift and change color.

I took a step closer to study it. I almost gasped out loud. Thousands of ticks swarmed in crazy busyness on the walls!

Reggie grunted again and I turned back toward him. He patted some blocks of wood that had been placed in a semicircle and turned upright like seats. He cleared his throat, coughing up phlegm. "Here."

I smiled a 'thanks,' but waited for him to sit down. I chose the block furthest from him. I didn't want any of his ticks jumping across to me.

Reggie turned his head sideways, like a bird. His one looking-ahead eye following every movement I made, as I unbuckled the guitar case, took out my instrument, and tuned it. Mik handed him a songbook, but he pushed it back. "You choose," he rasped.

I flicked through the hymnal and found a song. "How about 'There Shall Be Showers of Blessing'? That's been around a long time."

Mik nodded, and I strummed some chords. But as we sang Reggie bowed his head instead, as if he was praying. Had the music somehow upset him? His throat and mouth contorted in strange, quick jerks, and I heard a rumble come up from his chest. He suddenly lifted his head wolf-like, and howled, not in agony, but singing the words.

"Sh*ooowww*ers of blessing,

Sh*ooowww*ers of blessing we need.

Mercy drops round us are falling,

But for the sh*ooowww*ers we plead."

I marveled. "Reggie, you know the song!"

He cleared his throat again. "Used to be a choir boy. Haven't sung in years."

Mik read a chapter from the Bible; we sang two more songs, and Mik announced that he would pray. Reggie reached for an imaginary cap, and then he grew still. I glanced up at him and noticed tears running down his cheeks, and for a split second something flickered in his eyes. It was so beautiful, so beyond the word "beauty," it startled me. What had I seen? A light? A sparkle? Or was it Reggie's soul, that part of him reaching out to God? I stared at him, forgetting that Mik was praying.

I had often wondered what made someone beautiful. Was it the angle of their nose? The cut of their chin? But Reggie had just shown me the truth. A twisted and crippled body couldn't hinder real beauty, because beauty wasn't just a physical thing. I had heard people say that, "beauty is in the eye of the beholder." But maybe they should have said, "Beauty is within each one of us."

I sighed. When I looked at myself in the mirror, I saw a plain country bumpkin, a girl with no physical beauty or charm. I saw a nobody, a little dead bug on its back in a corner. Its stiff crooked legs sticking up in the air. Maybe with God living inside me, there was a hope.

I put the guitar back into its case, and, as we rose to leave, Reggie rose too. "Come again, Mik, and bring your sister. Do you have any more?"

Mik smiled. "I do."

"Bring them all."

We laughed, but once we were out of earshot, I turned to Mik. "What happened to Reggie, to make him bent over like that?"

"I did ask him, but I think he only told me part of the story. He said he got hit on the head with a baseball bat. I think he got into a fight. Anyway, did you know he was born in that shack? He has never lived anywhere else, except when he stayed in the insane asylum."

"He isn't crazy, Mik."

"I know. That's what the doctors said, too."

The next Sunday Mik asked Jana and Karina to come. Reggie was waiting for us, and he had washed his hands. We sang more songs; Mik read the Bible and prayed. But as we stood up to leave, Reggie put out his arm, stopping us. "Bring your mother next time."

Ma came down a week later, and this time Reggie looked presentable, having wet his hair and combed it. The Sunday after he even shaved. The one after that he wore a clean shirt. I couldn't believe that a half-hour visit, once a week, could make such a difference to a person.

About that time Pa heard about a film that was being shown in a town about twenty miles away. We had seen it before when we lived in the old farmhouse back East, and Pa asked if we would like to see it again. We voted a unanimous "yes." It showed what might happen when Jesus came back and took every Christian up to heaven.

We drove to the place, and it was packed. Jana and I grinned at each other. But as soon as the film began, I could barely breathe. When it finished, I felt weak. The main character in the film had been left behind, because she hadn't asked Jesus into her heart. That got me thinking. Was I a proper Christian or was I deluding myself? How could I be sure I had fulfilled God's criteria? Was asking God to be my boss enough to get me to heaven? What if I got it wrong? What if when Jesus came, I was left behind?

I checked inside my heart. Did I believe in God? Yes! Was I sorry for what I had done wrong? Yes! Did I believe Jesus died for my sins? Yes! Had I asked Jesus to come into my heart? No! I did it right there on the spot as we walked back to the car.

That film must have put an unease in Pa as well. In family devotions Pa told us his concerns. His eye glistened with intense earnestness. "I have this feeling in my heart that the time is short. Jesus will be coming soon, and the Bible says there will be great tribulation. We Christians will be persecuted, even killed. I feel in my heart that we should move even further away from civilization. I'm thinking of South America."

Ma nodded. "Linard, if we are going to move there, we need to learn Spanish."

Pa rested his hand on Ma's knee. "You're absolutely right, Lila. God gave me a wise wife. I'll see what I can do. There might be something at the university in town."

Pa drove into town the next day. That afternoon he returned, grinning. "You won't believe it," he said. "I stopped at the university office to ask about Spanish classes. A lady happened to be walking by and overheard my conversation. It turns out she runs free classes in the evening. It starts tomorrow, and it happens once a week. I signed the family up." Pa beamed. "Now I know we should be going to South America. God is opening the doors."

"This is wonderful!" Ma bubbled. "But who will babysit? All of us older ones need to learn."

"I've thought about it. I'll stay home and take care of the little ones, and the rest of you can go. You can do the talking for me when we get to South America, and I will learn it bit by bit."

Ma laughed. "Thank you, Linard. It will be good to do some proper studying again."

I looked from Pa to Ma, confused. Wasn't this mixing with 'evil' people? But I wasn't going to say a word. Every time I had opened my mouth, it had backfired on me. Maybe, this was the first step in getting to a university. I bit my lip and hoped.

The next evening Jana and I worked hard to look nice. We combed our hair, polished our shoes and wore our best pants and blouses. I could barely suppress a smile as I climbed into the car. Even Ma laughed as she sat in the driver's seat.

She found the modern building on the university campus and parked the car by the front door. There was a sign taped to the glass, with an arrow pointing to the right. We followed that arrow, and others, until we came to a large room full of people.

"Hola," the teacher called out as we entered the room. "Come in and find a seat. We will be starting soon."

We sat in a circle and Jana squeezed my hand. "Isn't this fun?" she whispered. I squeezed it back and smiled.

The teacher told us her story, and then introduced a young man who would be her helper. I pulled out my notebook, with pencil poised. The lesson that evening would be a review for me, as I had already studied Spanish for three years in high school. I sighed with joy anyways. I was finally inside a university, sitting in a university classroom.

The next week we split into small groups, and the young man sat down beside me. He smiled and handed me the first handout. I glanced up at Ma, to see if she had noticed. Pa had warned us not to make friends, that we were there strictly on business. But Ma was in another group chatting to the teacher.

The following week the young man sat with me again, and this time he asked me about myself. I felt my face go hot, and I hung my head in shame. "I, um, live at home with my parents. Um. I'm helping them out on the farm."

At the end of the session the teacher came up to me. She paused, studied my face, smiling the whole while. "Toma, I'm taking a painting class, and I would like to paint your portrait. You could come to my house for sittings. It will probably take me several months."

I smiled. "Let me ask my parents." But an unease began to rise up inside my heart. This was going to backfire somehow.

The lady nodded. "Let me know what they say next week, and then we can arrange a time."

I mentioned it to Ma, but she didn't respond. Later that evening I asked Pa, and he looked from me to Ma, and then back to me. "No!" he said. "Art is of this world, and I don't want you corrupted by it. It would only turn your head. Also, I hear there's a boy in that class, and that you have been flirting with him. I will not have my daughter acting like that. We have to flee this evil world."

He turned to Ma. "I don't think any of you should go to those classes anymore. I shall call up and say you're not going."

Ma nodded. "I agree, Linard. The last thing we want is for our daughters to date worldly young men. And, no one child of mine will get singled out from the others. Why didn't the teacher ask to paint the other children as well? What's wrong with them? Anyway, I've learned enough of the basics to teach Spanish to the children myself. We can hold our own classes on Saturdays."

I gawked at Ma. She had betrayed me to Pa once again. How could she construe that answering a guy was flirting? Maybe she had seen my face go red. If she had asked me, I could have told her that it was because I had no story to share, no life or future of my own.

Pa kissed Ma on the lips, ignoring me. "This is what I like about you, Lila. Resourcefulness."

I stumbled to my room and slumped on the bed. Why had I opened my big mouth again? Why hadn't I said, "no," to that teacher? I looked over at Jana, stretched out on her side of the bed. "I blew it, Jana. Pa won't let us go to the Spanish classes anymore."

I thought Jana might get angry with me, but she just shrugged her shoulders. "He's punishing us, Toma. Every time a guy talks to us, Pa pulls out his double-barreled shotgun. Then he expects us to thank him for driving off spineless suitors."

I laughed, and then I sighed. "I wonder if there will ever be a guy who will love us enough to fight for us."

Jana laughed. "Two guys, Toma. There's no way I'm sharing a husband with you!" Then she turned serious as well. "No one ever stopped Pa from seeing Ma. He did what he wanted. I feel like telling him that."

I shuddered. "Don't, Jana. Let's keep our heads down. We'll figure out how to get out of this alive."

"You call this alive?" Jana snapped. "We're not allowed to live."

I looked down at my hands and studied a deep cut on the tip of my finger. Why was God taking so long to come to the rescue? Every door to the outside world kept slamming shut. But maybe it didn't matter, with Jesus coming so soon.

CHAPTER 12

My brothers and sisters only had one more week of school, and I couldn't wait for summer vacation to start. I had worked hard rebuilding the house, helping Pa dig a well. But on top of that I had to cook supper each day, take care of the little ones each afternoon, and I took care of the one-acre vegetable garden. Maybe Pa could give me a break, tell my brothers and sisters to help.

Karina burst into the house after school that day. "Pa, my teacher told us that people came from monkeys. Is that true?"

I listened from the kitchen, peeling potatoes for supper. I raised my eyebrows. How was Pa going to respond? "Karina," he said, "it's a lie from the devil. The Bible says God created people. You just remember that."

Karina nodded, satisfied with the answer, and she ran outside to play. But afterwards I overheard Pa talking with Ma. "Lila, if they teach evolution in school, they deny that God exists. I thought that when we moved here, we would escape all this nonsense, but I see I was wrong. We must take the children out of school. You and I live protected here at home, but we are sending our children into corruption. I'm afraid it will destroy them.

Later, when I came in from milking, I found everyone sitting in the living room, waiting for me. "What's going on?"

Pa motioned with his hand. "Sit down, Toma. I want to make an announcement." I looked at him, and then at Jana. She shrugged her shoulders.

I hurried over and sat down on the hearth. Pa leaned back into the sofa, his legs stretched out before him, his Bible on his lap. "These are wicked times, my precious family. I sent you to school trusting you would learn what is true. Now I hear that this heresy called Evolution has reached into these mountains, and Karina tells me it is being taught in her class. Is that true for the rest of you?"

Jana and Mik nodded.

"Why didn't you tell me? It took your youngest sister to finally say something."

Mik raised his hand. "They do talk about it, Pa. But I know it's wrong. I let it go in one ear and out the other."

Pa listened, his face more serious than I had ever seen it. "My children, we moved here to escape evil and I have been sending you straight into it. I am sorry for that."

I had never heard Pa say "sorry," especially to his children. I stared at him, unable even to blink. A sense of reverence came over me, as if a miracle had happened. I could trust Pa now, and whatever decision he made, it would be good.

Pa continued. "The government says you must get an education, but that we can teach you at home. That is exactly what we will do. We will start our own school."

It sounded like a good idea and I nodded in agreement. "Who will teach it, Pa? I don't know of any Christian teachers around."

Pa smiled at me, his eyes twinkling. "Ma, you, Jana and me."

I drew in a sharp breath. Me a teacher? I worked hard enough already. I had to somehow dissuade him. "But, Pa, I don't know how to teach. People go to university to learn that."

Pa kept on smiling. "Toma, in the old days anyone who finished high school could teach, and you got straight A's. You are more than qualified. I think you should teach mathematics."

Boy, did that hurt! Pa had turned up his nose at my high school education, pulled me out against my will. Why was he bringing it up now? I had to think of another way to stop him. "Pa! I can't remember most of it. I did algebra three years go. Geometry, four."

"Don't worry, Toma. I will buy you books."

But this was all wrong. What kind of a school would we have? Pa had dropped out of university, saying he could never concentrate in class. Ma dropped out of university when she got married. Pa had made me drop out of high school. Now he was making my brothers and sisters dropouts as well.

"Will other kids come too?" Karina asked.

Pa beamed. "No. It will be just for us. You will stay at home and have school around the table."

"When will it start?" Jana asked, uncertainty in her voice.

"Tomorrow."

She gasped. "Tomorrow? But Pa, I graduate in a week. Please can't I finish."

Pa stared at her, his eyes stern. "All you have left are parties and those are evil. You are better off missing them."

Jana scrambled to her feet, disbelief and horror on her face. "But, Pa! I want to graduate!"

"Sit down, Jana! I can do what I want. I am your father, and don't you forget. The world will not set the standards and tell us what to do. God's ways are different. Do you hear?"

Jana dropped back down onto the couch, fighting back tears. But Mik leaned forwards, his elbows on his knees. "I want to be a mechanic, just like you, Pa. I don't need mathematics or science for that."

"That's my boy! Tomorrow I will take you all to your schools and tell the principals my plan. You can collect your things and say goodbye."

Jana lifted her hand, her eyes glistening with tears. "Please Pa! At least let me go to my graduation. I'll stay home until then."

Pa glared at her, but then his face softened. "Alright. It shouldn't do you much harm."

Jana tried not to smile, but her eyes sparkled through her tears. "Thanks, Pa."

Pa then turned to me, and tilted his head sideways, his face still looking soft. Jana must have put him into a good mood. "Toma, I want you to be my secretary. You did typing in high school. I will buy you a typewriter, so everything looks professional. We will incorporate this school and make it official. Then no one will bother us."

There he went again, bringing up my high school education. Couldn't he see he was hurting me? But Pa smiled at me and batted his eyes. What could I do, but give in. "Yes, sir."

The next day at 7:30am, Pa told the school bus driver the children were going to another school. At 8am they climbed into the car. Jana sat by the back window, looking out, holding back tears. By 8:45am they all tumbled back into the house, pushing their way in through the door.

I stood in the middle of the living room and watched them, overwhelmed. For the last two years I had lived in silence, doing jobs, staying out of Pa and Ma's way. I didn't know how to react to all this commotion. Pa did. He sat down on the couch and picked up his paper. "You start, Lila. I'll take over later."

Ma didn't even look at Pa. "That's fine, Linard." She cleared the picnic table, got some notebooks and pencils. "Alright, everyone," she called, "get changed. We'll start school right now."

Everyone hurried off, all except Jana. She stood before Ma. "What do you want me to do?" she asked.

"Get changed and sit at the table. You're still a student."

Jana's eyes grew big with horror. "I thought Pa said I was going to teach?"

But at that moment the rest of the children hurried back in, giggling, laughing, and shoving. I expected Ma to yell at them. Instead she thwacked a ruler on the table. "Silence! she said. "You will do as I say. You will respect me, just like you respected your teachers in school."

Everyone nodded and sat down instantly. Jana did too, but her face twisted in pain. She had to share a class with her younger brothers and sister. I couldn't think of anything more demeaning.

Ma reached for her Bible and set it on the table in front of her. She opened it up. "Our first lesson... the Bible. It's the most important book we can study."

I still stood there watching, still overwhelmed. Ma looked up at me. "What are you doing, Toma? You sit down too. You need to learn this."

I backed away from her. "I have to finish the hoeing."

"Hoeing can wait, girl. Sit down."

My mouth fell open. Why hadn't I fled the house? I glanced over at Pa to get some support, but he didn't look up. What was I supposed to do? Fight? But that would be disrespectful and a bad example to the younger ones. I sat down beside Karina, my face hot with humiliation.

Pa started clapping, slow and deliberate. He chuckled. "Bravo, Lila! You're a marvel. You really know how to keep these children under control. I don't think I will be needed. You're in charge from now on."

Ma's face went pale, and she said nothing in return. But every evening she studied her Bible, preparing a lesson for the next day. Every morning she smiled as she taught us what she had learned, outlines of the Bible, the Old Testament kings, and telling us which verses we had to memorize for that day. Every afternoon she rested, and we took over. I worked in the garden or did carpentry in the house. Jana looked after the little ones and tidied up. Mik helped Pa in the garage.

Finally, Pa bought a typewriter so I could make the school documents look official. One afternoon from his seat in the living room, he dictated to me what he wanted in the letter. I scribbled it down as fast as I could. He paused. "Toma, you should have taken shorthand in high school." Had he forgotten that I took classes to become a doctor, not a secretary? But I kept my mouth shut and kept on writing.

After we finished Pa turned around to where Ma sat at the picnic table with the younger children around her. "Lila, I think we should stop school for the summer. I want Mik to help me in the garage."

Ma sighed. "That's fine, Linard. When are you going to order us schoolbooks? I can't teach much longer without them."

"I'll get them soon. I used up the last of the cash to buy the typewriter. If Mik helps me rebuild the tractor, we can sell it sooner. Then I can buy your books."

"I can wait, Linard. Toma and Jana will need some too."

111

I marveled as I listened to their conversation. How had life turned so complicated? Pa took the kids out of school to educate them. But he had no money to do it. To educate them he had to pull them out of home school to get the money to do it. Would there ever be enough for books?

The next morning in family devotions Pa smiled at us. "I am pleased we can start a school. As soon as the paperwork comes through, we will be official. But there is one more thing we can do. I found some verses in the Bible for you girls."

My head jerked up. My heart skipped a beat. Pa was finally going to announce that Jana and I could get jobs and start saving up for university. He opened his Bible and read out the verse. "Every man who prays or prophecies with his head covered dishonors his head. But every woman who prays or prophecies with her head uncovered dishonors her head – it is the same as having her head shaved."

I couldn't take my eyes off Pa. What was he talking about? This wasn't supposed to be part of the plan. I wanted to go to university, not wear some stupid scarf!

But Pa put his Bible on his lap and kept on talking. "The Bible says that if a woman does not cover her head she should be shaved. I don't want that to happen to you girls. In family devotions and in church, you girls will wear head scarves."

Ma rose from her seat. "Linard! What are you talking about? I don't agree with you. That is a burden too heavy to carry."

I looked from Pa to Ma. Had I heard Pa right? Would he literally shave our heads? But then a movie came to mind. It had Ingrid Bergman in it, and she wore a scarf over her shoulders and head. The movie blurred her picture, making her look glamorous and soft. This scarf business might not be that warped an idea after all. Maybe a scarf would give me some elegance and how I craved elegance in my life. "I agree," I said. "If that's what the Bible says, let's do it."

Ma cried out in horror. "Girl, don't you ever know when to be quiet? We will be different. We will stand out."

Pa interrupted us. "Exactly! Toma's words encourage me. I have not talked over any of this with Ma, but I think you girls should look like girls as well. We must flee the worldliness around us. I don't want you wearing jeans anymore. The Bible says women should wear women's clothes, not men's. From now on you will wear dresses."

"What?" I babbled, trying my best to muster up a logical counter argument. "How can I milk a cow in a dress? How can I work in the garden or do carpentry? It's muddy and dirty everywhere."

Pa smirked. "If the Bible says it, you should do it. You just told me that, Toma."

I stared at him, speechless. I had been foolish enough to get caught up in my own fantasies. But, how could I fight the Bible? I loved it. I wanted to follow it with all my heart. But there was no one around to warn me that the thing which was most important to me could become my greatest vulnerability. No one cautioned me to stay away from those who used that vulnerability to gain control over me.

I fled to my room and Jana followed me in, her eyes snapping with anger. "Thanks a million, Toma! Look what you started."

I slumped onto the bed. I could never take back those words. "I'm sorry, Jana. I really am."

Ma burst in a few seconds later. "What were you thinking, girl? Do you always have to agree with Pa? You agreed about home schooling, about typing up the papers. Can't you keep your mouth shut? This time you have opened Pandora's Box, and I don't know if I can close it."

I pressed my hand hard to my chest, the pain pulsating again, but this time almost too much to bear. I didn't think I had that much sway in the family. I had messed up terribly and made things worse. "Sorry, Ma. I'm sorry."

Ma looked back at me as she turned to leave. "I'll try to talk some sense into Pa. Maybe he will relent."

A little while later I heard Ma, but Pa answered as I expected. "Lila, if we know that something is right, we must do it. We're not seeking praise from men, but from God."

That evening we girls made headscarves, cutting material into large squares, stitching up the edges. The next morning, we changed into skirts and nylons, and draped our expressions-of-obedience around our shoulders. I stared in the mirror at the piece of material. It looked like an ill-fitting tablecloth. We tromped into the living room, and Mik and Filip stared at us, sitting on the couches in their shorts and t-shirts.

113

Bemused smiles spread across their faces.

I reddened with shame, but Pa whooped with delight. "This is the way I like it, my girls looking like girls." He sat there grinning, surveying us from head to foot, as if it was a fashion show. "This is an important day," he said. "Let us begin with prayer."

He waited for us to sit down. He raised his eyebrows. That was our signal that we should cover our heads. I lifted my pale blue scarf, and then I helped Karina. But her scarf kept slipping off, and I could see frustration rising inside her.

I was the dumbest person ever to live. Why did I have to open my mouth? It was my fault Karina was suffering like this.

But Pa didn't seem to notice our struggles. He kept on smiling. "You look beautiful," he said.

Jana yanked at the scarf on her head, pulling it tight. "We're not doing this for you, Pa. We're doing it for God."

"That's right, Jana. But I can still enjoy your obedience to…"

"Linard, don't make us do this," Ma begged. "It is too much for us. Let us at least wear the small triangle scarves some women still wear. It will be more practical."

Pa's face hardened. "I don't care how you do it, Lila. Just make sure your heads are covered."

Ma took us girls shopping that afternoon. She bought us material and one dress pattern for us to share. That evening Jana and I cut out the pattern. We spread each on the cement floor. "We're going to look so ugly," whispered Jana.

I shrugged my shoulders. "That's the idea, I think."

Jana exploded, spattering spit in front of her. But no matter our feelings, we sewed those dresses and donned them three days later. I surveyed myself in the mirror. Big hazel eyes. A long thick braid hanging down over my shoulder. A bodice that fit snug around my waist. A long, gathered skirt that reached down to my ankles. I had changed from a modern teenager in jeans to a rustic pioneer from the 1800's. There was no way I could leave home looking like this. Forget about still wanting to become a doctor. Forget about running away.

I hurried outside to get Blackie for milking. The wind caught my skirt as I trudged across the field, and it billowed out like a tent. Blackie saw it and fled, only stopping when the fence barred her way. "Thanks for that honest evaluation," I called out to her.

I pulled my skirt tight around my legs and eventually Blackie followed me up to the milking shed. But when I sat on my stool, my skirt fell into the dirt. I tried holding it in one hand, but that made it impossible to milk. I tried throwing it over my shoulder, but it kept falling off. I tried holding it in my teeth, then tying it together with a piece of rope. Nothing worked, and Blackie turned her head, ears forward, looking back at me. Why wasn't I milking? "Sorry, Blackie," I groaned.

I finally found I could gather it up around my hips and fold it across my knees. It looked indecent, but I didn't care. No one could see me from the house. I grabbed the milk pail and squeezed the udders, watching the milk froth up in the pail... Something was wrong. Normal families didn't behave like this. Had we become a sect?

I hurried in from milking and found a dictionary on Pa's desk. I looked up the word. "Sect - A religious group regarded as extreme or heretical." I slammed the dictionary shut. *"No, God!"* I whispered. *"That's us!"*

CHAPTER 13

Autumn set in and with it the rain. The path to the outhouse turned muddy. During the day we could see where to go, but at nighttime we slipped and slid. After supper one evening, Ma sat down beside Pa. She put her hand on his arm, and he lowered his airplane magazine. "Linard, isn't it time we had a proper bathroom? Winter is coming."

"I suppose I could do something about it, Lila. But I'm broke. I haven't been able to sell the tractor Mik rebuilt. I could go to the bank and get a month-long loan. That would tide us over until it does."

Ma smiled, and early the next morning Pa drove into town. He got a $1,000 loan and bought what we needed to build a leaching field. I started working with him every morning, digging and leveling the field, laying down pipes. In the afternoons I taught. But two weeks later the tractor still hadn't sold, and Pa called a family meeting. "I have to find a $1,000 to pay back the bank. From this point on there will be no more school. We have to work and get that money."

I leaned forward. "But Pa, can't you return what you haven't spent? That would mean less to pay back."

"There's nothing left."

It didn't make sense. The leeching field only cost $200, food no more than a $100. Maybe the bills made it $400. What had Pa done with the rest? "Where did it go?" I asked.[3]

---

[33] Years later I found that Pa bought another Bellanca at that time.

Pa's nostrils flared. "None of your business." Then he turned to Mik. "I want you to start logging with me. Toma and Jana, I want you to bake bread. Ma can sell it at the Co-op. I will also sell some loads of gravel. One of our neighbors wants at least ten. If we get going now, we should just be able to do it."

Pa and Mik hurried outside, and I watched them through the kitchen window, as I kneaded bread. Pa clambered up the mountain, his chainsaw in one hand. Mik followed in a small rusty bulldozer, pulling at levers to steer a zigzag line.

The chainsaw sprang to life, and Pa headed for a tree. He cut a deep wedge, and then leaned against it. He pushed it with all his might. It slowly inched forward. It gathered speed. Crash! Branches splintered under its weight.

Pa revved his engine, cutting off the branches. Mik followed behind, pulling them away. Then Mik wound a chain around the trunk. He attached the other end to the back of the bulldozer. But Pa shouted something and ran over to Mik. He cuffed him hard and pushed him aside. Then he readjusted the chain.

All day long Pa treated Mik like this, and I watched from the kitchen window as Jana and I kneaded even more bread. Why did Pa have to be so angry? It wasn't our fault he couldn't pay his loan.

"Toma," Ma said, startling me. I expected her to shout, after all I had witnessed, but her voice was kind as she spoke. "I want you to make cottage cheese as well."

"Yes, Ma. But I don't know how."

She smiled as she spoke. "After you've milked this evening, I will show you what to do. I want to sell it at the Co-op."

I nodded. "For how much?"

"Seventy-five cents. Just like the bread."

I nodded again, even though it didn't make sense. How could bread and cottage cheese ever help meet a $1,000 debt? We might earn as much as a $150 in that time, that is, if everything sold.

We kept up the pace all day long. But in the evening, Pa kept on working. After he dismissed us, he started up his backhoe. He dug out bucket loads of gravel from the mountain behind the house and tipped the earth into his dump truck. The roar of his machinery echoed around the mountain. Then he drove off to deliver his load.

He always arrived back late in the night, with a wad of money in his greasy overall pocket. He would go to his desk, opened a draw and slide out a metal box. He unlocked it, slid the money in and locked it up again.

Pa did this every night, and on the seventh night he tipped the contents onto the picnic table. He counted it, and then looked up at us, his eyes wild. "We're not going to make it! Only a quarter is covered! We need to get those logs down to the sawmill. Mik, get dressed right now!"

Mik didn't answer. He trudged to his room and put his muddy work clothes back on. When he appeared a minute later, Pa pushed him out the door. "Get moving, boy!"

The two of them worked late into the night. The pickup and dump truck on either side of them, the motors idling, the headlights lighting up where they worked. When they finally came in Mik fled to his room, wiping away tears with his sleeve. I looked after him as he slid behind his curtained door. Pa had been after him, relentlessly. Maybe he would get over it by morning.

The next morning at breakfast, Mik was still pale. "Are you alright?" I asked. But he didn't answer.

Pa noticed our interchange. "Get your Bibles, everyone," he said. "I have a verse for you."

We pelted to our rooms in instant obedience, but Pa still glared at us as we took our seats. "Turn to 1 Samuel 15:23," he said.

We threw open our Bibles and found the verse. Pa read it, his voice firm and deliberate. "For rebellion is as the sin of witchcraft, and stubbornness is as iniquity and idolatry."[f] Pa looked up, making eye contact with each one of us. He spoke again, his voice louder. "Do you know what happened to witches in the Bible?"

I shuddered. I had just read about it in the Bible, and I raised my hand. "Pa, they were stoned!"

"That's right, girl. Witches were stoned, and it shows right here that rebellion gets the exact same punishment. I told you girls to work. All you have earned is $62. You have been lazing around. The money proves it!"

I sucked in my breath. His logic unhinged me. "Pa! Not all of the bread and cottage cheese are selling."

Pa leaned forward, pointing his finger at me. "This is what I am talking about! How dare you speak against me. The Bible calls this rebellion! Do you understand?"

I cowered before him. "Yes, Pa. I'm sorry."

He leaned back and narrowed his eyes. "Mik is working hard. I give him that much credit. But you girls… I'm disappointed. You will double the amount you make. I told you to produce."

"But, Pa, I already told you. Not all of it is selling."

Again, Pa shot forwards. "Rebellion in the ranks! This is witchcraft! Watch out, girl."

I visibly shook and shrank back into the couch. I stared at him in horror. *"No, God! This is wrong! Would he stone me for daring to speak? In the Bible, you call that murder."*

Pa then dismissed us and Jana and I fled to the kitchen. "Will he kill us?" Jana whispered.

"That's what he says."

"He's gone crazy, Toma. We're in big trouble now."

We worked like mad, keeping the quota Pa set. Mik worked like mad, keeping up with the trees Pa sawed down. But by the end of the day Mik still looked pale. Pa had been at him again and again. I wanted to ask, "Are you okay?" But I didn't dare.

Early the next morning, Pa's voice rang out, waking us up as usual. We gathered in the living room for Bible time. "Where is Mik?" Pa asked.

Silence.

"He must still be in bed, that lazy-head," Pa said. "Karina, go wake him up."

Karina leapt up from the couch and hurried off. "He isn't here," she called out a few seconds later. "He hasn't even slept in his bed."

All of us jumped up and sped to his room. We stared at his bed. His blanket lay on top, perfectly smooth, his pillow perfectly square.

Mik had never been that tidy. "Where is he?" we asked.

"Find him," Pa barked, and that shook us into action. We spread out in every direction, hunting in the woods, the attic. He might be hiding in the car. We couldn't find him anywhere.

We gathered in the living room, and Jana blinked back tears. "Mik must have run away," she said.

Ma rung her hands in agony. "Somebody! See if he took his clothes, and food." But Mik had taken nothing.

No longer could I hold myself together. I let out a wail. Jana and Karina joined me, and we cried out in unison. Pa had finally succeeded in breaking one of us. Mik was out there somewhere, alone and hungry, maybe even dead. "He's gone!" I sobbed.

Pa turned on us, his eyes wild. He pointed at us girls. "Get in the car," he yelled. "NOW! RUN!"

I jumped from the suddenness of his yell, yanked from grief to fear. We had just crossed the line, turned into wicked rebels. We shared the same fate as witches. There was no escaping our punishment now. PA WAS GOING TO EXECUTE US! Was there anyone out there who could rescue us?

Jana, Karina, and I ran to the car. We sat in the back seat, wide-eyed. Silent. Waiting. What would Pa do? Load his gun? Collect rocks to stone us? Get a rope to tie us and leave us in the woods? He showed up with keys in his hand.

"We must find that boy," he growled. "How dare he think he can run away? Keep your eyes open as we drive."

"Yes, Pa," we answered, the tension in our bodies visibly releasing.

We drove down narrow mountain roads, searching, calling until our voices grew hoarse. Three hours later Pa pulled over. He turned around, his eyes still blazing. "We've wasted enough time already! Karina, you will help Ma make bread. Toma, Jana, I want you outside. I had thought you girls shouldn't do heavy work, but in the old days everyone joined in."

"Can we change into jeans?" I asked.

"I can't believe it, girl!" Pa shouted, clenching his fists. "NO! Have you forgotten how rebels get punished?"

"Sorry, Pa. Sorry!" I begged, raising my hands to protect myself.

A half hour later we trooped into the house. Ma rose from the couch, her eyes puffy and red. "Did you find him?"

Pa didn't even look at her. "No."

Ma started sobbing into her hands. "My son. My son," she moaned. But Pa just turned and walked out the door. "Outside, girls! Get to work."

We dashed after Pa, and tucked our skirts into our belts, exposing our legs up to our thighs. We had to, even though it looked indecent. Experience had taught us that every time we bent down, we would trip over our skirts, catch them on branches. Pa pointed to the trees he had felled. "Roll those logs down to the trailer. Pile the branches."

We pulled away branches to make a clear path for the logs. But we couldn't roll them downhill. There were stumps everywhere. We found long metal poles instead and used them to lever each log, Jana at one end, me at the other. We finally managed and helped Pa load them onto the trailer with his backhoe. When we had finished, he jumped off. "I will take this load to the sawmill. You girls, get the next one ready."

We straightened up and wiped the sweat from our faces with the back of our arms. "Yes, Sir."

Finally, at dusk Pa let us go. We stumbled down the mountain to eat and wash. Our muscles ached. Blisters covered our hands. I slumped into bed as soon as I could, too tired to even pick up a book. "Toma, Jana, come here," Pa called, his voice harsh and urgent. "Right now."

We eased ourselves up and limped into the living room. Pa looked up from his usual place, still in his grubby overalls. A Bible lay open on his lap. I trembled inside. *"Oh God! What brutality has he planned for us now?"*

He eyed us up and down, at our crumpled flannel nightgowns, our damp hair and bare feet. I clasped my hands in front of me, hiding from his prying eyes. But his eyes crackled with anger. "I have every right to control you. Lot did. So can I."

I knew the story of selfish Lot, but Pa read part of it out to us anyways. It was about a mob of lustful men pounding on Lot's front door, wanting to rape his male guests. But Lot made a choice, a stinking choice. "Look," he told the mob, "I have two daughters who have never slept with a man. Let me bring them out to you and you can do what you like with them."g I hated Lot.

Pa jabbed his finger at the Bible. "You see?" he snarled. "I can do what I want with you two. You belong to me."

"Pa! No!" I cried, my voice shaking with fear. "It's only a story. It isn't a command."

"Are you questioning the Bible, girl? Everything it says is true. EVERYTHING. Do you hear? If Lot could do that to his daughters, I can too. You will do whatever I say."

I took a step back from him. "Please, no."

"You can't change the Bible, and don't try. Now, go!"

Jana and I fled to our room. My heart felt like it was being crushed. I glanced over at Jana. How was she taking Pa's sickening verdict? But it must have somehow gone over her head. Instead of crying, Jana slid under the covers and fell asleep. Had she not understood? Had she mercifully been blinded from the truth?

I hugged my knees close to my chest, staring out the window into blackness. *"God? Dear God? Pa is threatening to take our innocence. How could he even think of that? It's the most precious gift you have given us. He has no right. I can't just sit here and let him. Maybe I should kill myself..."*

I pressed my forehead hard into my knees. I rocked on the bed, barely able to breathe. But, God was the one who had given me life. It would be wrong to end it myself. Only God had that right. I squeezed my eyes shut. *"God, please kill me! Take me away before Pa hurts me."*

Nothing happened.

Maybe I could die like Jesus did on the cross. He cried out, "My God! My God, why have you forsaken me?" Then he let out his breath and gave up his spirit.

I hugged my knees tighter to my chest. Maybe it could work for me. *"God? Where are you? Why have you abandoned us?"* I breathed out my breath and held it out. I waited. Something inside me flickered out, just like a candle being snuffed out. Then everything went blank. Maybe I passed out.

The next day I woke up with the same deadness inside. I worked in

122

the woods, and even though the sky was perfectly clear, it felt like thick, dark fog. I couldn't see or feel the sun. That morning another word came to mind, "cult."

I looked up the word in the dictionary at lunch time. It said, "A religious group that uses devious psychological techniques to control its members." I stood there unable to move. Pa had just turned us into a cult. Was there anyone who could save us now? Negotiation was no longer an option.

I closed the dictionary in slow motion, put it back on the shelf. I shuddered with cold as I returned to the woods. I didn't speak with Jana as we worked side by side. I couldn't.

Two days later, as I headed out at dawn, Mik stood there just outside the back door, a rifle in his hand, a small backpack on his shoulders. He looked thinner than I had ever seen him, dark rings around his eyes. Neither of us smiled, and I unlocked the door. He stepped inside. I didn't speak, and he didn't seem to notice. "I'm hungry," he said.

I dropped the shiny aluminum milking pail and it clanged on the floor. I grabbed one of the loaves Ma had made for sale, cut it up, spread it with butter and jam. I didn't care about Pa's debt anymore. I didn't care if he murdered me. I handed the bread to Mik and passed him a glass of milk. I buttered another slice and watched him in silence. He ate in silence.

My siblings tumbled into the kitchen. They squealed with delight, threw their arms around Mik. "What's all this commotion?" Pa said, striding into the kitchen.

At the sound of his voice, everyone froze. Only then did Pa notice Mik. "You're back. It's about time."

Pa headed for the sliding door, as if nothing had happened. He paused in the doorway and turned around. He smiled, not at us, but at himself. "The loan is due in two days. I think I'll get an extension from the bank." He stepped outside, whistling, and shut the door.

I couldn't take it anymore. I ran to my room, buried my face in a blanket, put my fingers in my ears to block out his incessant whistling. The blanket grew damp around my face. I could feel something cracking inside. On the back of my eyelids, that blank white expanse shattered into jagged pieces. Was I going crazy? Was this how my life would end? But then in the distance I heard Karina call. "Toma, come. Pa wants us."

I stumbled to the living room and took a seat, just as Pa held up a wad of money. "I just sold the tractor," he said. "The man paid in cash. God provided for us in the nick of time, but I don't want the bank controlling us anymore. We must become more self-sufficient. Toma, you will stop teaching and plant more food. I will plough another acre of land..." I heard nothing more.

A few days later Pa ploughed up that acre at the bottom field. Mik and Karina helped me put in fence posts, to protect it from the cattle. But with two acres of garden and other chores, I could barely keep up with the work. Sometimes the children came out to help, but mostly I worked alone.

Six months later, as I watered tomatoes, lugging the five-gallon buckets up from the pond, I stopped to look up at the mountain behind me. Why I looked, I don't know. It was the first time in six months. I blinked my eyes as if waking up. I could see. I could smell. I could feel the sun.

Had I really been asleep all that time? Had it been a stupor? Whatever the case, I hadn't been off that mountain, or even off our property in all that time. Hadn't anyone noticed that I always stayed behind, that I hardly ever spoke?

How many words did I speak each day? I counted them up. "Good morning." "Good night." That made four. "Yes, Pa." "Yes, Ma." That made eight, and those I slurred and mumbled.

At dusk I slipped from the garden and walked down the driveway toward the gate. I looked up again into the darkening sky. *"God? Why didn't you take my life? Why am I still alive?"*

I opened the gate. SQUEAK. I shuddered and looked behind me. Had anyone heard I was leaving? I closed it behind me. SQUEAK. I turned right and dashed down the road. A few yards later I was hidden from the house by trees. I stopped and eyed the ditch, full of broken branches and rotting leaves. *"I'm already dead on the inside. Dear God, PLEASE let me die on the outside."*

No one passed me on the deserted road. No one would know

where I was. I stepped down into the ditch. It would make a good grave. Maybe God could make me faint, somehow collapse, and maybe I could die of exposure. I waited. Nothing happened.

Every evening I walked along that ditch. Every night I came back alive and read the same verse in the Bible. "'Comfort! Comfort my people!' says your God. 'Speak tenderly to Jerusalem.'"[h] Comfort? God speaking tenderly? That only happened in heaven. Why didn't God take me now? Why was he letting me suffer?

A week passed by, and still nothing happened. I turned the page in my Bible. Another verse caught my attention. "But those who hope in the Lord will renew their strength. They will soar on wings like eagles; they will run and not grow weary; they will walk and not be faint."[i]

Hope? Strength? These things didn't exist in my life. And as for running, I couldn't even crawl. I closed the Bible and stumbled outside, barefooted, and in my threadbare nightgown. I stood in the field, looking up at a full moon. *"God? You're asking the impossible. How can I hope when there is nothing to hope for?"*

"Run!" I heard someone call.

I looked around me, but there was no one. I didn't even recognize the voice. "Run!" it beckoned again.

Maybe it was God. Maybe he had just spoken. I had better run, just in case. I sprinted to the gate and back, then stopped. "Run," the voice called again.

This time I jogged, back and forth countless times, my chest heaving, hurting. Had I gone crazy? What if it wasn't God, just voices in my head? I slowed down. "Run!" the voice called again.

I picked up speed, but my legs didn't want to move. I made them anyway. I headed for the gate again, my chest feeling like it would burst. Maybe I could run myself to death. But, suddenly, for no reason at all, the pain vanished. My chest and legs stopped hurting. I could breathe.

"This is a second wind!" I whispered. That verse was about me. God didn't want me to die! He wanted me to keep running in life, even though I felt like giving up. That second wind would come soon enough, and I would get through it, soaring on wings.

I stopped running, and walked in huge circles, pulling at my night dress to cool myself off. Then it struck me. Even though Pa had

125

threatened me with murder and rape, he had never actually tried to harm me. He hadn't even come close. His words had only been words, horrible, manipulative words.

The moon disappeared behind a cloud, lining it with silver on all sides. A few minutes later it reappeared, and something flickered inside my heart like a flame being lit. I knew what it was. Hope.

CHAPTER 14

Winter came and the snowstorms in the mountains were especially harsh. No one could get on or off the mountain for days at a time, and to top it off we were running out of food. Almost everything I had grown in the vegetable plots had been eaten up.

Pa tried to sell a 6x6 he had bought, but nobody wanted to buy it. Why would they? It was a 1952 kaki green army truck with six wheels. Pa decided to sell our cattle instead. In between storms he sold some to a neighbor, and when the money ran out, he sold a few more. But he bought only enough food for a week. Soon all the beef cattle had gone and all we had left was Blackie, our milk cow.

"Please, don't sell her," I begged.

Pa scoffed. "I don't plan to. She gives us free food."

I sighed with relief, but not for long. Another snowstorm struck, an especially big one and I watched the store-bought food disappear. Soon all we had left was a half full, twenty-five-pound bag of flour. It wouldn't last long.

I marched up to Pa, where he sat with his airplane magazine. I stood in front of him, my arms folded across my chest. "Pa, we've run out of food. Even Blackie has hardly any feed left. She can't keep producing milk without it. We need to do something."

Pa looked up, his face unperturbed. "What do we have left in the house, Toma?"

I told him, and Pa nodded. "How much feed does Blackie still have?" he asked.

"A half a sack of bran, but the grain is almost gone."

Pa smiled. "Bring in the bran. You can mix it with the flour. That will stretch it out twice as long. Blackie can survive on grass."

I stared at Pa in horror. "That's cattle feed! We can't eat that."

"Oh, yes we can. God provides in mysterious ways."

"But Pa!"

"Get the bran, Toma. People are more important than animals."

"But what about Blackie?"

"Shovel snow off the field. There is plenty of grass underneath."

"Pa!"

"Go, Toma!"

I ran to the milking shed, picked up the sack of bran, and that morning Jana and I made biscuits, half bran, half flour. We heaped them up on a plate for breakfast, for lunch and supper. We skimmed the milk and made butter. We drank every last drop of milk. We did that every day, and in between meals, Karina and Filip helped me shovel snow off the grass.

Three weeks later, we were still eating biscuits. Blackie grew thin, her hip bones and ribs sticking out more and more. She produced less milk. Soon we would all be in trouble. *Dear God, please do something! At this rate we're going to starve.*

I took a deep breath. I had to reason with Pa once again. I stood before him, my hands clasped together, as if in prayer. "Please Pa, we only have enough flour for two more days. We can't survive anymore. Please, let me walk down the mountain and get a job."

Pa looked up. "No. We came here to get away from evil. No one would hire you anyway. God will provide."

I turned away. *How, dear God? Nobody knows what is happening here.*

The next day a man knocked on our kitchen door, holding three big paper bags in his arms. He looked like a businessman, in pleated pants and shiny black shoes. But how had he made it up the mountain? How did he even know who we were?

Pa sauntered to the door and slid it open. "Come in. I remember you. You're Mr..."

The man reached out his hand only, as he hung on to the paper bags. "Thorndike. We met in a grocery store a few months ago."

Pa chuckled and grasped his hand. "Actually, you stopped me and tried to witness to me, thinking I was a heathen." Pa chuckled again. "Anyway, what brings you up here in this weather?"

"I keep getting the feeling I need to bring you food. I do apologize if I am wrong. Here is what I bought just before coming up." He stepped into the house and handed Ma the bags.

She looked inside, and her eyes grew moist. "Thank you, Mr. Thorndike. This is much appreciated." She handed the bags to Jana and me. "Girls, you know what to do."

Jana and I peered inside and grinned at each other. We skipped to the kitchen while Pa, Ma, and Mr. Thorndike pulled up chairs, warmed themselves around the wood stove. Our eyes sparkled. Coffee! Now we could serve drinks. Cookies! Those went on a plate. Pancake mix! Eggs! Maple syrup! Bacon! We laughed as we reached for the mixing bowl and two frying pans.

I looked over at Mr. Thorndike, amazed. *"Jesus, you sent us a stranger. Thanks."*

Jana and I cooked up the bacon. It sizzled on the pan, filling the house with its wonderful smell. I smiled. The last time we had eaten bacon was at our old farmhouse. I opened the bottle of maple syrup and dipped my finger inside. I licked it and grinned again. Jana did the same, her eyes shining.

We cooked dozens of pancakes, piling them high on two big plates. Then we called everyone to the table, and instantly the sound of running feet filled the house. Everyone appeared, laughing, jostling each other, seeing who could get to the table first.

Pa laughed. "Come join us, Mr. Thorndike."

But Mr. Thorndike looked from Pa to us as he sat down at the picnic table, his eyebrows knit together. "Are you really that hungry?"

"Oh yeah," Mik said. "We haven't eaten in weeks."

Pa laughed again. "Actually, he's always hungry. He always says that

129

at mealtimes."

But I could tell Mr. Thorndike hadn't been fooled. He nodded his head slowly. "I see. I will have to come again." I hoped he would. How many people followed God like that?

The next day we had a particularly harsh storm and the roads turned to sheer ice. Again, we were stranded on the mountain for days, but one morning it turned warm. The roads ran with water and Pa called the family together. "I'm going into town right now to sell my small lathe to a machine shop. I want you to come with me and do the shopping. It will make a nice break for you all. But Toma, I want you to stay behind and keep the fire going. I want this house warm when we get back."

My heart sank, but I nodded anyway. I helped the little ones get on their shoes and coats and watched as they drove away. I walked slowly back to the house. Now I could do whatever I wanted, and no one would know. But there was nothing to do. No friend to telephone. No one to visit. I carried in firewood and washed the dishes instead. I picked up my guitar and sang some songs. No one could see me; so I wept.

But the day wore on, and still the family hadn't returned. The temperature dropped. The driveway turned to ice. I slid to the road and checked that too. It had frozen smooth. The family would never make it up.

I tramped inside and the telephone rang. "It's me, Pa," said a voice at the other end. "We're stranded at the bottom of the mountain, but we're okay. We're visiting friends right now. Get the snow chains I use for the tractor. Put them on the Army 6x6. Then come down and get us. I'll be waiting at the bottom. Hurry up."

I stared at the telephone as I hung it back on the wall. I had never driven the 6x6, never put on snow chains, never driven down a mountain on ice. *"Help me, dear God,"* I whispered.

The first thing I had to do was find the ignition key. I hunted in Pa's bedroom, on his desk, and in his toolboxes, but I couldn't find it anywhere. Maybe inspiration would come a bit later. I would work on the snow chains next.

I dragged them from the garage one at a time and laid each one in front of a tire. Then I hauled myself into the cab. If I could put the 6x6 into neutral, I might be able to push it forward a bit, to on top of the chains. Maybe I could fit them on. Maybe I could jumpstart the 6x6.

I studied the gearstick, the knobs on the dashboard, and found a white button saying, "Ignition." *"Help me, dear God,"* I prayed again and again, as I stepped on the clutch, and pressed the gas pedal several times. Then I pushed that little button. For all I knew, it meant, "self-destruct."

The motor shook into life and I patted the steering wheel. "Thanks for not blowing up!"

I moved the 6x6 forward a yard, put it into neutral, and pulled the emergency brake. I had learned that much over the years. "Now for the next step," I muttered. But the snow chains were heavy, and my mittens kept sticking to the frozen metal. In the end I tore off my mittens and pulled the chains over the wheels barehanded. My fingers froze, and I had to stop every few minutes, warming them in my armpits.

Finally, I clipped the ends of the chains together, but they hung over the wheels like oversized bracelets. I tried to pull them tighter, but in the end, I gave up. Just maybe they wouldn't fall off.

I climbed into the cab and put the 6x6 into gear. The snow chains began to clink. A good sign. As long as they clinked, I would be alright.

I crawled down the driveway and along the bench. But when the road started descending, I came to a stop. If the 6X6 decided to slide, no amount of snow chains could rescue me now. "If I perish, I perish," I muttered and released the clutch.

Foot by foot I crept down the mountain, keeping away from the cliff. The clink of snow chains rang in my ears. But suddenly, the clinking stopped, the 6x6 kept moving, straight for the cliff. "I'm sliding," I shrieked, and yanked at the steering wheel. But the 6x6 refused to respond. "I hate you, Pa," I howled out in agony.

What did I say? I didn't hate Pa. It was a reaction I still had from the past. Hate only destroyed; it never saved. *"Help me, Jesus,"* I cried out instead. *"I want to live!"*

At that instant the 6x6 stopped, the right front wheel on the edge of the cliff. Could it be angels pushing with their shoulders to keep me on the road? I peered out the side view mirror hunting for their gleaming white bodies, but all I saw was snow. Maybe they were invisible.

I turned the steering wheel, and one inch at a time, the 6x6 edged away from the cliff. I could hear the snow chains clinking again, and ten minutes later I rounded the last corner. Pa stood at the bottom waving his arms and I came to a stop in front of him, not even bothering to climb out.

Pa opened the driver's door and I slid over to make room for him. He looked at me, wonder on his face. "Toma, I forgot to tell you how to start the 6x6, and that you shouldn't turn it off when you put on the snow chains. How did you know?"

"I prayed, Pa."

A minute later we arrived at his friend's house. I stepped inside. Music! An almost empty plate of cookies on the table. The smell of hot chocolate. Hot chocolate! We hadn't had that in years. "It's time to go," Pa called out.

I looked at the empty mugs on the table. Just one cup of hot chocolate would have been reward enough, especially for risking my life. But the wave of human beings surging toward me decided my fate, and I left the house without saying, "hello," or "goodbye." Being alive would have to be enough.

We squished into the 6x6, and Pa took us up the mountain. Ma sat beside him and he glanced over at her. "Lila, I am impressed with Toma. She took good initiative. She's got a good head on her shoulders."

I turned my head and looked out the window, putting my hand up to hide my face. I raised my eyebrows and smiled at the trees. Finally, Pa approved of me! But Ma said nothing in response.

A couple of days later a neighbor dropped by. He had seen how the 6x6 coped on the ice, and he wanted to buy it straight away. Pa smiled at me. "It was that good driving of yours, Toma. Well done!" I grinned at him, feeling warm all over. Finally, Pa liked me!

The next morning, I skipped from the milking shed, whistling, carrying a half-full pail of milk. My single long braid bounced down my back. My dress swished with every step I took. Pa had accepted me. I was so happy.

I kicked off my rubber boots and stepped into the house, red cheeked and breathless from the frosty air. Ma watched me from the fireplace, her face unfathomable. Something wasn't right. I escaped the house as soon as I could. There was plenty to do outside.

But Pa had set up a new regime. Every afternoon all of us children had to spend two hours on our beds. Pa and Ma expected total silence, and in that stillness, I heard Ma call my name. I ran to the living room and found her standing in the middle, her lips pressed together, her eyes emotionless. Pa sat on the couch, reading his magazine. I stopped before her and stood at attention. "Yes, Ma'am, you called?"

Ma surveyed me from head to foot, and I felt uncomfortable as she took in my details, a tear in my skirt, a stain on my bodice, my hair a bit untidy. What did she want?

She finally spoke. "You're getting proud, girl. You walk around with that long braid of yours, thinking you're someone special. I'm going to cut it off. Do you hear?"

I couldn't say a word. I stood riveted to the spot, my arms pressed hard to my sides. I couldn't think of what she meant. How had I been proud? I served her hand and foot. I jumped when she snapped her fingers at me.

Ma crossed the living room, over to Pa's desk. Her sewing box sat beside it. She picked it up, and I watched her pull out her large silver scissors. She opened and shut them as she turned back toward me, and the swish, swish sent shivers through me. I could only assume I had somehow transgressed, even though I had no idea. Pride was a terrible and deceptive thing.

Ma stopped in front of me, and we stood eye to eye. "Turn around," she said, and I did. I had quit fighting a long time ago.

She grabbed my braid and pulled it away from my back, not even bothering to undo it. Instead she lifted the scissors up above my shoulders, trying to cut my braid in one big swipe. She failed. My braid was thick, and she couldn't get through. Instead she worked at it bit by bit, yanking my head this way and that. But with every snip, something different happened in my heart. Snip. Hair has nothing to do with pride. Snip. Pride is in the heart. Snip. She's setting me in my place so that Pa sees that she is better than me. Snip. I'm going to look ugly. Snip. Don't worry. It's only hair. Snip. It's only hair.

Ma put down her scissors, a faint smile on her lips. She handed me the severed braid. "Here, girl. You can go."

Pa looked up from his paper and laughed. "You could sell that for a fortune, Toma."

I gawked at them. Was this a "Les Misérables"[4] story instead? Had I got it entirely wrong? They wanted to sell my braid for cash. Would they want my front teeth as well? I held out my braid to Pa. "You can have it."

But Pa shook his head, and I stared at him, bewildered, my hand still outstretched. Why had he rejected it? Maybe this was another of their lemming tests, to see how I would react. Didn't they know they had already broken my will? I would have done anything they asked.

I backed away and walked stiffly down the hall. In my room, I placed my braid on top of the drawers, and adjusted it, making it curl like a capital "G." I had worn braids, even as a toddler. Long hair had always been a part of my identity. Did they really have to tear away this last bit of me? I was a faceless member in the family now.

I picked up Jana's hand mirror and studied myself. My hair stood out this way and that, uneven, no matter which way I turned. I looked an ugly mess. Then Jana glanced up from a book she was reading. "What happened to you?"

Something suddenly clicked inside my head. I didn't need a braid to be Toma, to be myself. Ma in her concern to protect her marriage, had just set me free. She had cut off the last of my affections. I laughed. "Ma just cut my hair. It was time for a new look!"

I still gazed at my reflection but noticed something else. *Hang on, dear Jesus. I don't hurt. My heart should be breaking in two. Could it be that Pa and Ma can't touch me on the inside anymore? Could it be that you are the one who determines who I am?*

A song we sang in our early morning family devotionals rose up in my heart, a slow and simple tune.

---

[4] Victor Hugo, Belgium, 1862.

"I will arise and go to Jesus.

He will embrace me in his arms.

In the arms of my dear Savior,

Oh, there are ten-thousand charms."[5]

"Jesus, are you saying I can go to you and no one can stop me? Are you saying you love me, and no one can stop you? This is amazing. I am safe in you, despite what happens to my body."

I paused, still staring at myself. *"I can even choose what to think. No one can control my thoughts. I can soar on wings like an eagle and no one can pull me down. I am free, even though nothing has changed. This is my second wind!"*

I had to get away and be alone, but Pa and Ma would never let me out. The only other way to escape was through the bedroom window. I opened it. The cold wind hit me, but that wasn't going to stop me. I threw off my slippers and slid outside. "Where are you going?" Jana said.

"Out."

I dropped the four feet to the ground and hugged my thin sweater to my chest. Barefooted, I dashed to the milking shed, the only place sheltered from the biting wind. I leapt across the snow, my frost-bitten toes not feeling a thing. Once inside, I wanted to dance, to soar in my newfound freedom. I hesitated. Pa had told me dancing was wrong.

No, it wasn't! I read the Bible, and it said it was good. I stretched both arms into the air, imagining one hand resting on Jesus' shoulder, the other holding his hand. I took a step and pointed my toes, the song in my heart guiding my feet. My skirt swayed in rhythm, swishing around me. I twirled around, again and again, Jesus and me in silent dance.

---

[5] Lyrics by Joseph Hart, London, 1759.

CHAPTER 15

The winter storms kept on raging, and Mik had to hike down to Reggie's every other day to make sure he had enough wood in his shack. "I have to bring it right into his house," Mik told me one day. "The steps to his shack are covered in ice. He could fall if he went outside."

I grimaced. "I can imagine he uses a lot of wood. There are holes in his shack, all over the place."

Mik pulled on his boots and mittens. "Yup. I tried to fix a few, but it didn't make any difference. He needs a new shack." Mik stood up and headed out the door, but an hour and a half later he burst back in, his face red. "Reggie is sick," he gasped.

Ma whipped around from teaching school. "What do you mean, Mik?"

"I found him in bed, and the fire was out. When I asked him what was wrong, he pointed at his feet. Ma! I checked them. They're completely white. I think he has frost bite. I lit the fire for him and got it going. He needs help right now."

I stared at Mik, horrified. Even though my toes had decided not to fall off, they hurt like anything most of the time. I didn't want Reggie to have to go through that.

Ma jumped up. "I must ring Reggie's sister first. Jana, you stay home and take care of the little ones. The rest of you come with me."

We stood around Ma as she telephoned his sister. When Ma broke the news, we could hear his sister's voice over the phone. "Please go down right now, Mrs. Rose," she wailed.

"I will. I'll let you know what's happening."

We raced down the mountain, sliding over boulders, sometimes falling head-long in the snow. We couldn't get there fast enough. But when we stepped into Reggie's clearing, it looked so peaceful, just like a Christmas card. It felt all wrong.

Ma picked her way up the ice packed steps and opened the door a crack. "Reggie, may I come in."

Reggie didn't answer, and Ma flung the door open. We tumbled inside, gathering around his bed. He turned toward us, his looking-ahead eye dull and sad. Ma reached out and laid a hand on his forehead. "Reggie, you're sick. You have a fever."

"I'm cold," he mumbled.

Mik dashed to the woodstove. "I'll put on more wood."

I stooped down with him as he unlatched the door. The fire had almost burned out. "Look, Mik," I whispered, pointing to the stove. "No wonder Reggie can't keep warm. There are no dampers on this stove, or in the smoke pipe. He needs to feed this stove every hour to keep it going."

Mik studied the stove and leaned back on his haunches, resting his arms on his knees. "I should have noticed."

"I should have too, Mik."

We looked at each other and said nothing more. How could we have been so blind? No dampers meant air flowed through unhindered, making the fire burn hard and fast. Only dampers could control the intake of air, make the fire last for hours.

While Mik rekindled the fire, Ma inspected Reggie's feet. She had wanted to be a nurse before she had children, and I watched as she slowly ran her hands over his feet. She finally looked up. "Reggie, you need to go to the hospital. You could lose your feet."

Reggie looked at her, his one eye earnest, his voice catching. "If I go, my sister won't let me come back. She almost didn't when I got sick last year. I had to keep begging until she gave in."

Ma nodded, as if she understood. "We'll get you back here

137

somehow. I'll talk with your sister."

"No!"

Ma pulled his shredded quilt up to his chin. "Maybe we can get a doctor to come out here." But Reggie didn't answer. He just closed his eyes. So Mik stayed with Reggie to keep his shack warm. The rest of us hiked back up the mountain. Maybe a doctor could come that afternoon.

As soon as we arrived Ma telephoned Reggie's sister and asked her to send a doctor down. While we waited for a reply, I made cheese sandwiches for Mik, and Reggie if he wanted. The rest of us had barely finished eating when Reggie's sister telephoned again. The doctor would be there at 2:30pm, and he would be driving in. Driving? How could he do that? There was no road into that valley.

We trotted down again to make sure we were on time, and Ma pulled up the only chair in the shack. She held Reggie's hand in both of hers. "Reggie, the doctor is coming. You might need to go to the hospital."

"I'm not going."

But the doctor was still coming, and we had to wait. The rest of us sat down on the floor. (At least there was one benefit in having a freezing shack, all the ticks had moved away.) We leaned against the walls close to the stove. We waited in silence and listened.

A half hour later we heard an uneven roar. We hurried outside, all except Ma. We looked in the direction of the noise and saw a red jeep coming up the middle of the creek! It lurched from side to side, weaving between big boulders. It splashed in water up to the middle of its wheels. As it pulled up out of the creek, we could see the grocery man at the wheel. Beside him sat a man who looked younger.

The grocery man stopped, and the passenger door opened at once. The young man strode toward me, a black bag in his hand. "I'm Dr. Coleman. Are you Mrs. Rose?"

I shook my head and pointed to the shack. "She's my mother. She's inside."

The doctor stopped and surveyed the shack. I could see the disbelief in his eyes. But he didn't say a word and hurried up the stairs. "Dr. Coleman, here." The door flew open, and he stepped in.

The rest of us waited outside, but it didn't take long for the cold to seep into our clothes. We clapped our hands and stamped our feet. "Want to get in?" the grocery man called from the jeep. "It's warm in here."

"No thanks," we called back in unison.

Pa and Ma had taught us that accepting help from others degraded our honorable name. We were strong. We were self-sufficient. We were survivors. We didn't need anyone's sympathy or pity. "Let's get some firewood," I said. "It will warm us up."

We fanned out into the woods to look for dead branches. We hauled them back and Mik chopped them up. It didn't take long to start feeling warm. But we kept on going until we had collected enough wood to last Reggie a few days.

As we finished Dr. Coleman and Ma stepped out. Once on level ground and out of earshot of Reggie, Dr. Coleman turned to Ma. "He needs hospitalization. He won't survive in this shack. I've never seen anything like this before." He paused. "But neither can we make him leave. He has to go willingly."

Ma nodded. "It will be hard to persuade him, but I will try."

Doctor Coleman smiled, but his smile looked weary. He climbed back into the jeep and looked back. We waved "goodbye" as they descended into the creek. Then we filed into the shack. I noticed that Ma had added more wood to the stove.

Ma sat down beside Reggie again. "Reggie, the doctor says you will die if you stay."

"I'm not leaving."

"But, Reggie, we don't want you to die."

"I don't want to miss another spring."

Ma reached out and held his hand. "Reggie, I promise, you will be able to come back."

"No!"

Ma looked up at Mik and Jana. "I want you two to stay here tonight and keep the fire going. Otherwise, I don't think he will survive the night."

Mik and Jana nodded, determination in their eyes. "We will need to get sleeping bags first," Jana said.

Ma nodded. "Put lots of wood on the fire. That will give you enough time to run to the house and back."

"Yes, Ma'am!" They packed the stove full and dashed out of the shack. We followed a few minutes later.

Early the next morning, Ma and I hiked down. I carried breakfast in a backpack for everyone. But when we opened Reggie's door, Mik and Jana were still wrapped up in their sleeping bags. They looked weary to the bone. "We took turns staying up," Jana croaked. "We couldn't get it warm in here. We had to keep the fire roaring all night. But I think Reggie's alright."

Ma sat down beside Reggie again. He searched her face with his one good eye. "Am I really that sick?"

"Yes."

"You promise I can come back?"

Ma smiled and held his hand. She sat there a few minutes before standing up. "Mik, Jana, I want you to stay here again. Toma and I will go back. I need to make some telephone calls."

An hour later Ma and I strode up to our house and shook the snow from our dresses. But Ma didn't sit down to rest. She telephoned Reggie's sister straight away. Afterwards, she flopped on the couch, sighing as if she would split. "I think we'll need lots of help carrying Reggie to the jeep. The jeep will be there this afternoon and take Reggie straight to the hospital."

Pa looked up from his airplane magazine. "I'll take care of the little ones. All of you should go."

Ma smiled. "Thanks, Linard. That's kind of you."

"It's the least I can do. Reggie is our mission field."

That afternoon Ma, Karina, and I trekked back down. We gathered more wood and brought it inside, while Ma packed Reggie's things. But when we heard the roar of the jeep, only Ma stayed inside with Reggie. I glanced back as I closed the door. In that instant I saw a man lying death-like under shredded quilts. Ma sitting beside him, her skirt brushing the floor, her hair pulled back in a bun, her head bent as if in prayer. The sun shining through cracks in the walls, dappling the room with shafts of light. It almost looked like the doorstep to heaven.

Outside, the jeep bumped into view. Its harsh redness and jerky movements jarred with the holiness inside Reggie's shack. This time Reggie's sister sat beside the driver. Her white hair was perfectly made up, her cheeks rosy. She clung to the door and dashboard, steadying herself as best she could.

When the jeep finally stopped, Reggie's sister slowly climbed out. She stared at the shack, her mouth open in horror. "How did we survive? How did my mother and father manage?" Then she started in surprise, noticing us. "Where is your Ma?"

"Inside with Reggie," Jana said.

Reggie's sister dabbed her eyes. "My poor brother. I can't bear him living here."

"He says he likes it," Mik said.

"Reggie doesn't know any better," she replied, and then she bustled up to the shack.

Karina held her hand as she made her way up the steps, and we followed her inside. We watched as she bent down and hugged her brother. "Let's go home," she said.

But Reggie refused to look at her. He kept his looking-ahead eye fixed on Ma, who still sat there holding his hand. "This is home," Reggie rasped.

Reggie's sister threw her hands in the air. "This is a shack! I'm taking you home."

Ma stood up. "I've packed his things."

We gathered around Reggie and slid our arms under his body. I could feel the bones in his ribcage, and when we lifted him, he hardly weighed a thing. Between us we carried him down the stairs to the jeep. We laid him on the back seat, filling the legroom space with his things, so he wouldn't roll onto the floor.

Reggie's sister climbed into the jeep. "Thank you, Lila," she said. "Come and visit. Bring the family. That will cheer him up."

We waved as the jeep turned around and inched its way into the creek. Ma suddenly sighed. "He will never come back, poor man." I

141

wanted to cry.

We visited Reggie in the hospital as soon as we could. "I'll be going home soon," he told Ma, his one good eye fixed on her.

Ma smiled. "When you get better, Reggie."

But when he improved his sister moved him into her house, and we visited him there. Reggie sat on a couch, his feet propped up on a stool, a quilt wrapped around him. His sister stood behind him and tucked in a loose corner. How she loved taking care of her brother. And Reggie looked well. He had gained weight. His hair was washed and combed, and he wore a clean, ironed shirt. But his lips had turned down; his head was bowed.

I could only imagine how he missed his shack, being able to sit by the river with no one around. I pulled out my guitar and we sang a few songs. How I hoped that would cheer him, bring back happy memories. Afterwards Mik opened his Bible and read a few passages. Then he closed in prayer.

Reggie's sister instantly jumped up, her eyes sparkling. She readjusted his quilt, but Reggie pushed her hand away. "Leave me alone." He turned to Ma, his voice raspy and weak. "Take me home."

Ma shook her head. "I can't, Reggie. The doctor says you need to stay here."

Reggie looked away, but the pain in his eye said everything. "He could live with us," Mik said. "That would be closer to the valley than here, and we could take him down once in a while."

"No!" Reggie's sister and Ma cried out in unison.

Back at our house, Pa met us at the door, a scowl on his face. "You've been dilly dallying around long enough, coming and going with Reggie. His sister is taking care of him now."

"No, God!" I pleaded in my heart. *"Please don't let Pa take Reggie from us."*

Mik reached out his hands. "But Pa! Please! He is our friend."

"We can't go running after every sick person in the world. I want you to help me build a runway in the field. I want to fly the Cessna out. I've already walked it, and I think we can do it."

Pa looked around at us all. "I want to buy a bulldozer and begin work at once. I've been thinking about our lives. I have been delaying following God, and South America keeps coming to mind. We can flee there and be missionaries at the same time."

Mik kicked his foot at the floor. "But Reggie is a mission field."

"He doesn't need us anymore. Look at all the help he gets."

Mik didn't answer, and we drifted to our rooms, to get changed into our work clothes. "I'm tired of all this leaving business," Jana whispered. "What's wrong with this place? Doesn't Pa realize there is evil everywhere?"

I shrugged my shoulders, then nodded. I didn't want to go either. Even though it was hard on this mountain, for some reason it felt safe. Maybe it was because I understood the rules, harsh as they were. I knew just where I stood or didn't stand. But feeling safe and being safe were two different things. It must have been true for Reggie as well. He felt safe in his shack, but it was killing him. If he hadn't gotten out, he would have died. But then, he died emotionally.

All this thinking hurt my head. It was easier to work hard and help Pa build the runway. It was easier to help him put his Cessna back together than to fret about escaping evil. And, it was just plain exhilarating to hold the airplane wing while Pa pulled at the propeller for the first time. It proved that there was hope for broken things.

Once again Pa climbed into his aircraft and tested the flaps. His face beamed as his sat in the pilot's seat. Our faces beamed for his delight. We watched him taxi to the top of the runway and take off. We watched the trees at the end of the runway sway under the wind of the propeller. That runway was barely long enough! But Pa didn't loop around the field and dip his wings and I turned away in disappointed silence. Something must be wrong.

We drifted back to jobs in the house, and an hour later the telephone rang. Ma answered it. "I'm going to the airport," she said. "That was Pa. He said he isn't going to land on our runway. He hit a branch as he took off."

Three hours later Pa and Ma returned, and we all gathered around them in the living room. "Pa," Mik said, "that runway must be too short. How are you thinking of making it longer?"

Pa chuckled. "I'm not going to extend it. It was just an experiment. At least I got the Cessna out."

I stared at Pa in disbelief. An experiment? I had thought this was God's will. "But Pa! We worked so hard. Now it's all a waste."

Pa grinned. "I have been thinking. Let's call it a road. I can sell plots of land on the other side, and we can use the money to get to South America. I want to buy an airplane big enough to take us all."

At that moment the telephone rang. Pa picked it up and handed it to Ma. "It's Reggie's sister."

Ma hardly said a word, but when she finally put down the telephone, she looked over at Mik. "Reggie is back in the hospital. They don't know what's wrong with him."

Mik jumped to his feet. "Let's go right now."

Pa cleared his throat. "No! Sundays are your day off. You can go then."

"But he might not make it."

Pa shrugged his shoulders. "We have work to do. He won't go anywhere soon. I want us to start surveying the land. Our job is to get to South America. There are plenty of people out there who need help."

Mik threw his hands in the air. "Then why are we sitting here! Wasting our time!"

"Be patient, Mik. Be patient. I just got back."

"I am being patient! Why don't you ever do anything?"

I thought Pa might explode, but he just chuckled and turned toward Ma. "Lila, let's have some coffee."

We only started measuring the land two days later, and Pa worked us late that day. I ran to the milking shed just as it turned dark, and Blackie was already waiting for me. Mik slipped in, without me knowing, startling me. His voice wobbled as he spoke. "He's dead, Toma. Reggie's sister just called. He's dead. We didn't get to see him."

I stared at Mik, not able to milk, grief welling up in my heart. We didn't even get to say "good-bye." "When did he die?" I whispered.

"This morning. Why didn't they tell us sooner?"

I blinked back tears. "I don't know, Mik. When is the funeral? I want to go."

Mik nodded. "In three days. Let's ask Pa."

I kept on milking once Mik had gone, watching the milk froth up, listening to the swish as it squirted into the pail. I pulled at the udders, each the size of my thumb. Why had I believed Pa? He had just made it up that Reggie would live. If Mik didn't have the courage to ask if we could go to the funeral, I would.

I tramped inside, but Mik was already talking with Pa. "Please let us go to Reggie's funeral," he asked.

Pa lounged on the couch as if nothing heart-breaking had happened. "No, it's a workday."

Mik took a deep breath. "Pa, please. He was our friend."

"Please let us, Pa!" I begged. "We'll work harder to make up the time."

Pa looked from Mik to me. "Alright, but only out of the generosity of my heart. What considerate person organizes a funeral in the middle of the week? They should have thought of those people who have to work."

The funeral day arrived and we quit work early. We slipped into an almost empty church and sat at the back. After the service we followed the coffin out, to the cemetery behind the church. I stared at the hole they had dug for Reggie and backed away from it a few paces. *"Please, Jesus! I don't want to die like Reggie, a prisoner!"*

Reggie's sister burst into sobs. "He was so healthy," she wailed. "Why did he die?"

I watched her weep, and then I noticed daffodils blooming behind her. I looked around the cemetery on all sides. Daffodils were in bloom everywhere. It suddenly made sense. *"Oh, dear God, it's springtime. Reggie died of a broken heart."* I burst into tears, not just for Reggie, but for myself as well. My heart was broken. Would I die?

Back at home I ran to the lower garden and hid between the furrows of newly planted peanut seeds. I lay on my stomach and covered my face with my hands. The dampness of the ground, the smell of warm earth, the buzz of flies filled my senses. I stayed there and didn't move. It felt safe, a place where no one could find me, and if they called from the house I wouldn't even hear.

I lay there for quite a long time, breathing in wholeness. I sighed and looked up at the mountain behind the house. The clouds had turned black. They raced up the side of the mountain. Suddenly a mammoth black funnel shot out. It struck the trees.

A proper tornado! I had never seen a real one before. I jumped to my feet and stared. It was untamed. Wild. Powerful. It went where it wanted. But what if it hit the house? What if it headed in my direction and picked me up? I threw myself down on the ground again.

A few seconds later the tornado pulled up. I leapt to my feet and sprinted to the house. "A tornado!" I cried. "It just hit the mountain."

My siblings and I ran up the mountain to find the place where it had struck. But as we ran thoughts began mulling in my mind. God had protected our house. Our neighbor, Joel McKay, was right. The man who built our house had put it in a good place. God had protected Reggie even though he didn't think so. God would protect me too. I, too, was in the place where God had placed me. I would be safe.

CHAPTER 16

Summer came, and we hiked into the mountains every day searching for blackberry patches. We found them in gullies and meadows. We circled the mountains hunting for more, and all the time the grass and trees rustled in the breeze. I listened and wondered. It said in the Bible that God spoke through the wind. Was God speaking to me?

One day as we headed home, our buckets full of blackberries, a mud-spattered white station wagon bumped down the road, dust billowing up behind it. For several months now that station wagon had taken to driving up and down our mountain, and we edged off the road, waiting for it to pass. A bearded man sat behind the wheel, a fair-haired woman beside him. Some children stared at us from the back. They looked just like the other hippies we had met on occasion at the Co-op in town. Wild, but somehow refined.

The man lifted his hand in what looked like a peace sign. We waved back in the normal way. "Why are hippies moving here?" Karina said. "I've counted four different cars already."

Mik grinned. "Actually, they're everywhere. When I drove into town yesterday, I heard some of the guys talking about it. They said they're selling those hippies their land at super high prices."

I gasped. "Mik, that's cheating!"

"Not really. Everyone is happy. The hippies think they're getting a good deal. The locals sure are, and they're are getting rid of their useless land."

"Like what?" Jana asked.

"Oh, land that has no access to a road, or that faces north, or is so steep you can't even stand on it."

Jana blinked as it registered in her mind. "Well, I suppose that's business."

Mik kicked a pebble on the road, and it sailed into the woods. "Yup. And guess what? The guys said they don't think the hippies will stay. They think most of them will leave in the next couple of years. It isn't easy roughing it out in the mountains."

Another car approached us, a green one this time, and we clambered off the road again. This car looked in pretty good condition and the family inside did too. The man had short hair, all of them wore bandanas, and they all looked tidy. But we knew they were hippies alright. Their license plate gave them away. It said they came from out west.

The next morning, after I had made more jam, I strode outside to weed the garden. That same green car passed the house again, the whole family inside. I wondered, how did all those hippies survive, perched on their useless bits of land?

A while later that green car returned, and this time the man was alone. I waved, and I thought he would keep on driving. He stopped in the middle of the road, across from where I was weeding. I straightened my back as he looked my way. He shifted his gears, and the car engine roared as he backed up to our gate. He climbed out and opened it. I dropped my hoe, heading his way.

The man drove through. "Hello?" I called.

He strode toward me, his gait quick. "I know this sounds strange," he said, speaking even quicker. Then he paused, as if hunting for words. He looked at the ground and shifted his weight. He cleared his throat. "I need to ask you a question."

"Yes?"

The man looked up again. He smiled, a quick nervous sort of smile. "What makes you tick? I drive by here every day and you're always happy and friendly. I need to know why."

I took a double take. No one had ever asked me that question or told me that I stood out. That question demanded an answer. Only one response came to mind, even though it felt inadequate. "Well... I... I mean... we're Christians."

At that moment Pa hurried up, wiping his hands on an oily cloth. "How may I help?"

The man extended his hand. "My name is Max. We moved down the road three months ago."

I interrupted as Pa shook his hand. "Pa, he asked what makes us tick."

Pa and Max laughed, and Pa raised his hand toward the house. "Come in for coffee, Max. We can chat inside."

Forget about the weeds. Forget about being responsible. There was no way I wanted to miss this conversation. After all, that question had been leveled at me. A stranger had noticed that I was different. Could it be that God had sent that stranger with a message for me? I couldn't dare believe it. I was a nobody in this world.

I followed as Pa led the way, passing the garage. Max looked inside. Mik was bent over an engine, covered in black grease. We stepped in through the sliding door, and Max spotted Jana. She was just sliding bread into the oven. He looked at Ma sitting at the picnic table, teaching Karina. Filip was tracing letters. He noticed Peter playing quietly on the floor.

Max's face lit up. "This is amazing,"

Pa smiled and introduced Ma. "This is my wife, Lila."

Ma rose, dismissed school, and sat down with Pa and Max. I strode to the kitchen to wash my hands. "We have nothing to serve him," Jana whispered to me.

"How about the bread?"

"That will take half an hour."

"Ask Ma."

Jana edged up to Ma, and Ma nodded her head. "Max," she said, "do you have time to wait for the bread to bake? We could have it with some homemade jam and butter."

Max grinned. "I have plenty of time. This is amazing."

"But we don't have any butter," Jana whispered to me.

Yesterday's milking was still in the refrigerator. I pulled it out, skimmed off the cream that had settled on top, and ladled it into a glass gallon jar. I closed the lid and grasped it at both ends, shaking it back and forth, just like a baby's rattle. It would only take half an hour to turn the cream into butter.

Ma looked up and shook her finger. "Toma, give that to Karina. I want you to make us some coffee."

"Yes, Ma'am."

Max laughed. "This is amazing. Your children obey you."

"Democracy rules in this house," said Pa, "and my name is Democracy."

Max laughed even louder, and I could tell he liked the joke. But it wasn't a joke. Not to Pa. Not to us.

Pa reached over and drew Ma to himself, his arm around her shoulders. "Lila, Max here wants to know what makes us tick."

Ma smiled. "That's easy. It's Jesus."

My eyebrows flew up. An excellent answer. But a visible tremor ran through Max, a startled look crossed his face. "Well! I didn't expect that answer, but if it makes your family like this, I'm all ears."

Ma smiled again. "Tell us about your family first. What brought you here?"

Max told us how they had moved to the mountains three months earlier, and that thousands of unhappy people had left the Coast, wanting to get back to nature. They wanted to live without electricity, enjoy the basics of life, and news had spread that these mountains were perfect. People could hide and escape civilization.

Max sighed. "We're trying to grow our own food, but it's hard work. We thought we would be happy once we moved here. We're even more miserable. But every time we drive by your house, your children are friendly and hard at work. I was wondering - why?"

As Pa and Ma told our story, Jana and I served coffee. Afterwards we took turns with Karina, shaking the glass bottle of cream. We sat in a row at the picnic table passing it on every two minutes. Soon the cream went thick. It turned into flecks of yellow butter, and finally into a lumpy mass.

The timer went off, and Jana sped to the oven. She coaxed the bread from the baking tins. I washed the lump of butter in a bowl of cold water and added a bit of salt. The bread smelled wonderful as Jana sliced it, and I watched delicate spirals of steam swirl up. I took the slices and spread the butter on top. It melted straight into the bread. Jana topped it with blackberry jam.

We filled a plate with the steaming bread and Jana carried it into the living room. Max's face lit up. His eyes grew big, as if he had just witnessed a miracle. "This is amazing," he whispered.

An hour and a half later Pa and Ma walked Max back to his car. They waved him off and ambled inside. Pa chuckled and looked around at all of us children. "The Bible says, 'Let your light shine before others.'[j] That is exactly what we are doing. We are showing the world what it means to be Christians."

Max came back the next day, this time bringing his family. A few days later he brought his friends, the hippies in the mud-spattered white car. We met them on the driveway as they got out of their cars. "This is Don and Megan," said Max, and he extended his arm like a presenter.

They all shook hands with Pa and Ma. Then Max and Don turned to Pa, asking him about digging a well on their land. Ma led Megan off to the front porch. Jana and I hurried to the kitchen to make coffee for everyone. But when we approached the porch, we could hear Ma telling Megan how to become a Christian. Jana and I backed away. Coffee could wait.

Fifteen minutes later Ma and Megan slipped into the house. I looked at Megan and her face had changed. She had that same spark, beauty in her eyes that Reggie had when I first met him, except hers didn't disappear a split second later. What had happened? When she arrived, she looked just like any other woman, now she shined like a stunning beauty. This only happened in fairy tales.

"I just became a Christian," she said, smiling.

I watched as she sat in a daze on the couch. Was this what Jesus did? Did he so completely transform a person, that they even looked different? The beauty God gave really did have nothing to do with the angle of a person's chin or the straightness of their nose.

I sighed. I felt like a scurrying little bug, even though Jesus lived in me. Maybe I just had to trust that what had happened to Megan was already happening in me. I didn't have to hide from people, thinking they somehow saw me as a hideous wretch, someone who elicited their pity. I was God's precious daughter, and he hadn't made a mistake when he created me.

Pa, Max, and Don came in a little while later. Don looked at Megan, concern clouding his face. "Are you alright?" he asked. Megan nodded and smiled.

The men sat down, and Don and Megan told us their story. They lived in a teepee, a proper one like the Indians used. They had no water, no sanitation, and ticks crawled everywhere. With this combination, when winter came, they both came down with pneumonia. They lay in the teepee too sick to cook. If Max hadn't helped them, they wouldn't have survived.

We listened, our eyes growing big. How could all these things have happened, and we never knew anything about it? But I suppose no one put up signs on the outside of their houses, or shacks, or teepees, saying, "Help us, please! We're not managing."

All of us felt compassion as they finished their story. Don and Megan did look particularly thin. They looked tired as well. "Would you like to join us for pancakes," Ma asked. "It's nearly supper time."

"That would be wonderful," Don exclaimed. "I never thought I would say it, but it is good to be in a proper house."

Jana and I leapt to our feet. We knew that was our cue to make mountains of pancakes. We hurried to the kitchen and pulled out the ingredients. "This is really exciting," Jana whispered.

I smiled at her. "Yup! It's so nice to have people around."

Jana laughed. "People? Then what am I? A green Martian?"

I grinned. "Yup!"

We cooked dozens of pancakes, three batches in the end, and carried them to the table. Everyone squeezed in tight, laughing as they shimmied and shoved. But Megan seemed oblivious. She couldn't stop smiling. "Are you alright?" Don whispered again.

She nodded, her face clouding. "I just became a Christian."

Anger flashed in Don's eyes. As soon as he could, he gathered his family and they headed out the door. I watched them, my heart sinking. If Don was anything like Pa, he would protect his family from any perceived danger and forbid them to ever come again. He would even talk with Max and dissuade him from coming as well.

The minute they left Pa sat down hard on the couch. "I knew this was happening, and I did nothing about it."

"What, Pa?" Mik asked.

Pa put his head in his hands. "I knew they lived in a teepee. I knew something was wrong. The few times I passed them, delivering gravel, I thought they looked too thin. But they were hippies, and I thought that's what they wanted. I didn't even bother to stop and ask if something was wrong. I just judged them."

Ma reached over and put her hand on Pa shoulder. But Pa continued. "They could have died, and it would have been my fault. God brought them across my path, and I turned away."

Ma looked at Pa, compassion on her face. "Thank the Lord that he gives us second chances. Linard, they didn't die. And Megan is a Christian now."

Pa looked up. "I'm still very sad. It says in the Bible 'Be perfect, therefore, as your heavenly Father is perfect.'ᵏ I have failed God yet again."

We sat around Pa, silent, our compassion toward him overflowing. I could forgive his hard-heartedness, not just toward those hippies, but toward me as well. If he could feel remorse for turning his back on those strangers, one day he would realize what he was doing to us. I could forgive him, and I could wait.

The next morning, we got on with life. But suddenly, we heard the gate squeaking. We ran outside to see who it was. The mud-spattered white car! It drove up to the house.

Don stepped out, a grin on his face. Megan joined him and laughed. Pa reached out to shake their hands, sadness still in his smile. He asked if they would like to come into the house. They did and sat on the couch.

Don began. "Last night I was angry when I heard Megan had become a Christian. I told her we would never come back."

I looked from one to the other. So, why were they here? Had Don somehow convinced Megan not to believe, and they wanted to set us straight?

Don continued. "I couldn't sleep last night, and… well… what you said is right. I asked Jesus into my heart."

Megan reached over and grasped his hand. "We both became Christians yesterday. It's so cool!"

We laughed. We clapped our hands. This was a miracle beyond belief. A man who had fought it, had suddenly changed. I studied Don, just as I had Megan. That same sparkle, beauty, filled his eyes. He looked over at Megan and kissed her on the lips. This was truly a happy family.

We started to see them regularly, and the same weekly transformation that had happened in Reggie began to take place in Don. The beard disappeared. He found a job. He cut his hair. He cut it even shorter. They sold their tepee and land. They bought a proper house. Jesus had completely changed their lives.

It didn't take long for Don, Megan, and Max, to spread the word. They brought along more friends. "We have devotions every Sunday," Pa started telling everyone. "Come and join us. Stay for lunch afterwards. The girls make good soup and bread."

"We would like that," they said.

So, the next Saturday Jana and I cooked a huge pot of vegetable soup, just in case anyone showed up. We baked four loaves of bread. Then on Sunday, at around 11am, two families arrived. They trooped into the house. We packed ourselves on the couches, the hearth, and an old carpet on the floor.

Pa started with prayer. Then I played the guitar and led us in a few songs. Pa read the Bible, and each of us shared a thought. We sang another song, and Pa ended in prayer yet again. That was it. Then we had lunch.

Our new friends liked it and spread the word. The next Sunday three families came, a few weeks later, four. Pa started preaching short sermons each time. Within six months we had six families coming, and those young couples started asking questions. They wanted to know how to raise their children. They wanted to know how to have good marriages.

Pa and Ma nodded and smiled, sharing the secrets of their success. They told those young parents to teach their children the Bible, protect them from evil, and to expect obedience and respect. They told them that in marriage they should love one another, and that was the best gift they could give their children.

I prayed for those couples, that they would listen to what God wanted them to hear and be protected from everything that was wrong. I prayed that those people would also see what Pa and Ma had left out. First, that everyone deserved equal respect. That included children, regardless of their age. Second, that every person was created in the image of God. No one had the right to own another person, to do what they wanted with them. That included children, regardless of their age.

I prayed.

CHAPTER 17

P a usually did the grocery shopping, and one day he came home with two live geese. We gathered around and looked at the crate in the back of the car. Two orange beaks poked through wooden slats. Beady eyes stared at us. Filip reached out his hand to stroke their feathers, but when it squawked, he jumped away. "Why did you get them, Pa?" he asked.

"For Thanksgiving. Last year we had pea soup. Once is enough in a lifetime." We laughed, recalling the day. All we had in the house that day was a package of dried split peas and some flour.

I stooped down to get a better look at the geese. "Toma," Pa said, putting his hand on my shoulder, "I want you to look after them."

"But I already look after Blackie and make sure the chickens are locked in every night. Why can't someone else do it?"

"I trust you. Now run to the house and get Ma's scissors. We need to clip their wings."

I dashed back a couple of minutes later, holding Ma's instrument of torture, and Pa and I carried the crate to the pond. He pulled out a goose, held it firmly between his knees. He spread a wing across his lap. "Toma, snip off the tips of the feathers."

I hesitated. "But Pa, if danger comes, they won't be able to fly away."

"They will be safe in the pond. Danger or no danger, I don't want my roast dinner flying away." I laughed at Pa's joke and snipped off three inches of feathers. The goose didn't seem to mind.

I expected Pa to spread out the other wing, but he let the goose go. "Don't we need to clip the other one?" I asked.

"No. If we cut both wings, it can still fly."

"How?"

"Because the wings would be the same length."

I looked up at Pa, taken a back. He spoke with certainty, as if he was teaching me a lesson. I clipped the second goose, and, as Pa let it lose, it flapped its wings and tried to fly. It only managed a few yards. Pa chuckled. "See?"

I watched the geese and then I looked at the scissors. It was as if I suddenly woke up. Pa had clipped my wings by making me feel helpless. Snip. I had to maintain our ethnic roots by never intermarrying with a native. Snip. I had an obligation to obey Pa, regardless of consequences or implications. Snip. I wasn't good enough to find a job. Snip. I had to constantly remember that rebellion was punishable by death. Snip. I must trust no one other than Pa. Anyone else would lead me astray.

How was I supposed to stand against this? Pa really thought he was doing the right thing. But somewhere in there I knew he was mixed up; I just wasn't wise enough to figure out how. But at least those geese had each other. They carried on with life, built a nest among the reeds, and soon they laid five eggs. I kept an eye on them as I did my chores, and, a month later, I noticed three little fluff-balls sitting in their nest. I dashed to the house and told the family, and all that morning I sat among the reeds with one or other of my siblings watching the goslings learn to walk.

Fillip was with me when the last two eggs wobbled in the nest. We watched little beaks breaking through the shells, and Filip wriggled up close to me. "Why doesn't the mummy goose help them out?"

"The pecking makes them strong."

"Why?"

"It helps them survive in the world."

"But what if they can't get out?"

"They will, Filip. God put it inside them to know what to do."

Man! Did I hope God had done the same for Jana and me, and that at the right time we would know how to get out!

Every day I kept an eye on those birds, thankful that their nest was away from the edge. No wild animal could get close to them. But two weeks later the gander went missing. "I'm going up to search in the woods," I told Pa. "Maybe he's wandered up there." I strode up to the edge of our property and found scattered goose feathers by the barbwire fence.

"No!" I cried. That gander had been killed on our land and I hadn't heard a thing. I would have tried to save it if I had known. After all I was responsible. I stumbled down the mountain to confess to Pa.

I found him under a pickup truck he had just bought, attaching an exhaust pipe. "Pa, the gander is dead! An animal must have killed it up in the woods."

Pa wriggled out from underneath and wiped his oily hands on his overalls. "Joel McKay said he sighted wolves. That must be what happened. We will have to build them a shed."

I stared at Pa in shock. "Pa!" I cried. "You should have told me!"

"I thought they'd be okay in the pond."

"But they're my responsibility, Pa. You told me to take care of them."

"I didn't think it was important."

"Pa! Wolves are important!"

"Alright. I'll go to the lumber yard and get you what you need. You can build a shed."

"I have to build it today. The wolf might come back tonight."

Pa left almost immediately and came back with a pile of boards, plywood and tarpaper. I set to work, feverishly measuring, sawing, and hammering. "I should have thought of building a shed," I chided myself. "I shouldn't have listened to Pa and believed that the pond was safe. They had their wings clipped, poor things. I clipped them. How could they have escaped?"

But I wasn't the only one in pain. The living goose swam around in circles on the pond. All day she honked for her mate, and the five little goslings bobbed this way and that, cheeping in confusion, trying to keep up. I glanced at them again and again, as I nailed together bits of wood. I had to finish the shed that day! The wolf would certainly come back, searching for another easy meal.

By evening I finished the basic shed. All I still needed was to cover it with tarpaper, but I could do that the following day. I ran to the house. "I need some help herding the geese into the shed," I called.

There was a sudden patter of feet and all my brothers and sisters appeared, their faces sad as well. We tramped outside in the dusk and lined up like a human wall, guiding the goose and goslings toward the shed. It took us a while. Then I shut the door. But I had shut it a day too late.

The next morning, I let out the birds and the mother goose headed straight for the pond. She swam in circles, honking, still calling for her mate. I gazed at her, seized with grief all over again. Geese paired up for life and if one of them died, they never sought another mate. Why had I believed Pa? My error in judgment had cost a life. Now that mother goose would never have any more babies. She would never have another friend.

I worked in the vegetable garden from morning till evening, and all that day the goose swam in circles, her babies trying to keep up with her. Her honks echoed among the trees. "I'm sorry, goose," I kept repeating. "I'm so sorry."

But then, a new kind of ache rose up inside my heart. "Where is my mate?" honked the goose. *"Where is my mate?"* I sobbed.

A week later I rose before dawn and slipped outside in my thin summer nightdress. I couldn't bear those honks anymore. They rang in my ears day in and day out, but they rang in my heart all night as well. Down by the pond I stared up at the sky. *"I want a husband, Jesus. I too want to be loved. I want to be kissed, hugged."*

I looked up into the blackness. A breeze sprang up. I shivered as it tugged at my night dress. It felt like a human hand. I stretched out my arms and let it caress me. *"Jesus, if you don't give me a husband,"* I whispered, *"I give myself to you. My body. My longing for love and children."*

I stood there waiting, my arms still outstretched. I waited some more. Any minute now God would take away those passions, just like he had before. He would free me from my emotions and fill me with sweet and perfect peace. After all, I had just given him my most precious gift. I didn't need those feelings. I could live free.

But nothing happened, and the breeze died down. I lowered my arms, and they hung limp by my sides. I felt no different inside. Maybe this was a thing of mind over matter. I would just have to choose to squash my emotions. They didn't count anymore.

That morning I made an announcement in family devotions. "I just want to tell you, I won't be getting married. I want to belong completely to God."

"Toma, what are you talking about?" Ma cried out. "No one is asking for your hand in marriage. Don't say such a foolish thing."

Pa looked at Ma and me, his face uninterested, as if I was telling him which pair of socks I was going to wear. "Sounds good to me."

Ma turned on Pa. "Linard! What are you saying?"

Pa didn't flinch. "Let her do what she wants," he said, his voice still flat.

My eyes grew big. Pa's response should have been to ask me how I came to my decision, to ask me to reconsider. Instead he slowly opened his Bible, turned the pages, cleared his throat. He read with authority.

"When a young woman still living in her father's household makes a vow to the LORD or binds herself by a pledge, and her father hears about her vow or pledge but says nothing to her, then all her vows and every pledge by which she bound herself will stand."[l]

Pa looked up. "Toma has chosen well. I will not revoke it. Other Christian leaders agree with me. Fathers have that right. God wants us to protect our families."

"Linard! Do you want an old maid on your hands until you die? Not me!"

Pa shrugged his shoulders. The conversation was over. I fled to my room and reached for my Bible. *Jesus, what just happened?* I babbled, the pain in my heart clearing my thinking. *You never actually told me to stay single. I just kind of said it, to make it easier for me. But now Pa has agreed with me. Help!*

I opened my Bible in a panic and read, "The one who sent me is with me; he has not left me alone, for I always do what pleases Him."[m]

I filled with confusion. *"Dear Jesus, I don't know what is pleasing to you? Do you want me to stay single for the rest of my life? Do you want me to always obey Pa? Do you want me to never leave home?"*

That morning I let the goose and goslings out of the shed, and they didn't run straight for the pond. The goose didn't even honk. I watched her waddle over the grass, leading her babies on. If that goose could find peace, so could I. No matter what I had said, stupid or not, no matter what Pa had said, God would do what was right.

Around that time, Mr. Thorndike came for a visit, the one who had brought us food when we were hungry. But this time he brought a young man in his late twenties, someone who looked polished and educated. But this young man didn't smile as he entered our house. He studied me instead, even before he sat down. He gazed at my sun-bleached hair, my stained dress, my dark brown sneakers with my big toes poking through. I cringed at my messiness and fled to the kitchen. Jana joined me a few seconds later.

Mr. Thorndike introduced the young man to Pa and Ma. "Linard and Lila, this is Alan. I brought him over because there aren't many godly young women around. Maybe one of your daughters might be interested in dating him. I told Alan about them, that they are hardworking and beautiful, submissive, pure. Mr. Rose, would you consider it?"

I gasped. Did Mr. Thorndike think Jana and I were eligible? What a compliment! Others could see something good in us as well. But, I had just told everyone I wouldn't get married. I couldn't very well go back on that, and I didn't want to mess up my heart anyways. It was too hard to keep it steady and calm.

I sighed. I didn't have to worry though. Pa would send Mr. Thorndike and that young man packing out the back door. Pa would keep his daughters secure, that was for sure. Instead Pa invited them to sit down! Had he suddenly changed? How many times had he told us that dating was wrong? Why? Because nowhere in the Bible was it ever mentioned. Pa also assured us that he was the one who had the right to choose our husbands. Didn't the patriarch Abraham do that for his son?

But, from what I had read in the Bible, and I had already read it through twice, Pa had picked out the only example of it ever

161

happening. God had given no such command. In fact, he had said the exact opposite. God once told five sisters that they could marry anyone they pleased, as long as it was within their tribe, and that was only so that their inheritance would stay within the clan.

I worked in the kitchen, thoughts whirling in my head. No matter what Pa thought, it didn't take away from one fact, Mr. Thorndike had called us women. Women! Grown-up. Capable. Not voiceless children.

I glanced back at Alan with his nice clothes and shiny shoes, his neat haircut. Yet, if dating led to marriage, I would make a pretty poor match. I didn't know how to dress. I didn't even know what I liked. I didn't know how to make my hair look nice. I had never worn makeup. I didn't know how to hold a conversation with someone outside the family anymore. If ever there was an uncut diamond, it was me. I would bring that young man shame.

Unless he was willing to work with me and help me become who I should be. But who wanted to take on a job like that? The outside could be transformed in a day or two, but my inside would take much, much longer. In the Bible, when Moses freed the slaves from Egypt, it only took a day to change from slave to free, but it took them forty years to learn how to live in that freedom. It was a terribly big job.

I looked at Jana. She grimaced. "Let's get out of here," she whispered.

"We can't, Jana. Pa and Ma are expecting us to serve them. Let's get in and out as fast as we can."

We crept into the living room, our heads bowed down. Maybe our guests wouldn't notice us. But I glanced up once and caught Alan's eyes, and our gaze held for just a second. Again, he didn't smile. I fled.

Once in our bedroom, Jana and I sat down on our bed, our hands on our laps, awaiting the verdict. We listened to the conversation in the living room. Was this the point where Pa decided our fate? I could almost hear him saying. "Oh, you can date Jana. I still need Toma at home."

"So, Alan," Pa said, "you want to date one of my daughters, and you like that they are pure. Are you?"

Jana and I exploded, spattering spit in front of us. We threw our hands over our mouths. Pa was about to roast that young man, and what a roasting it would be. I had never heard him go this far. I would NEVER want to be in that young man's shoes!

Mr. Thorndike cleared his throat. "Alan is working in a church part time…"

Jana jumped up. "I can't take it anymore. I might want a boyfriend, but this is awful. No one has asked us what we think?"

"I agree! Let's get out of here, just in case Pa says 'yes.' We'll have a good head start if he tries to catch us."

Jana and I lifted the bedroom window, climbed out, and fled up the side of the mountain. We found two boulders next to each other and sat down to watch the house. Jana cupped her chin in her hands. "I wonder what kind of a husband he would make?" But, neither of us answered the question.

We watched the back door for over an hour, and eventually Jana stood up, rubbing her bottom. "It's getting cold. I suppose we can stay in our room, and, if there is danger, we can jump out the window."

"Yup. We can run into the woods and hide. They will never find us there."

Jana laughed, and we slinked back to the house, just in time to hear the last of the conversation. "Please consider it, Mr. Rose," that young man said, his voice earnest.

We heard a shuffle as they rose to their feet, the rumble of the back door as it slid open on its runners. Jana and I stared at each other, our eyebrows raised. That young man was still alive! How had he survived? If he could, so could I.

A fierce determination filled my heart. Pa could decide where we went as missionaries; he could even decide what we wore, but I wouldn't let him choose my husband. I would rather stay single all my life.

I marveled at this new-found strength. "Jana," I said, as I headed for our bedroom door, "I'm telling Pa I'm not interested." But as I strode into the living room, Ma spoke up. "Linard, I am not happy. I don't know if that young man would be right for our girls."

I crossed my arms. "I agree."

Pa chuckled. "Well, that settles it."

163

CHAPTER 18

Almost a year went by. Most days we talked about the end of the world and about the safest place we could flee. But South America was such a big place. Pa couldn't decide where we should live. Brazil? There was a huge displaced persons' community there. We could buy an airplane and fly. Peru? We could buy a ship and sail there through the Panama Canal. It would be a place to live while we sorted ourselves out. Mexico would be the easiest. We could convert a bus into a mobile home, and simply drive.

Then Pa heard of some missionaries who lived in the Amazon jungle. They were acquaintances of someone we knew. Now, at least, Pa had a real live contact. He started telephoning around. He located them and got in touch. In family devotions one morning he grinned. "I have some good news."

All of us sat forward, eager to hear. We had travelled across South America in our hearts, getting excited with each new idea. Pa laughed. "I just heard from those people in the Amazon jungle. They're back in the States on furlough. They told me they have a son in Bible School. This boy might be happy to visit us and tell us firsthand about their mission. I plan to telephone today."

I looked at Pa, and my heart suddenly jumped, but in two opposite directions at once. Maybe this was the open-door Pa had been seeking all these years. How I wanted him to fulfill his dream. But then Pa mentioned this Bible School. Maybe I should let go of being a doctor and go there instead. They offered a class in tropical medicine. Maybe that was all I needed.

But I didn't dare hope. It might all fall flat. I had better fill my mind with other things. So, after devotions I hurried outside to harvest potatoes, to gather cow plops from the field, to mow the grass, and to mend the milk shed. I escaped the two-hour rest curfew, and only came in that evening, my mind empty and safe. I congratulated myself on my success.

But Pa made another announcement at suppertime. "I telephoned that boy at the Bible School. It turns out his name is Luke, and the school is 2000 miles away. But Luke is willing to come for a few days and tell us about the mission field. I will send him a bus ticket this week."

I stared at Pa, trying to discern his heart. Would he pull out at the very last minute? After all, he had invited a young man into our house, and didn't that go against his principles? But Pa held true, and Luke came as planned.

Pa picked him up from the bus station one afternoon, and when Luke stepped into our house, we had our first glimpse of someone who grew up overseas. I expected him to look serious, have a deep tan, and wear old-fashioned hand-me-downs. Instead, he had a guitar strapped to his back, and a beat-up suitcase with curled-up stickers all over. He wore bell bottom jeans, a polyester shirt.

He grinned as he shook each of our hands, starting with Ma and all the way down. He even bent down double to grasp Peter's hand. But Pa interrupted Luke and patted him on the shoulder, father-like. "Come, Luke. Let's sit down. Tell us about the Amazon jungle. What are the needs down there?"

Luke ambled to the couch and laughed. "You know, it was hard to get used to living here in North America. When I first came two years ago, what shocked me most were the signs. They were everywhere. 'Don't walk there.' 'Don't sit here.' 'Don't put your bike there.' I couldn't move without a sign telling me what to do. In the Amazon jungle they leave you alone. They let you do what you want."

We sat forward in our seats, attentive, and Luke grinned. "It's a good place to live, even though it has great needs. One of the greatest is to get in and out of the mission station. We have a small landing strip, and sometimes airplanes fly in."

"Airplanes?" Pa interrupted. "How big?"

"Oh, four, sometimes six-seaters. There is a mission agency that flies into remote places, bringing in supplies, or taking sick people out. But there are times when they can't make it in for months at a time. It's pretty tough when supplies run out, especially at the clinic."

Pa's eyes sparkled. "Luke, I could do that. I can fly. I have a Cessna 150 at the airport."

Luke's eyes grew big. "That's exactly the kind of airplane they fly."

Pa hit his knee and laughed. "I'm glad you came, Luke. Already God is doing amazing things."

They talked about airplanes, and the rest of us listened. But all the while a question burned in my heart. As soon as the conversation started lagging, I spoke up. "Luke, please tell us about that Bible School."

Luke grinned. "It's a good place. Lots of the teachers were missionaries at one time, and they are really good. It isn't an expensive school either. All the students have to work for an hour and a half each day, and that helps keep the cost down. I think it's only $850 a year. But I need to tell you one thing. In classes the boys sit on one side of the room, girls on the other, and you can't date until your second year in Bible School."

Pa clapped his hands. "That's my idea of a sensible school. I'm glad there are others still out there who think like me."

A few days later, after Luke left, I found Pa sitting in his spot on the couch again. I stood before him, my hands clasped behind my back, my face still, my voice even. "Pa? May I go to that Bible School?"

Pa glanced up from his magazine. "If God provides." He eyed me for another second or so, and then went back to reading.

I gawked at him, taken aback. Had he finally accepted that he should let us go? Had he noted that Luke had turned out well, and that going to Bible School could be beneficial? But I didn't dare show how much I cared. Pa might change his mind. "Thanks, Pa," I said, keeping my voice calm.

A few weeks later one of the plots of land sold on the other side of the runway. I sidled up to Jana that afternoon. "Wouldn't it be great if Pa sent us to Bible School? With the money he could send us both."

Jana scrunched up her face. "I don't want to go to some Bible School in the middle of nowhere. Why should Pa decide where I study? I want to make my own decisions."

The next morning in family devotions, Pa cleared his throat. "I have some good news for you all." I looked up at him, holding my breath. He was going to tell everyone that I could go.

He smiled. "I just read a quote by a man called Saint Augustine. He said, 'Love God and do as you please.'" Pa paused and looked around at us all. "I love God, so I can do whatever I want. I just found an airplane in Germany, coming up for auction. There's enough money from the sale of the land to buy a ticket to get there. The timing is perfect. A real answer to prayer. Now I know God will give us that airplane."

"How much is the ticket?" Mik asked.

Pa leaned back, and smiled, stretching out his legs in front of him. "About a thousand dollars."

Every single one of us gasped. "Pa!" Mik said. "I don't think it's right to spend that kind of money on a ticket. Isn't there anything closer?"

"No. This is the one God has for us."

"But Pa," I reasoned, reaching out my hands, trying to somehow rearrange the crazy thinking in Pa's mind. "That ticket will cost more than a year's tuition at Bible School. You could send one of us to study for that."

Pa lifted his nose and looked down at me. "God speaks to me, not you, Toma. He put me in charge of this family. I will decide what happens to you. I will decide where that money goes. Is that clear?"

"Yes, Pa."

The rest of that day Jana and I made soup and bread for the Sunday service the following morning. We worked side by side in silence. We were prisoners to Pa's whims, and he wasn't going to let us leave.

I glanced over at Pa every now and then, as he sat on the couch. It looked as if he was preparing a sermon. At the right time God would rescue me. At least, in the meantime, we had plenty to do living like missionaries on the mountain.

The next day cars, pickups and vans pulled into our driveway. I watched the young families pour in through the kitchen door, laughing and joking. There were more than usual that day. I hurried to the bedrooms to gather all our pillows. Some of us would have to sit on the floor.

Ma greeted the guests, but Pa remained where he was, sitting on the couch. He didn't even look up. Instead, his head was bowed, and his Bible open on his lap. His face appeared serene, as if he was in deep thought.

Our guests hushed their children and tiptoed around to find a place to sit. I could sense electricity in the air. It was clear, Pa was having a vision from God, right there in front of us. We were in for a treat.

I looked at Pa, happiness suddenly bubbling up inside me. When we had company, Pa always turned funny. He was caring and talkative. It was as if he needed outsiders to keep his balance. He was helping them, but without knowing it, they helped him.

All of us squished together, leaning forward, trying to keep as quiet as possible. Who wanted to disturb Pa when God was speaking to him? Talk had been going around the group before the families even arrived that day. I had heard they wanted to start a church in our house. They wanted Pa to be their pastor. He would be perfect.

I perched on the hearth with my guitar ready to play the first song. I waited for Pa to look up at 11am, the time church was supposed to begin. Minutes passed, and the excitement grew. Pa turned a page in his Bible. Everyone watched.

"Pa," I whispered. "It's time to start." But he didn't look up. Instead, he turned another page and then one more. At 11:15am Ma reached over and touched his arm. "Linard, everyone is here."

Pa cleared his throat and shifted a bit, but he kept on reading, as if he hadn't heard. I shifted too, disquiet rising within me. This wasn't a vision. Something was wrong. Why was Pa acting like no one was here? He had wanted to be a pastor and his dream congregation sat in front of him, a house full of eager young couples.

I looked at the floor, not wanting to catch anyone's eye. I heard the movement of bodies, as people shifted. Suddenly a man stood up and helped his wife to her feet. I watched as they headed down the hall to the boys' room, where all the children played with blocks. I heard them whisper to their child.

"I don't want to leave," the child wailed. "What about church?"

"I don't know," the father whispered, and the child began to howl. The parents tried to sooth him, but they couldn't stop his distress. In the end they hurried past us and out the kitchen door. We could still hear the howls when they climbed into their car.

Ma waited another minute and finally stood up. "If anyone would like to stay for an early lunch you are most welcome. The food is ready."

"We need to get going," most of the couples said. They gathered their children and hurried out in silence, looking at Pa with hurt, confused faces. Pa had been like a father to them, talking with them, giving them advice, helping them out when they needed it. He was the father most of them had wanted. Now, something else was coming out.

Only two families stayed behind, and we headed for the kitchen in silence. Jana and I served. The soup and bread smelled good, but our guests could hardly eat. They played with their spoons and nibbled at their bread.

Suddenly, Pa stood up and strode into the kitchen. We looked at him surprised, but he refused to look at us. He still refused to speak. I passed him a bowl of soup and he returned to his seat. The last two couples put down their food. They fled out the door with their children.

I stared at Pa. What had come over him? He had told us dozens of times how much he loved those people. Now he acted as if he hated them. But Pa didn't seem to notice or even care.

The following Sunday only two families showed up, telling us the others had decided to go to other churches. Again, Pa acted in the exact same way. He read his Bible and refused to look up. Those last poor souls left a few minutes later. The Sunday after nobody came, and, suddenly we were on our own again.

A week later Pa flew off to Germany, and a week after that he returned. He sat on the couch looking relaxed and happy, as if he had been on vacation. He chuckled as we gathered around. "I left Germany thirty years ago. We had lived in a DP camp. I learned to speak the language. It was amazing how quickly it came back. On the flight home I spoke to the stewardess and she didn't have a clue I wasn't German." Pa chuckled again.

"What about the airplane?" Mik asked. "Did you get it?"

Pa yawned and stretched his arms above his head. "No. There is another one out there, somewhere. God will get us to the Amazon jungle." He yawned again and stood up. "I need to get to bed. This jet lag is getting to me."

Mik kept his eyes steady on Pa. "Maybe God doesn't want us to go there. Maybe he wants us to stay here. Maybe he doesn't want you to spend all that money for nothing."

"Mik, no one has to ask God if they should become a missionary. It's a command every Christian should follow, and hardly anyone does. We are different. Do you understand?"

Mik rose and walked out the room. Jana and I followed. "I'm leaving as soon as I turn eighteen," he whispered to us.

I looked at Mik. He was almost grown up now. He could leave against Pa's wishes if he wanted. But the question was, would Pa bless him? I hoped so. I didn't want him damned for the rest of his life just because Pa didn't feel inclined to give it. He didn't deserve it.

Pa began planning his next trip almost immediately, this time a survey trip to the Amazon jungle. I joined him at the table, as he poured over a map. "Pa, there is still enough money from selling the land to send one of us to Bible School."

Pa kept his eye on the map, his finger pressed on the Amazon River. "No, there isn't. I want to make sure we get to the right place. I need to find us a house." I backed away from him, saying no more.

Pa bought his tickets and left us again. But two days later the telephone rang. Ma jumped to answer it. "Linard," she exclaimed, "where are you?"

All of us children gathered around, and when she hung up, we waited for her to speak. She looked at us, her hand still on the receiver. She said nothing for a few seconds. "Pa's coming home tomorrow. He's okay. That's all I know."

As soon as Pa stepped in through the door, he sat down on the couch and grinned. We gathered around him, sitting at the edge of our seats. "What happened, Pa?" Mik asked. "Was there a military coup?"

Pa chuckled and put his hands behind his head. "No. Everything was fine. Patience, Mik! Let me start from the beginning. The flight was good and the food excellent. I had a glass of wine on the plane, the first one in years." He stopped and smiled to himself.

"He acts like he went on vacation," Jana whispered to me.

Thankfully, Pa didn't hear. "We landed at the international airport," he continued, "and taxied down the runway. At the far end, where the airplane had to turn around, a grandfather and his grandson, a little boy on a tricycle, stood there. They were only yards away, and the airplane nose swung over their heads. I could see their faces as they watched us go by. It was amazing. In this country we have fences for everything. They have the right idea down there."

Pa grinned. "At that moment I knew I didn't need to explore any more. I booked the next airplane home, while still at the airport. That gave me a day to look around the city and find a hotel for the night."

"But Pa," I said, my voice rising, "you already knew that. Luke told us that when he came. He said there were no rules. Instead, you could have sent one of us to Bible..."

Mik cut me short. "Pa, did you find us a place to live?"

"No. I will do that when we actually move. There is no rush right now. As I walked around the city, I noticed that the cloud cover was really low. I will need to get an instrument rating to fly in zero visibility and a twin-engine rating as well."

Mik knit his brows together. "Why a twin-engine rating?"

"If you have two engines on an airplane, if one fails you can still get to your destination. And if you're flying over a remote place, it is absolutely essential. Now I know how to prepare. I have a lot to do to get ready, and I still need to buy that airplane. Isn't this exciting?"

Jana leaned over close to me. "He doesn't care about the mission field," she whispered. "All he cares about is airplanes."

I too felt numb in heart and brain. We would still be here another couple of years at least. *Dear God! Stop him! He's throwing our lives down the drain, just so he can better himself. How long do we have to wait? Can't you send someone to reason with him? Isn't there someone he respects?"*

Late that evening, I overheard Pa talking with Ma in the kitchen. "Lila, all this Bible School stuff is turning Toma's head. She's growing restless."

"She's a young woman, Linard. What do you expect? I was already married and had two children at her age."

"That might be true, but Jesus didn't leave home until he was thirty, and she must follow his example. Toma has plenty of time."

I just about stopped breathing. *"NO! NO!"* I cried. I shoved my head into my pillow and sobbed. *"Jesus! Will he keep me a prisoner for another nine years? How can he demand what he never did himself?"* I sobbed myself to sleep.

The next morning I awoke, my breath still catching. I sat opposite Pa in family devotions. Bitterness mushroomed inside my heart. He looked happy. I was sad. He told us he had slept like a baby. I hadn't. Could it be that my anger toward him wasn't hurting him in the least? Could it be that I was only hurting myself?

Somewhere in the Bible it talked about bitterness. I hunted it down. "See to it that no one falls short of the grace of God and that no bitter root grows up to cause trouble and defile many."[n] I pulled in a shaky breath. The Bible was clear. Nowhere did it say, "Poor thing, I know how you feel. You have every right to be bitter." It said that bitterness caused trouble. And, it certainly wasn't right to fight wrong with wrong.

But how could I get rid of it? The only solution I could find was in Philippians 4:6. "Have no anxiety about anything, but in everything by prayer and supplication, with thanksgiving, let your requests be made known to God, and the peace of God which passes all understanding will keep your hearts and minds in Christ Jesus." I would tell God all my problems, in detail. I would make sure I found things to thank him for, like thunderstorms, like watching our dog nuzzle baby chicks in his paws. I would try not to worry, and trust that God was big and strong, and that he would take care of me. If I could do that, bitterness would flee.

Spring came, and life ticked on without change. Pa ploughed the two acres of vegetable garden. We worked, and Pa studied for his twin-engine rating. But when he got it, he decided to delay in getting the next one. He told us, "I can always wait for clear weather to fly."

I sighed. Nothing was going to happen anyway. We would stay stuck on the mountain for the rest of our lives. But the next Monday afternoon, during our daily enforced rest, I opened my Bible. The first words I read said, "You have stayed long enough at this mountain. Break camp..."⁰

A tremor ran through my body, and I read it again. This verse was for me! It matched my situation almost perfectly. I was on a mountain. I had been there a long time, almost four years to be exact. And, now it was time to leave! *"God,"* I prayed, *"I know this is from you, but you will have to do it. I don't have the money to leave. I don't know where to go. I don't even know how to get going. I will wait on you."*

A week passed and nothing happened. Two. Then three. Doubts crept in. *"Did I misunderstand you, Jesus? Or was it wishful thinking?"* But a month later Pa summoned us together in the middle of the day. We gathered around him on the couches. "I have decided we should move. If we are going to get to South America, we must sell this house. I can't buy an airplane otherwise."

I sat there, staring at Pa. He was doing what God wanted, without even knowing. God had moved him into a course of action. And, if God could do that, he could do anything. I squeezed my eyes shut. *"You did it, God!"* I cried, joy welling up in my heart. *"You did it! We're breaking camp, and I didn't even have to say a word! I can't wait to see where we go!"*

CHAPTER 19

Pa sold most of our possessions at an auction he held in our field. He bought a Twin Beech, a twin-engine propeller airplane, and learned to fly it. Not long after he put our house up for sale. It sold at record speed.

Pa then called us together. "I think we should visit Grandma and Grandpa before we fly to South America. I want to test out the airplane, and I need more practice. It would also be good to see them."

Ma smiled. "Linard, that sounds like a sensible idea."

We spent our last night in that mountain house, on the floor in sleeping bags. I slid into mine and covered my head. I grinned at God in the darkness. *"I can't believe it,"* I whispered to him. *"You did it. We're breaking camp. It can only get better now."*

Pa woke us the next morning, well before dawn. I leapt to my feet and couldn't stop smiling. We threw our night clothes and bedding into cardboard boxes and slid them into the back of the pickup. I placed my guitar, some household things and food on top of the boxes. Pa whistled the whole time. He opened the pickup door for Ma to climb in. The younger ones crowded in around her. He laughed. "Now for the next adventure in our lives. This could be the greatest one yet."

Ma smiled back, a smile I had never seen. Had she too been praying to get off this lonely mountain? I had never thought that she might feel a prisoner as well, that she had suffered just like the rest of us. No wonder she had acted as she had, a dying person with squashed hopes and dreams.

I looked back at the house. How I loved that house. I had put in four years of hard work to finish it up. But it had been my prison as well. Maybe God was saving all of us in this move. "Goodbye forever," I whispered.

The older ones and I climbed into the car. I drove, following Pa down the mountain. We arrived at the airport just as dawn tinted the night sky and stopped in front of an airplane, a big white one with wide blue stripes down the sides. Pa jumped out and pulled a key from his pocket. He unlocked the airplane door and lowered it. It turned into a pair of stairs. Man! This was going to be travelling in style.

Pa straightened up and smiled. "Alright, everyone, get everything into the back of the airplane. Toma, Mik, park the car and pickup truck behind that hanger." He pointed to one a few hundred yards away. "Lock them up. I got permission to leave them there."

I looked up at Pa, not comprehending. *"Please, no, God. Don't let Pa bring us back."* But I followed Pa's instructions and grabbed a box of our clothes from the pickup. I followed him up the stairs of the airplane.

Pa turned left toward the cockpit, where the pilot and co-pilot sat. We turned right to store our things. We walked down the aisle. "Pa, there aren't enough seats for us all," Karina called.

He glanced back. "That's okay. It's all about our combined weights, and we are well within the limit. The little ones can sit on laps for landing and takeoff. The rest of the time you can move around."

We nodded, thankful for the clarification, and dashed outside once more. A few minutes later Mik and I parked our vehicles behind a hanger and jogged back. We climbed in and Pa pulled the stairs up. He locked the door.

"This is scary," Karina whispered to me.

I tried to sound brave. "We'll be okay." But I too had sudden doubts. Pa was practicing his flying with his entire family in the plane. If he went down, so did we. But Pa walked back up the aisle, whistling, patting the younger ones on the head. He climbed into the cockpit, and Mik into the co-pilot's seat.

The rest of us sat in silence as Pa did his pre-flight tests. The marker lights on each wing tip began to flash, lighting up the airplane

175

cabin at intervals. Suddenly an engine cranked into life, then the other one a few minutes later. I felt their vibration run through my body. I felt the whole airplane shake.

Pa gunned the engines and the airplane moved forward. The radio crackled into life. "You're free to go," it said.

A thrill of excitement ran through my heart. Those words were meant for me as well. Everything would be okay. God was setting us free.

Pa then turned the airplane onto the runway and we gathered speed. We lifted off. I looked out the window at the receding ground, at the sun rising over the horizon. We were flying. I was flying, like on the wings of an eagle! *"God! I'm free,"* I silently shrieked. *"I'm free!"*

About ten minutes later Pa turned around. "This is your pilot speaking. You may unbuckle your seatbelts. Enjoy the flight." Then he grinned. "I need your help, everyone. Keep an eye out for other airplanes. We don't want any midair collisions."

"Yes, Pa," we called, and began searching the skies.

All morning we gazed out the windows into clearness, but at lunch time giant clouds began to form. By the early afternoon the clouds grew thick, and we flew above them. By mid-afternoon only a few large patches of earth could be seen below. "We should be okay," Pa called out. "The weather report says it will stay like this." But by late afternoon and only 300 miles from our destination, the patches disappeared altogether. We flew over a solid carpet of white.

A little later Pa turned around. "Everyone, see if you can find a break in the clouds. This isn't good. I'll have to radio the nearest airport and see if they can guide me through before it gets dark. I should have gotten that instrument rating."

I could see Pa twiddle some knobs as he turned on the radio. "We are in need of assistance," he called into it. "I repeat, we are in need of assistance."

The radio crackled. "Roger that. What is your situation?"

"There are no breaks in the clouds. I can't get through."

"Roger that. How many souls on board?"

Pa hesitated. "My family."

"I repeat, how many souls on board?"

Pa told him.

"Repeat that please."

Pa did, and the radio went silent. Suddenly it crackled. "What do you think you are doing?" the air controller shouted. "You're over the passenger limit."

I held my breath as the conversation went on. "Some are children," Pa said, "and I thought the weight..."

Pa never finished the sentence. "Children! You're carrying children? Who do you think you are, risking lives like that?"

Had Pa twisted another rule? But it didn't matter at that moment. We had to get away. If Pa landed there, he would most likely get into trouble. *"Help us, God,"* I whispered.

As the airport controller began giving instructions, Pa whipped around. "Toma, switch places with Mik. I want your eyes up here. See if you can find me a break in the clouds."

I dashed to the cockpit, squeezed past Mik, and slid into the co-pilot's seat. I looked in all directions, at the solid white blanket. "I don't see anything, Pa."

"Keep looking."

Thirty seconds later I spied a hole off to our right, not big, but big enough. I poked Pa hard on the shoulder, and he looked to where I was pointing. He turned the airplane sharp around. "No more assistance required," he called into the radio and turned it off.

But even as he spoke, the hole grew smaller. Pa dove through it, the wings disappearing at the edges. And by the time we leveled out underneath, the hole had closed completely. Pa laughed, his voice shaking as he did. "Toma, I knew you could do it."

I looked over at Pa. His hands trembled as he turned some knobs. His face was gray. He swallowed. "That was close. If I had landed there, they would have confiscated the airplane, probably thrown me into prison, and left you stranded at the airport without a penny. They don't care about anything but their rules."

I shuddered, clutching the co-pilot's seat. I couldn't imagine what we would have done if that had happened. Would those people have left us penniless? Homeless? We needed Pa to survive. There was no way I wanted to lose my Pa, no matter what he was like. I loved him. What did I say? I loved him.

If he could follow God without even knowing, God would use him to do what was right in my life. Anyway, love had nothing to do with trust. They were two separate things. I would trust God for Pa, but I didn't have to trust Pa. I didn't have to be afraid.

We landed at a small airport in the dark, 175 miles from Grandma and Grandpa's. Pa unbuckled his seatbelt and stood up slowly. His face was lined. "We will drive the rest of the way. I need to find a telephone."

Pa left us in the airplane, and the younger ones fell asleep. An hour later he reappeared with a small four-door sedan. We packed into it with all our possessions, but we fit in so tight we could barely move. We ached and tried to shift a half-inch this way and that, just to alleviate our cramps.

We arrived at Grandma and Grandpa's sometime past midnight, and Grandpa was waiting outside. He hadn't changed one bit since I had last seen him. He still had his flat-topped crew-cut, the same hairstyle he had worn as an officer during WWII. He waved and swung open the gate.

We untangled ourselves and hobbled toward him. Grandpa wept as he hugged us one by one. He looked at Pa. "Welcome home, son."

A few seconds later Grandma appeared at the side door, in her dressing gown and tattered slippers. She made her way down the stairs, her arms outstretched. She hugged us and stroked our faces. We hugged her back, our arms wrapped around her waist.

She finally turned toward Pa. "Why do you have to live so far away?"

Pa just chuckled and gave her a hug. "Hi, mother."

The next morning, I woke to the sound of rain and crept into the kitchen to look at the time. It was 7am and Grandma was up, taking a last pink curler from her hair. I hugged her, and she pushed my hair behind my ears. "My darling Toma, why did you cut your beautiful hair?"

I didn't want to tell her the truth and shrugged my shoulders instead. "I needed a change, Grandma."

She shook her head and led me to the sunroom. The table was already laid, and my eyes grew big as I took it in. There was ham and donuts, and Grandma's special sour-dough bread. There was cake, raspberries and grapes. I could have danced for joy. "This is wonderful, Grandma. We haven't had anything like this in years."

She pushed a plate in front of me. "I know. Sit, my precious granddaughter, and eat."

I smiled at her as she sat down beside me, taking hold of my hand and stroking it. She looked at the thick yellow callouses on my palm and her eyes grew moist. "I bought a set of stainless-steel pots for you, for when you get married."

My heart sank. How could I reveal that I had announced to the family I wouldn't be getting married, and that Pa had agreed with me? How could I tell her Pa wouldn't let us date anyway, and that she would be hanging on to those pots an awfully long time? I tried to look cheerful. "Thanks, Grandma. That's awfully nice of you. Could you keep them until I do?" Grandma nodded and handed me the plate of donuts.

Soon my siblings appeared, one by one. Each hugged Grandma, and, when they saw the food, they squealed with delight. Pa came next. "It's raining," he said, pulling back a lace curtain to look outside. "We made it just in time, but I hope it stops. We will need to get going soon."

"But you just got here," Grandma said, her voice rising. "Can't you stay a few days?"

Pa narrowed his eyes. "Do you always have to lecture me, mother?"

Tears welled up in Grandma's eyes. They rolled down her wrinkly cheeks. But Pa didn't seem to take any notice. "I have to use the telephone," he said. "I need a bigger airplane. This one is too small."

We stared at Pa, stunned, but Grandma pointed down the hall. "Use the one in the office, my son."

Pa looked at her, at us all as we sat around the table, delicacies piled on our plates. He snorted and walked out the room. But as soon as he had gone, Jana threw her arms around Grandma. "Don't cry, Grandma. It's raining outside. We can't go anywhere anyways."

Grandma wiped her tears and smiled. "You're right, my dear. Let's thank God for this food and the time we have together." We bowed our heads and she prayed. *"Good Shepherd, thank you for being able to prepare this food for my wonderful grandchildren. Thank you for Linard, that you opened his heart to bring my grandchildren here. Keep them here as long as you want. Above all, please help my grandchildren find your path, to grow in deep love for you. Protect them from evil, and from anyone who would harm them. And help us to be thankful for every moment. This I ask in your precious name, Amen."*

"Amen," the rest of us chorused.

It rained every day after that. Four days in and Pa found an airplane, but it was parked at an airport 1,400 miles away. Six days in and Pa paced the floor. The rain kept bucketing down, but I gazed at it, thankful. God had heard Grandma's prayers and had sent angels to hold the storm in place. Pa couldn't leave, even if he wanted to. I really could trust God for him.

But Pa didn't see things the way I did. He kept pulling back the curtains and looking outside. "Winter is coming! We have to get out of here! Why didn't I get that instrument rating?"

The following night Pa shook us awake. "We're leaving right now. The rain has stopped." I looked at the clock. It was 3am.

Grandpa was up and already dressed. Grandma was in the kitchen making sandwiches, still in her pajamas, with an apron on. Pa rushed in. "Hurry up, mother! We have to go right now."

She looked up at him, tears running unhindered down her cheeks. "Linard, what are you doing? Look at your children. Toma, Jana and Mik have already grown up. Can't you see you're hurting your family? Please, don't go to the jungle."

Pa clenched his fists. "Don't you meddle with my family. You know nothing. God told us to go, and I will obey."

I drew in a sharp breath and fled to the car. Jana was already there. "Why is Pa so mean to Grandma?" she whispered. "He would kill us if we treated him like that."

It was still dark when we arrived at the airport, but Pa took off anyways. He wanted to get out before anyone asked him questions. We flew all day and landed at the airport where we had left our vehicles.

"What now?" Mik asked.

Pa ran his fingers through his hair. "We will drive up to the airport where I bought that airplane. I'll fly this one up later. The exchange should only take a few days."

"Where will we stay?" Ma asked.

Pa grinned. "I will buy some tents. The weather is still good down here."

I looked at Pa, taken aback. Why did we need tents? We would only be staying a few days. But Ma smiled, her face full of light. "That's good, Linard. We will call it a vacation."

Pa laughed. "Some people still have to work."

That night we slept in our clothes in the airplane cabin, and the following day Pa bought four bright orange tents. Two for us children. One for him and Ma. Another for our stores. Then we drove another six hours to the airport with Pa's new airplane. We found a campground and pitched our tents. We swam in the lake and cooked hotdogs around a fire.

I sighed as we laughed, joked, and played hide-and-seek. We hadn't had a vacation in seven years. And Ma felt it too. She leaned over to Pa and kissed him on the cheek. "This is wonderful, Linard. Just what we need."

The next morning Pa drove off to inspect the new airplane, and we idled away as we hiked and swam. It felt so good to have no responsibilities, to have no jobs that needed to get done. But a full week later and still Pa hadn't done an exchange of airplanes. Ma called us together, "Children, vacation is over. We're going to restart school."

We cleared the picnic table and Ma pulled out some schoolbooks. Every morning we sat together, me teaching algebra to Mik and Karina, Jana teaching Filip to read and write, then Ma teaching everyone history. Every afternoon, Jana and I kept camp, took care of the younger ones, made supper, and Ma rested. Every evening we went on a long hike.

Two weeks ticked by and still nothing had changed. But there was a two-week limit on staying at the campsite. Pa came back early that evening, and we packed everything up. We spent the night in a dingy motel, in a single room with two double beds squeezed in. The next morning we set up our tents in the exact same place.

"God, what are you doing?" I blubbered that night. *"I thought you had set me free, but this is even worse. We're homeless now. Please do something."* But another two weeks passed, and we stayed in the motel again. We moved back to the campsite yet again.

Then, finally Pa told us his news. "We exchanged airplanes today, but the one I got needs a lot more work than I had thought. Mik, I want you to come to the airport with me. I will need help repairing it."

Mik grinned. "Sure thing, Pa. Now I won't have to do school."

Pa chuckled. "This will be school. I will teach you airplane mechanics."

The two of them left early the next morning, and the rest of us got on with living. Life on the campsite carried on as well. Campers came and went, mostly staying for one or two days. But one man stayed a week, and it didn't take him long to realize we were different. "Hey, you weirdoes" he shouted out. "Are you gypsies?"

I shook my head.

"Don't answer him, Toma," Ma said.

But that man was right. We did look weird. Our skin had burned dark. We girls wore long dresses. The boys ran around without shirts. We acted weird too, holding family devotions around the picnic table and singing songs, doing school, speaking another language. "Go away," the man shouted. "This place is for normal people."

Other campers emerged from their tents. "Tramps!" they shouted. "Can't you afford a house?" "Scum!" "Drifters." They laughed and clinked their beer bottles together.

I kept my back turned. Did they think we lived like this by choice? I wished we had a house. I wanted a safe place, where we didn't have to fight with snakes and spiders, where my pillow would stay clean. *"God,"* I whispered, *"we used to be respectable. Now we're a laughingstock. Please, please get us out."*

That night I lay in my tent, and I could hear those people still clinking their bottles, still laughing, gathered around a small fire. We had united them in friendship. *"God, maybe one day they will learn that we aren't scum."* I paused, regrouping my thoughts. *"At least now I know how it feels to be homeless. I know what it feels like to be laughed at. I suppose those things are good to learn, and the only way to learn them is by living it."*

I watched the light of the campfire flicker on our tent. Then a song from Handel's Messiah started ringing in my ears. I had listened to it as a teenager. But this time the words, instead of the tune, caught my attention:

"He was despised and rejected of men, a man of sorrow and acquainted with grief…"P

I could relate. I hadn't done anything wrong, yet those people rejected me. But I had done the exact same thing. I had rejected God in high school. Now I understood just how he felt. It hurt like anything.

I reached out my arms and touched the flickering tent above me. *"I'm so sorry for hurting you like that."* I held my hands there, touching light, touching God. He forgave me. He loved me. I could do the same for those people out there, gathered around their fire.

The weeks marched on and the weather grew cold. We went about life wrapped in our sleeping bags, rubbing our hands together, holding school in a tent. We huddled together trying to keep warm. My twenty-first birthday came and went in that mess, and the absurdity of it all hit me hard. *"God? I'm not married to Pa. He can't legally hold me. Why am I wasting my life?"*

But I got no further in planning an escape. A stupor settled over me. I couldn't think or even stand up straight. I existed. We all just existed. But not Ma. She went crazy, especially when Pa left her for days at a time, travelling around to find replacement airplane parts. She raged; she hit us, and then she hid in her tent. Now we had lost our mother as well.

But a moment of clarity filtered into my heart. God wanted me to stay. If Jana and I left, who would look after the little ones, hug them, feed them, and mend their clothes? Who would try to make a home for them? With absent parents, my brothers and sisters would certainly die, and that wasn't an option in God's eyes. I had to let go of my own desires and hold onto the fact that I was saving lives.

After two-and-a-half months of living in tents, Pa came home early one evening. He grinned. "Guess what? I just bought us a place."

None of us moved. We stared at him. "What are you waiting for?" Pa said. "Pack up the tents. We're leaving now."

CHAPTER 20

I t took only forty-five minutes to pack and throw everything into the back of the pickup. We squished into the double cab, stacked one on top of the other. There was no other way. Pa had already sold our car for cash. *"Dear Jesus,"* I prayed, *"Pa bought us a place! I've almost forgotten what it feels like to have four walls and a roof over our heads. And radiators! A bath! I can't wait."*

We drove down the highway and I stared at the houses along the way. Christmas decorations had already gone up, and the houses looked warm and happy. But, I wondered, were those homes happy? A house didn't automatically guarantee joy. Maybe I was happier than the people inside those houses, with nothing but a tent over my head.

A half hour later Pa pulled off the highway and drove up to a huge grey tin barn. There was nothing shiny or happy about it. A small white, cement block building, about fifteen-foot square, stood next to it. Pa stopped in front of the barn and turned off the ignition.

"Where is the house?" Karina asked.

"This is it," Pa said. "You can set up your tents in the barn. At least you can lock the door and stay dry. This is more than I had in the war. You don't know how fortunate you are."

No one moved from the pickup. We stared at the barn. "The war is over," Jana whispered.

Pa heard her and chuckled. "It will only be for a month or two."

"God!" I cried out in my heart. *"What's happening? We can't live in a*

barn. It's degrading. It's inhumane."

But we couldn't stay in the pickup forever. We climbed out and followed Pa to the barn. He pulled a key from his pocket and opened a padlock. But when he pushed open the door the whole front of the barn yawned open. The door must have been thirty feet high. Pa flicked on a switch and a single light bulb turned on.

We looked around in the semidarkness. The walls, with metal beams and corrugated iron, rose up into a shadowy roof. The floor was cemented at the front and was sand at the back, and there were bits of broken machinery thrown here and there. Even poison ivy grew up the inside of one wall. *"No God!"* I cried. *"Please, stop Pa right now."*

God didn't. But, why not? If he was in control of everything, how could this be part of his plan? If he had moved Pa so that we left the mountains, how could he have let Pa make us live in a barn? Was he not supposed to have made things better?

The sound of a train broke my stupor. I turned around. A goods train was just chugging by, only 150 yards from the barn. Its wheels squealed. It blasted its horn. But that didn't matter to Filip and Peter. They clapped their hands and started counting carriages. "One, two, three…"

I stared at them, taken aback. How could they find something to enjoy? If they could make a choice, I could too. I looked above the train, at the evening sky. *"God, it's wrong for Pa to make us live in a barn. But, please make something good come out of it."*

"Linard," Ma said, her face grey, "show me the office."

We followed her and Pa the ten yards to the cement block building, and Pa pulled another key from his pocket. He unlocked the door and threw it open, beckoning Ma to go in first. We followed Pa and stood in the middle. The walls and ceiling had been painted white, and there was a desk, a chair, and a bookshelf. I stared at the furniture, and memories flooded back. Oh yes! This is what normal people kept in their houses.

Ma sat down on the chair straight away and ran her fingers along the armrests. "I will sleep in here with Filip and Peter. Linard, you can sleep in the barn with the older ones."

Pa laughed. "I'm sleeping with you, my bride. The big kids will be alright."

"Alright?" Jana whispered to me. "What's alright about living in a barn?"

Pa heard her and laughed again. "Okay, everyone, let's unpack."

We hurried to the pickup and started dividing things, carrying them to the office or barn. We set up our tents inside the barn, and Filip helped me push tent pegs into the sand. He smiled. "This is fun."

"God! GOD!" I cried in my heart. *"This is beyond horrible. What kind of a childhood is this for my brothers and sisters? At least I grew up in a house. I had a bed. They have nothing. Not even toys."* But I smiled at my brother. I would make his life as normal as I could. It might be in a barn, but I would try my best.

That night Jana, Karina and I cuddled in a tent, but I didn't feel any safer. With no way to padlock the door from the inside, and with the highway running parallel to the tracks, with trucks and cars passing all the time, any weirdo could have stopped and caused trouble. I listened, making sure no one turned up the drive.

The wind picked up and the whole barn creaked. I could hear trees swaying outside. I looked at the tent, with its sides sloping down, with hardly a movement in the fabric. We would have lost our tents by now. House or no house, this was better than outside.

A flash of lightning suddenly lit up the barn. The light came in through two small windows I hadn't noticed. A second later thunder cracked, and rain came down in torrents. It hit the tin roof so hard we couldn't hear each other speak, even when we shouted.

All night long the storm raged on, and we girls huddled together. Trains chugged by. Cars zoomed by. And all the time the song, "He was despised, rejected," kept playing in my head. But this time the last phrase touched me most. "A man of sorrows and acquainted with grief." God knew what it meant to grieve. He knew what it felt like to suffer at the hands of others. He understood.

The next morning Mik pushed the barn door open and we looked outside. Deep puddles stood everywhere, but we stepped out anyway, sinking into mud. "I can't wait to turn eighteen," Mik said. "I'm getting out of here. Pa is treating us like animals."

I looked at Mik. He towered above me, but his shoulders drooped, just like an old man. "Where will you go?" I asked.

"I don't know. I'll figure something out."

We wandered around the barn, and I noticed a wall of bushes to one side. I walked around them and pulled back suddenly, shocked. A huge chasm spread out at my feet with sides that fell vertically down. Scraggly trees grew at the bottom. Green stagnant water surrounded them. It stank of rot. "This is dangerous!" I cried. "Peter is only four. He could fall in and die."

Mik studied the chasm on all sides. "It looks like a disused sand pit. I wonder if Pa knows."

Pa called us a few minutes later, and we jogged to the office, taking our muddy sneakers off by the door. Inside Pa sat on a window ledge and Ma on the chair. She still wore her red flannel nightgown, and we sat on the floor by her feet.

"Pa," Mik said, "did you know there's an old sandpit next to the barn?"

"This is a disused quarry. That's why I got it so cheap."

"But Pa," I broke in, "the younger ones could fall in."

"Then it is your job to keep them out."

My mouth dropped open. Didn't he care if his children got hurt? But all I could say was, "Yes, sir."

Pa yawned. "I slept like a log. Wasn't it good to be under cover last night? I think that winter has finally set in. But being this far south I don't think we will get snow. We have been fortunate with the weather till now. This is good training for the mission field."

We listened in silence, all of us dirty, uncombed, and hungry. Pa took no notice and looked out the window. "We need a strategy," he said. "I thought the airplane I bought would be good for the jungle, but it needs too long of a runway. No jungle landing strip would ever be that long. I will sell it and buy a better one. Anyway, I still need to get my instrument rating. We have plenty of time. I also want to start collecting airplane equipment and store it at the back of the barn. What a blessing I got this place."

Blessing? If everyone around us lived in cardboard boxes, a tin barn would have been a blessing. This was humiliating. But, I had seen plenty of people feel sorry for themselves and blame it on others. I had noticed that they always complained, and no one ever wanted to be around them. I didn't want to become like that. Even though Pa had put us into a terrifying situation, it was still better than camping outside.

"First things first," Ma said, "I want a mattress, and we need a bath."

"We need an electric hob too," I said. "We can't cook over a fire in the rain."

"And a Laundromat," Jana added.

Pa raised his arms, as if in surrender. "Alright, alright. First I want Mik to dig a hole behind the trees."

"Breakfast first," Ma said, interrupting Pa. "Girls, I'm hungry." But Ma herself didn't move. She looked out the window, her face like a stone, her mouth a thin line.

Jana and I turned and hurried to the barn. Filip hurtled past us. "I need to go," he said, and headed out back.

"We have turned into animals," Jana moaned.

What could I say? We rummaged through the pile of cardboard boxes. Breakfast was on its way. Bruised apples. Crushed bread. A jar of oily peanut butter.

We carried it into the office and made sandwiches on the desk. But Ma took no interest. She sat, her face still turned away, staring out the window.

Suddenly we heard Filip cry out. Everyone, except Ma, tumbled out of the office. "He must have fallen into the pit," I cried.

I expected his voice to sound frightened, but it didn't. We followed it to behind the office instead. "Water!" he cried, jumping up and down. He pointed to a faucet gushing at full strength. "I just turned it on!"

We cheered. Pa hooted. "Amazing! God is looking after us."

I laughed and bent over, letting the water run through my fingers. I washed my face and dried it in my skirt. Thankfulness surged through every corner of my heart. At least we would be able to stay clean.

Pa drove off a half hour later, a smile still on his face. He came back two hours later with a double mattress for him and Ma, a four-hob cooker for us girls. He bought a heater for the office, an old tin tub, and rolls of rubber runners about a foot wide and many yards long.

I pointed to the rolls. "What are these?"

Pa patted one. "They're old conveyor belts. I thought I should buy them. We'll find a use."

At that moment Ma stepped from the office, dressed, and tiptoed toward us in her blue flowered sneakers, stepping around puddles. She looked in the pickup, her face still expressionless. "Linard, we will use those rolls as paths. They will go from the barn to the office. We won't get muddy then."

"An excellent idea, Lila. I knew God was leading me. Big kids, you know what to do."

We four big ones reached in, but each of the rolls felt like it weighed a ton. It took two of us to lift one out, carry it to the right place, and unroll it. We stretched them out from the office to the barn, around the barn to the toilet and bath area at the back, and still there was more left over. We carried the leftovers to where the bath sat in the sand. We cut the roll into shorter strips and lay a floor under and around the bath. We stood back and gazed at our work. For an outdoor bathroom, it didn't look too bad!

Pa and Ma drove off later and came back with the pickup piled high with furniture. We swarmed around it, untied the ropes, and carried a large secondhand table and loads of chairs into the barn, an old wringer washing machine to behind the office. *This feels strange, God,"* I whispered. *"We're moving into a barn as if it was a house. Is that alright?"*

Pa's eyes sparkled, and he whistled as he helped. "Isn't God good! He gives us everything we need."

I stared at Pa. His definition of 'good' certainly needed reexamining. Sure, God was good, but was he?

Sunday came, and we had breakfast in the barn, cornflakes and milk, and again Pa's eyes sparkled with delight. "I saw a church down the highway. Let's see what it's like. What an adventure we're having!"

But Ma looked at him, her eyes lifeless. "I'm not wearing a head scarf anymore."

Pa started. "Lila, don't say that! You know what the Bible says."

Something horrid flicked across Ma's face. "Try making me," she whispered.

I did a double take. Boy, was she brave, standing up to Pa. But Pa's eyes grew big, his nostrils flared. "Lila! You will do as I say!"

But Ma didn't flinch. Her eyes never left Pa. "The girls won't be wearing them either."

A look of confusion crossed Pa's face. He shook his head and let out his breath. "Let's go to church anyway. Maybe God will forgive you."

We climbed into the pickup, Pa and Ma in front, the rest of us in the back. I couldn't stop smiling as we drove down the highway. *"God! Ma is waking up. Finally, someone is standing up for us."* I smiled even more as the church came into view, a modern building with a metal spire on top. I knew there would be bathrooms with flushing toilets, toilet paper in holders, chairs with cushions, and warm radiators. I couldn't wait.

We filed into the church, and Pa led the way. He marched us to the front, and the congregation watched as we sat down. We filled an entire pew. Then the pastor asked Pa to stand and introduce us.

Pa cleared his throat. "My name is Linard Rose, and this is my family. We are here for only a short time. We are preparing to go as missionaries to the Amazon jungle." A murmur ran through the church as Pa took his seat. I could see he enjoyed the affirmation.

The service ended, and we followed Pa out. The pastor shook our hands. "I'm Pastor Weber," he said. "I like to visit all our guests. Where are you staying?"

My heart flipped over. *"God, don't let Pa tell him!"*

But Pa smiled and squeezed Pastor Weber's hand. "We live down the road. Come over for coffee this afternoon?" He gave directions to the barn.

Jana and I stared in horror. "What's Pa doing?" Jana whispered into my ear. "Did he forget that we live in a barn?"

I shuddered. "I don't know. But we had better tidy up before he comes."

Jana looked at me, wrinkling up her face. "How do you tidy up a barn?"

I paused. "I don't know." But as soon as we got home, I found some old shoelaces and tied back the sheets I had hung across the windows. Then I tried to sweep the cement floor. Jana ran around zipping up tents.

Pastor Weber arrived a couple of hours later and parked his car behind our pickup. Jana, Karina and I watched him from behind the barn door. How would he react when he saw how we lived?

He opened his car door and stepped onto the rubber runner. He looked up. "Hello, girls," he called, catching sight of us. "Which way do I go?"

I gawked. There wasn't a stitch of condemnation on his face! Maybe he always visited people who lived in barns. We waved for him to come, and Pastor Weber threw out his arms as he balanced his thin body on the runners. His white hair glowed in the setting sun. Maybe God looked like this man.

He stepped into the barn and didn't even look around. He looked in our faces and smiled. "I'm happy you came to church this morning. God will honor you for what you are doing."

Pa showed up and led Pastor Weber to the office. But the pastor's words stirred in my heart. Here was a man who cared about us, saw through our problems and still accepted us. I kept repeating his words. "God will honor you for what you are doing."

If that was true, it meant that even though Pa thought he controlled us, he didn't. We could follow God on our own. Doing what God said didn't suddenly happen when we relocated to the Amazon jungle. It happened right there in the barn. It was all up-side-down. I smiled. *God, this is wild. You're not upset about where we live. Even Jesus was born in a barn. What you want is my love, and for me to serve you right now.*

A week later we awoke in the morning, with ice on the inside of our tent, and a strange pattering sound coming from above, as if something light was landing on the roof. I shivered in my sleeping bag. Whatever it was, I wasn't going to find out. I snuggled in closer to my sisters.

The barn door creaked open a few minutes later. "Everyone alright?" Pa called out.

"Yes," we answered in unison, poking our heads from our tents.

Pa chuckled. "It's snowing outside. An inch already. Good thing we aren't camping. Get dressed and come into the office. It's warm in there."

Pa pulled the barn door shut and we dressed in our tents. "Man, is it cold," I heard Mik say, his voice shaking as he spoke.

"You can say that again," all of us chorused.

We rushed to the office and gathered around the small electric heater. Pa laughed. "What great missionary training. We are learning to make do."

"Linard," Ma cried, her lips blue, "we can't survive the winter like this."

"Lila, I have bought you everything you need. Now I have to get on with the airplane. If God wanted us to have a house, he could have given us one. I've wasted enough time already."

Tears rolled down Ma's cheeks. "Linard, why won't you listen to me?"

But Pa turned to us children instead. "All of you, I want you to clean out the back of the barn. I noticed some pallets. Line them up. I want to stack my things on them. And Mik, you're coming with me."

"Yes, sir," we replied, and did what Pa said. Afterwards, we hurried outside and warmed ourselves in the sun. The snow had mostly melted by then. But as we stood there, we heard the office door bang open. Ma burst out and ran down the driveway. Had she gone crazy? Was she running away?

She stopped at the side of the highway and started shouting. She had gone crazy! What were we supposed to do? But then I spotted a young man walking past, carrying a small backpack across one shoulder. The man stopped and walked back toward Ma. They talked for a few minutes and then headed our way. Ma invited him into the barn. "Jana, Toma," she said, "cook us lunch. This hitchhiker is hungry."

Ma and the young man stood in the doorway and watched as Jana cracked eggs into a bowl and I cut up an onion to fry. They stood there a minute, and then Ma turned to the young man. She told him about Jesus. The young man listened, his face serious as she spoke. And, when Ma asked him if he wanted to take Jesus into his life, he nodded. By the time we had finished making scrambled eggs with toast, the hitchhiker had become a Christian.

We handed him a plate of food, and as he ate Ma plied him with questions. Where was his family? Where was he going? How long had he been on the road?

Pa and Mik arrived back soon after that, and we children hurried out to greet them. Pa climbed out of the pickup smiling. "Look what I got," he called out. "Some real bargains here."

Pa then noticed the hitchhiker. He nodded his head and Ma explained. Pa chuckled. "Ma, you really do have that missionary spirit."

Ma nodded. "I want to let this young man sleep in the barn tonight. He has nowhere to stay. He slept in a ditch last night."

Pa laughed. "Fine by me. There's no holding you back, is there, Ma?"

"You can't do that!" I wanted to scream out. "It might be a barn, but it's our bedroom! It's wrong to let a stranger sleep with young women and children."

I looked from Pa to Ma. They would be safe in their office that night. They could lock their door. But if something bad happened to us, they wouldn't know until it was too late. Only God could save us now. *"Please, please, don't let that man hurt us, dear Jesus. Please put your hedge around us. Please watch over us."*

We helped Pa move his boxes of airplane radios into the barn, and that night the hitchhiker had supper with us. He unrolled his sleeping bag in the far corner of the barn and used his backpack as a pillow. He settled down and then was still. A few minutes later I could hear his even breathing.

Was he pretending, just to put us off guard? I didn't dare sleep. I mustn't sleep. Someone had to protect my siblings. I stayed awake in my tent, fighting the urge to sleep, straining my ears, listening, praying. But I lost the battle and awoke at dawn.

I chided myself as I checked my sisters, to make sure they were okay. I crept outside and listened by Mik's tent. He too had survived the night unscathed; his breathing gave away that he still lived.

But the young man decided to stay another two nights, and I simply couldn't stay awake any more. I jerked from deep sleep in the early hours of each morning. I checked my siblings, and each morning I breathed out the same prayer. *"Thank you, Jesus. Thank you, for keeping us safe!!"*

After this, Ma made it a habit to invite in every hitchhiker who passed our barn, or anyone Pa and Ma passed on the road. They always offered them a place to sleep, and most of the hitchhikers accepted without hesitation. At first Jana and I begged Pa and Ma to stop, telling them it wasn't safe, but they refused to listen. Pa said, "God gave us this barn for a reason. Who else can minister to those hitchhikers so effectively? Those people feel comfortable with us."

What more could we say? Jana and I gave up trying to reason with Pa and Ma. Instead, each time another hitchhiker stayed, I lay awake in my tent like a sentinel. I could do nothing else.

Nothing ever happened, and every single hitchhiker treated us with respect. They never once touched us. Maybe they had been specially chosen by God. Maybe they were angels in disguise. I couldn't tell. But after those people had regained their strength, they shouldered their backpacks and walked away.

Not us. An entire year passed by, and we still lived in that barn, Pa and Ma in the office. But we had an outhouse now, and we children had moved out of our tents. We slept in bunk beds at the back of the barn. We even built a room in one of the corners and Pa put a woodstove in. It became our living room, dining room, and school, and sometimes on freezing nights, our bedroom.

One morning we gathered in the office for our daily family devotions, and Mik closed his Bible with a bang. We turned to look. "It's my birthday tomorrow. I'm leaving," he said.

We turned in unison to watch Pa's reaction. He said nothing. He did nothing.

Mik walked out the next day with nothing but the clothes on his back, even though it was winter again. He slept on the ground by the railroad tracks that night. "Please, Pa," Jana begged. "Help him. He won't survive.

Pa threw up his hands. "Alright. Alright. I'll take him into town to look for a job."

I shuddered at his words. How many times had Jana and I begged for him to let us go, but he always refused? As soon as I could, I fled behind the barn. I leaned against the corrugated iron wall and slid to the ground. I stared at the sky, at my silent Father in heaven. *"God, what about me?"*

A strange kind of stillness settled over me. I already knew the answer, even though I kept on forgetting. This wasn't a time to indulge in self-pity. I heaved myself up and went back to the barn, to sew clothes for my family on an old-fashioned treadle, to cook supper, to teach mathematics to the older ones, to clean the outhouse, to give some kind of dignity to my younger brothers and sisters. I had to protect them, keep them alive.

Not long after, Mik packed his clothes into a car he had just bought. He closed the trunk and grinned at us. "This is it! I'll be back soon for a visit." He drove away free.

Yes, I wept. I sat behind the barn again. I sat there a long time.

CHAPTER 21

In early spring, as we ate our supper one evening, Pa pushed his plate away, more deliberately than normal. His eyes looked dead serious. "I need to make another survey trip to South America. I realize I was hasty the last time."

I turned my face away. *"He hasn't kept a single promise, God. What do I care about his plans?"*

But surprisingly, Pa did go, and when he returned ten days later, he sat on the floor in the office, his back against the wall. We sat with him. I expected him to talk about the food and wine, but he didn't. He had a serious joy about him. "It was amazing," he said. "I met a missionary couple while there. We started talking, and they told me about what they do. One story really moved me. They shared how a single missionary lady got sick at a mission station out in the jungle. They only found out when they visited her. They got some natives to carry her out on a stretcher."

I listened, horrified. "She could have died out there all alone," I cried.

"Oh yes. She won't be able to go back either. But the saddest thing is that there is no one to take her place. I felt so bad for those natives. I told the missionary couple that I have two daughters who could go, and that I would get you there."

I stopped breathing. What had Pa just done? Sure, we were able, but that didn't make us willing. He was only doing this to make himself look good. Maybe he even thought it would take him off the hook.

Anyway, what chance did Jana and I have at surviving, if that missionary lady almost died. Pa had just put a death sentence on us.

Jana stared Pa straight in the face, crimson splotches appearing on her neck. "I don't want to go."

"I already said you will. The missionary couple actually cried out for joy. They told me it was an answer to prayer."

Jana's splotches grew bigger. "Why don't you go yourself?"

I cringed at her boldness, but Pa didn't seem to mind. "I can't. My job is to get the family there. Anyway, imagine the opportunity you will have to serve."

Jana's voice rose in distress. "I'm already serving!"

Pa stood up. "Enough of this. I need to rest."

All of us older ones left the office, but as we closed the door behind us, Ma cried out. "Linard, you can't make decisions like that without me! Those are my girls as well."

We stopped dead in our tracks. "Lila, they can help out for a couple of years and then come back."

"They could die out there. Are you crazy? You yourself said a missionary lady almost died. How safe would two young women be, alone in the jungle?"

"It is the right thing to do. The girls are available. There is a need. It is obvious God's hand is in this. Anyway, I don't know what to do with them."

Jana and I stared at each other. The truth had finally slipped out. Pa wanted to get rid of us. Jana's breath caught. "Toma, if we died out there, I bet he wouldn't shed a single tear. Instead he would boast that his daughters had become martyrs."

I nodded, and we drifted apart, she to a book she had borrowed from the church library, and I to the far end of the barn. I sat down on one of Pa's instrument boxes and stared at the corrugated iron wall. The lump in my heart began pulsating again. Why couldn't I tell Pa to stop pushing us around? Jana had courage. What was wrong with me?

I studied the flecks of different colored greys in the metal. *"God? Maybe you want Jana and me to go to South America. Maybe you want us to die. Maybe it is your will. It would certainly save on funeral expenses."*

198

That evening, as we gathered around the table for hot dogs and baked beans, Pa brought up the subject again. "I know Ma is against this, but I think it is right. Girls, I will buy your tickets next week."

Pa looked at Ma, trying to make eye contact with her, but Ma turned her head. Pa looked at Jana and me. I couldn't smile. I looked down at the floor instead, and a vision of Jana and me in the jungle unfolded before my eyes. I saw us squatting in a bamboo hut, with rain pouring through and flooding the floor. I saw Jana and me laying sick on mats and breathing out our last, only to be found when our bodies had bloated and started decomposing.

I wept that night. Our fate had been sealed. *"God, I so wanted to get married and have children of my own. That will never happen now."*

The next Sunday morning when we went to church, I sat on the pew behind Pa and Ma, my head bowed down to my chest. I couldn't sing the songs at the beginning of the service, about salvation and victory. I couldn't even look up to hear the sermon. But Pastor Weber must have seen my grief, and he stopped speaking. Instead he said, "If anyone would like to come forward for prayer, please do so right now. Could we have some music, please?"

The pianist stood up and hurried to the front. I too stood up and pushed past my siblings. I kept my eyes focused on the carpet and refused to look at Pa. I knew just what he was thinking. How dare I go up without his permission.

I fell on my knees by the pulpit, my hands clasped in prayer, my eyes closed. I felt someone touch my shoulder. I looked up. A lady from the church was kneeling beside me. "What can I pray for you, Toma?"

"I don't want to die."

Her eyes grew big. "Are you sick?"

I shook my head and looked down at my hands, unable to say anymore. How could I tell her what Pa had done, how he was forcing us to go to the jungle? Would she understand that I had no choice? Children obeyed their parents, especially older daughters who still lived at home. Wasn't that what the Bible commanded?

She put her arm around my shoulder and prayed. *"Dear Father in heaven, please sort out whatever is wrong. Please help Toma to see your hand in her*

199

life. Please take care of her in every way. In Jesus' name, Amen."

I blinked at the lady as something clicked inside my mind. There were things in life far worse than dying, like going to hell, like living with someone who hated you, like breaking your neck and never being able to walk again. The fear in my heart drained away. *"God, help me to trust you again. It seems I keep forgetting that lesson. I know you will do what is best for me."* I squared my shoulders and walked back to my seat.

Pa cornered me in the parking lot after church. "Why did you go forward and make a fool of yourself? You embarrassed me. If you have a problem, you come to me, and don't proclaim it to the whole world. What was it all about anyway?"

I didn't want to tell Pa, but I didn't want to lie either. I looked down at my feet. "I don't want to die."

"What are you talking about, girl? No one is killing you." I glanced up at him, as he towered over me. I didn't tell him the whole truth.

The next morning Pa came into the barn, as I was tidying up after breakfast. He unplugged the cooking hob and picked it up from the wooded box where it sat. I looked at him, confused. "What are you doing, Pa?"

"I just found another airplane instrument. I'll sell this at the pawn shop, so I can buy it."

"But, Pa? You already have at least two hundred." I pointed to the back wall. "What will we cook on?"

"We all have to make sacrifices, Toma."

I stared as he slid the hob under his arm and carried it out to the pickup. I watched him drive away. I stood by the open barn door and looked up at the sky. *"God, it looks like I'm cooking outside again. Maybe going to South America isn't such a bad idea after all."*

Later that morning Pa came back, whistling, carrying a small black box into the barn. He showed us older ones his treasure, and grinned. "This altimeter will be useful for when we go."

He stashed it in the pile with his twenty other altimeters, instruments that told the altitude of an airplane. He rearranged them and headed back to the office. But a few seconds later we heard him bellow, "You did what?"

We charged to the office and opened the door. We found Ma sitting on the bed, a library book on her lap, her face bright red. Pa leaned over her, his fists clenched. "How dare you!" he shouted.

Ma gazed up at him with steady eyes. Her voice was even as she spoke. "You wouldn't listen to me, Linard. I won't let my girls go."

"You can't do that."

"I just did, and I told those missionaries that my girls are going to Bible School. They understood."

"That's a lie!"

"Is it?"

We knew better than to stand at the door and slipped away before Pa and Ma noticed. Back at the barn we could still hear their muffled voices, rising and falling in intensity. Then, after a while the office door slammed shut. The pickup roared into life, and we watched Pa skid out of the driveway. He zoomed down the highway. "I hope he's okay," Karina said.

Ma came in a little while later, her face expressionless and pale. "It's time for school, everyone." Pa came back hours later, his face expressionless as well.

The following Sunday we went to church. But this time Pastor Weber asked a different question during the service. "Does anyone have a testimony they would like to share? Something God is doing in your lives?"

Several people raised their hands, and Pastor Weber pointed to them one by one. They stood where they were and shared their stories. Ma put her hand up at the end, and Pastor Weber called her by name.

Ma stood up, but then she pushed her way toward the center aisle. She strode to the front with long determined strides and continued to climb the stairs to where Pastor Weber stood by the pulpit. He looked at her, his eyebrows rising. He suddenly smiled and stepped back from the microphone.

I gazed at Ma and Pastor Weber up on the platform. They looked like they came from two different worlds. Ma's bright flowered shawl, something she had picked up at the flea market. Pastor Weber's smart grey suit. Ma's long gathered skirt, her hair pulled back in a bun. Pastor

Weber's bright tie and shiny black shoes. I looked over at my sisters. We all looked almost identical to Ma. Only Pa and the boys looked normal.

Ma stepped up behind the pulpit. She leaned into the microphone, but she never took her eyes off Pastor Weber. "I am in great need, Pastor Weber. You all know how we live in a barn. How my husband has determined that we should go to the Amazon jungle. I have accepted all these things, but now my husband has determined to send my girls there this week, alone and unprepared. He refuses to let them go to Bible School to get the training they need. Please pray for him, that he will change his mind, and that God will provide the finances for my girls to go."

"Man Alive!" I shrieked inside. *"I can't believe Ma just said that."* I glanced at Pa and I dreaded what he might do. The whole church fixed their eyes on him. But Pa looked straight ahead, his face pale and hard. Not a muscle moved in his face.

Pastor Weber nodded. "We will pray for you and your family, Mrs. Rose." He lifted his arms in the air. *"Almighty God, you have heard this woman's cry…"*

At the end of the service Pa stood up, and we followed him out as usual. He acted as if nothing had happened and shook people's hands. But person after person came up to me and Jana and patted us on the shoulder. "God will do something, just you wait and see."

Pastor Weber shook my hand. But when I looked down at my feet, overcome with shame that the whole church had been dragged into our disputes, he reached over and lifted my chin. He smiled, his eyes full of compassion. "Cheer up, Toma. God is at work."

I half-smiled back. But he still held my chin. "I'm praying for you, dear," he said.

Praying for me? A nobody. A fearful, weak girl. But, suddenly a whiff of hope nudged its way into my heart. I smiled, a three-quarter smile this time. "Thank you," I whispered.

Pastor Weber could see this hope, and his eyes danced with joy. He tilted back his head and laughed. "Everything will work out alright, Toma. Everything will work out."

I followed Pa back to the pickup, and we drove away from the church, seemingly at peace. But, once we were out of earshot and down the road, Pa exploded at Ma, then at Jana and me. "I'm not sending you to Bible School. Do you hear? You are going to South America." But Pastor Weber's words came to mind and I felt a deep calmness. "I'm praying for you," he had said, and I knew he would keep his promise.

Jana and I looked at Pa, but we didn't know what to say. "Do you hear me?" he yelled.

"Yes, Pa."

The next morning Pa stormed into the barn. Ma was teaching school, and Jana and I were mending clothes. "Alright," he shouted, "if you want to go to Bible School, go. But you can only go to the one that Luke went to. At least there they have strict rules."

Pastor Weber's words echoed in my heart yet again. "I'm praying for you," he had said. He was fighting for us as well.

Ma looked up at Pa, her pencil poised. "I want Karina to go as well. I regret not getting Mik there."

Pa looked like he would explode. "No! Who will help you with Filip and Peter? You know you can't manage on your own. Anyway, she's too young."

Ma's pencil still hung in mid-air. "I disagree with you, Linard. She is ready to take her GED[6]. She has just as much of a right to go as the big girls."

Pa glared at her, the veins on his neck bulging out; his nose flared, but he didn't respond. Instead he jumped in the pickup, slammed the door hard, and skidded down the driveway yet again. I wondered, how much more he could take.

As soon as I could, I wrote a letter to the Bible School, asking if they could send me an application form and catalogue. I had to get it off before Pa changed his mind.

Jana looked over my shoulder as I wrote. "I don't want to go to a missionary training school. I'm not sending a letter. I want to make my own choice."

I looked up at her, not understanding her logic. "Jana, it's better

---

[6] GED – a high school diploma equivalency exam.

than nothing."

"You're just letting Pa control you every inch of the way."

I shrugged my shoulders. "Maybe God wants us to go."

Jana drew away from me. "Don't you start sounding like Pa! One of him is enough!"

The next day I showed Ma my letter and asked if she had a stamp. She read it. "Toma, why didn't you ask for your sisters? You are responsible for them. Don't be selfish and think about yourself. The only way you will get there is if all three of you go. Do you understand that, girl?"

I nodded and retreated to the barn, my heart heavy. It took me another two weeks to find the strength to rewrite that letter. I told Jana and Karina the morning I sent it. Karina grinned, Jana scowled, sarcasm etched in her voice. "Whoopee-doo," she said.

Three weeks later, a package arrived from the Bible School. My hands trembled as I tore it open at the mailbox, pulling out a catalogue and three application forms. I flicked through the application right there at the edge of the highway. Did they want my SAT results? I had failed them so miserably. No! My high school transcripts would be enough!

I ran to the office and showed Ma the package. She flicked through the catalogue and forms as she sat on her bed. "Toma, it will take a miracle to get you girls there. I need to do some more thinking."

She did. A week later, when Pa left for another trip, to buy more airplane parts, she called us all together. But we stood there uncertain. Would she rage and hit us, now that she had been left alone once again?

She pursed her lips instead. "Your Pa will be gone for the next two days," she declared. "I found us a job so we can earn some money for Bible School."

"But Ma!" I begged. "Pa doesn't want us to get a job."

Ma turned on me. "Are you telling me what to do?"

I backed away. "No, Ma'am,"

"Good. The peach farmer down the road wants his peach trees hoed and we can start tomorrow."

"We?"

"Yes, we're all going."

I didn't want that! If Ma came, she might implode. I reached out my hands beseechingly. "It will be hard work, Ma. We can go by ourselves. We will be okay."

She silenced me with a wave of her hand. "I'm going." But I couldn't understand why. She didn't like work. We did almost everything for her.

At dawn the next day we all walked the half mile to the farmer's house, keeping to the grass at the edge of the highway. We older ones carried water and sandwiches. The wind from passing trucks almost blew us over. But I still felt a tinge of excitement. I had never had a proper job.

Ma marched up the stairs of the farmer's house and banged on the door. We stood at the bottom watching her. A minute later the farmer opened his screen door, still chewing his breakfast. He looked startled. I could only assume he hadn't expected to see a band of women and children at his front door.

He handed us each a sharpened hoe and pointed to the nearest field of peach trees. "Do that one today. I'll be in the house if you need me."

We nodded and tramped to the end of the field. We dropped our things in a pile. The peach trees before us stood only eight feet tall. "Let's have a race," Karina called out. "See who can go the fastest."

Jana laughed. "Race yourself. I'm not wearing myself out at the start."

Karina whipped her hoe down onto a weed and sliced it off. She wielded it in a frenzy. But the sun was already hot, and there were no clouds in the sky. Karina slowed down a minute later. The younger ones dropped their hoes a half hour later. They hopped from one small shady spot to another, chatting and keeping up with us.

But soon even they grew quiet in the heat. The only noise was the scrape of hoes and the grunts that escaped our lips. I looked up to check how the others were coping. Jana's hair hung down in strings, sweat dripping from the ends. Karina had a scarf on her head, and it sagged to one side in a damp little mess. But Ma was the one who impressed me most. She too was beet red, but she had kept up with us.

205

I got back to work, and a book I had read in high school came to mind, "The Grapes of Wrath," by John Steinbeck. It showed me how migrants had to work, year in and year out. There was a time when I felt pity for them. Now I respected them with all my heart. They put up with hell, just to stay alive. They refused to roll into a ditch and die, just because life was tough. If they could do it, so would I.

Lunch time came, and we finally sat down, each of us sitting in the shade of our own peach tree. Jana handed out sandwiches, and we ate in silence. Afterwards, we inspected our hands. All of us had blisters, some still bulged with liquid inside, and others had burst, filling up with dirt.

After a while we heaved ourselves up. We older ones and Ma picked up our hoes and continued to work. At 5pm the farmer strolled over and pulled out a leather wallet. "See you tomorrow," he said, as he handed Ma some bills.

Ma didn't answer. Instead, she folded the money and put it in her purse. The farmer stared at her, and then he gathered the hoes, bundling them onto his shoulder. He went one way. We went the other, staggering home in the evening sun.

"I don't want to come back," Karina groaned. But my mind was elsewhere, and I barely heard her voice.

It looked like the farmer had given Ma twenty dollars. Let's say I got a fifth of the money, which meant I earned about four dollars a day, or twenty dollars a week. It would take me four years to get enough money to go to Bible School, that is, if I left out the fact that I still had to eat. *"God,"* I reasoned in my heart, *"there must be some other way."*

Pa returned unexpectedly that evening, just as Filip vomited in the barn. I ran to the office and knocked on the door. "Pa! Filip is sick," I shouted.

Pa came straight over to look at him. He put his hand on Filip's forehead. He asked him to open his mouth. "Filip, why are you sunburned? You have sun stroke. What were you doing?"

Filip looked at Pa, his eyes filling with fear. "We went to a field."

Pa looked over to the rest of us, his face sad and drawn. "What's going on here?"

Jana told him everything.

CHAPTER 22

Not long after, Pa came into the barn. "I don't think your Ma can take much more," he said. "Filip and Peter are constantly under her feet, yet she refuses to let them sleep in here. She says the barn is no place for children. I have to do something before she goes crazy."

All of us looked up from the jobs we were doing. I was crocheting an afghan from old sweaters I had unraveled. Jana was knitting some mittens. Karina was sewing a potholder. None of us answered him. Ma had to deal with far more than her fair share in life. Between losing her home in WWII and losing it again to Pa's schemes, who wouldn't find it hard to cope with life?

But Pa didn't seem to notice our silence. He kept right on talking. "I have checked around and I hear there is a house for sale about six miles from here. The highway department is building a road, and the house needs moving, or else it will get knocked down. We could buy it and move it here."

He shifted his hands to his pockets and pulled out the pickup truck keys. "I already called the highways office," he said. "Come on, everyone. They will show us the house in half an hour."

We piled into the pickup, even Ma. I sat in the back with Filip on my lap, staring out the window at passing peach fields and farmhouses along the highway. Then we drove up a long driveway to an old-fashioned white farmhouse. It was only one story high, with windows in the attic, and ancient pecan trees surrounding it. It looked so pretty, so welcoming, so perfect, compared to the barn.

Pa stopped the pickup, and we tumbled out. We strolled around the house, looking in through the windows. A few minutes later a man appeared, a key in hand. He shook Pa's hand. "This house is a good deal, Mr. Rose. It's sturdy, has cladding on the inside and out. It will be easy to move."

The man unlocked the door, and we stepped inside, moving from room to room. It felt so foreign and strange. A living room with a radiator. A kitchen with a sink and stove. A dining room. A bathroom with a toilet and bath. Even a toilet roll holder. There were doors with locks, and screens on the windows. This was how normal people lived. I had forgotten already.

We found the stairs and headed up. Ma followed us and glanced around. "This is good, Linard," she said, her voice in slow monotone. "You and I can sleep in the living room downstairs. All the children can sleep up here."

Pa put his arm around Ma. He smiled at her, tenderness in his eyes. "That settles it," he said.

He and Ma headed downstairs, but Jana and I remained. We looked at each other. "All of us?" Jana whispered. "But it's only two tiny rooms! How can all of us fit up here? There isn't even enough room for our bunkbeds."

"We will have to use our sleeping bags again," I said. "But anything is better than that barn."

Jana shrugged her shoulders. "I don't know, Toma. At least we have space in there. At least we have proper beds and drawers. We will have to go back to cardboard boxes for our clothes."

I looked at Jana. She made plenty of sense. But Ma needed a house, and, come to think of it, I just wanted to be at least half-way normal again. We headed downstairs and wandered around each room again. I looked more closely this time. There was wallpaper on the walls, wooden floors, and white ceilings. Even electric sockets! I studied them, admired them.

I looked out the window. Ma was sitting alone in the pickup truck, looking straight ahead, her face grim. I drew a sharp breath. *"God, Ma isn't doing very well. Please show Pa that he has to buy this house. Please help Ma find happiness again."*

Outside, Pa was talking with the man in charge. "Can I lock up now?" the man said. "I need to get back to the office. I'll tell them you like the house."

"Thanks," Pa said. "We'll leave in a few minutes as well."

They shook hands, and the man drove off. But as soon as he had left, Pa called us together. "Right," he said, "I want to know if this house is attached to the foundations." He took us around to the back and pointed at a hatch. "Toma," he said, "slide in and check out the foundations. You have a good eye for detail. Tell me what you see."

I gawked at Pa. Why couldn't he go in himself? I was wearing a dress! But I nodded and gathered my skirt, bent down and slid in headfirst. Pa handed me a flashlight.

I elbowed myself in, pushing away cobwebs from my face. I looked around. Everywhere the soil rose up like a hill toward the center of the house. The only clear path was around the foundation. I shimmied forward. But the darkness, the dank smell, the weight of the house above me, with nails poking down through the floor like teeth, somehow crushed me. *"God,"* I whispered, *"it feels like a grave! Like I'm being buried alive! I don't want to live like this."*

I drew a deep breath. Jesus was with me. I was okay. And, he would help me see what I was supposed to see under that house.

I finally crawled out and shook loose dirt from my dress and hair. I looked over at Pa. He was leaning against the house, cleaning his nails with his jackknife. He smiled. "Well, Toma, what did you see?"

"Pa, the only things holding the house in place are the water and sewage pipes. It isn't bolted down."

"Just as I hoped. We have a lot to do now."

We headed back to the pickup and piled in. Pa revealed his plan as we drove back to the barn. "First, we need to choose a place where we can put the house. Next, I need to find a house moving rig. Then we can move it." I listened from the back seat, perplexed. Was it really that easy to move a house from A to B?

We drove up our driveway, and Ma pointed to a grove of pecan trees that stood at the far end of our property. "I want the house there," she said. "It will be away from the barn." Again, her voice sounded lifeless, hopeless.

I stared at the back of Ma's head, at her tight little bun held secure with pins. She had actually spoken twice that day, cared about what was happening. That was more than she usually did.

Pa smiled at her and rested his hand on her knee. "Good idea, Lila! It will make this place look like an old homestead, with its own business next door. We will get started at once."

We children and Pa strode out to the pecan grove, but Ma headed back to the office. We helped Pa measure where the foundations should go and pounded in marker posts. We children dug out the soil making long deep ditches, and Pa came every afternoon to inspect our work.

After work, Jana and I always made supper, heated up water for everyone's bath, and then washed the dishes afterwards. Only later in the evening could I pull out the Bible School catalogue and read through it. I sat on my bottom bunk, hunched over, considering the course options. I would apply for the three-year accelerated course. That way we could get to South America sooner.

Finally, one evening I slid down on the piece of carpet I had laid in the sand by my bed and used my bed as a desk. It was time to fill in that application form. I picked up a pen, my hands shaking from exhaustion and not wanting to make a mistake. But line by line, over the days, I worked my way through that form.

Jana glanced down from her top bunk from time to time, but she refused to fill in her form. She read a church library book instead. One evening I poked her arm. "Jana, when are you going to fill in your application form?"

"Leave me alone! Why should I do what Pa wants?"

I backed away. Didn't she realize that this was our only option, and we had to seize the opportunities as they came? "Please, Jana," I begged, but she refused to reply.

The next day Pa came early to inspect the foundations. We dropped our shovels and watched his movements. "Good news, children! I just found a man who has a house moving rig. He is retired, and his wife doesn't want the rig on their driveway anymore. He said that if we keep it for him, we can use it free of charge. And, when we're ready, we can borrow his truck. It's a good deal."

I wiped the sweat from my face and half-smiled. Finally, things were coming together. And, when the man pulled the rig onto our drive an hour later, I burst out laughing. The rig was enormous, with incredibly long metal beams, and four sets of double wheels running down each side.

We dropped our shovels and ambled over to admire it. "How in the world are we going to get a house on top of that?" Karina asked.

Pa grinned. "We will jack it up."

It took us a couple more weeks to finish the foundation, and Pa started planning the route we should take. He spread out a map on the table in the barn, and followed the different routes with his finger. "I think we should take the back roads," he said.

I leaned over and studied the map. "Why, Pa? The highway runs straight to the barn."

Pa looked up at me and grinned. "True, but I would have to buy a permit and get a police escort. It all costs so much money. Don't you worry. It will be fine."

The very next day the rig man arrived, and he helped Pa hook the rig to the truck. He gave Pa some instructions and left us with a smile. But, not a minute later Pa clapped his hands. "Let's move that house today!"

Jana, Karina, and I helped Pa get ready. We filled the pickup with shovels, picks, a sledgehammer, and jacks. We then followed him, right behind the rig, down the highway and up to the house. Pa pulled out a tape measure and measured the foundation, marking off four crosses, two at the front and two at the back.

He grasped the sledgehammer and wielded it like a lumberjack. Thud. Thud. Thud. Four holes in the right places, so that the beams could slide right through. Pa then backed the rig, maneuvering it into place. But the beams slid in no more than two feet. Pa revved the engine, trying to force them further, but the truck only stalled. "What's going on?" he called back.

211

I bent down to look. "I think you hit the soil under the house. It's piled up in the middle. I had thought you could push it aside, with all the weight of the truck and rig. What are we going to do now?"

Pa climbed from the truck and folded his arms. "This is really bad news. It looks like we will have to abandon the house. What a waste of time and money."

My heart sank. Would we ever get out of that barn? But then the picture of Ma came to mind, of her sitting in the pickup, almost deathlike. She was the reason we were moving this house. I couldn't give up now. "We can still do it!" I cried out. "I'll dig a ditch for each beam."

Pa shrugged his shoulders. "Okay, Toma, you can try. I'll give you two days."

I grabbed a small pick and shimmied underneath. Forget about fears of being buried alive, I had to do this for Ma. I loosened the soil, pushed it to one side, down toward the foundation. Jana and Karina stood by, but they soon grew bored and joined me.

Scratches crisscrossed our hands and arms, as we caught them on the nails that protruded from the floor above our heads. "You know, I would be helping you right now, if I could," Pa said as he bent down to look. "But my chest is too big to fit in there."

"It's okay, Pa," we called. And it really was. I figured out why, as we worked. Pa and Ma, without meaning to, had done us a great favor. They didn't like to work, and they expected us to do it. Not only that, they often didn't tell us how to do it, and yet they still expected us to do it well. In a backwards kind of way, they instilled in us a confidence. We had to take initiative. We had to use our heads. And, we had to knuckle down and just do it.

In the end it took us three days to dig those trenches, and when Pa tried backing the rig in once more, the beams slid in all the way. We clapped and cheered. "Well done!" Pa called. "I didn't think it was possible. Now, everyone, shimmy underneath and detach those pipes. This lady comes home tomorrow."

We stood up straight and saluted Pa. "Yes, Sir!"

I smiled again, as I detached the pipes with Jana and Karina. Without meaning to, Pa and Ma also had given us the opportunity to learn how to never give up. By doing nothing, they built in us determination.

A verse came to mind. "All things work together for good to them that love God." *"I don't understand how you do it,"* I whispered to God in my heart. *"How do you always take what is bad and make something good?"*

The next morning Pa opened the barn door early. "Rise and shine. Today we move that house."

He threw a pair of his stained overalls on Jana's bed, two more on mine and Karina's. "Girls, I don't want you wearing dresses today. It will be dangerous, and they could get caught under the wheels. Put these on."

I stared at the overalls, squirming at the idea. I didn't want to wear Pa's grubby clothes. It was degrading enough having to wear dresses. But we had a job to do. Getting Ma into a house was way more important than how I felt about clothes. "Okay, Pa," I called.

Mik arrived at 6:30am and by 7am we were at the house, placing jacks at the end of each beam. Each of us children stood by one, and we turned the crank until the beams touched the bottom of the house. "Stop!" Pa called. "I'll take over now. Each of you stand at your corner. Keep an eye on things."

The jacks squealed as Pa turned the cranks, a half-revolution at a time. I stood at my corner expecting the house to crumble, but it rose, one inch, then two, one foot and then another. It stayed together as if still on its foundation. Soon there was enough room for Pa to back all sixteen wheels under the beams and get them into position. He jumped from the truck and switched a knob on each jack. He lowered the beams onto the wheels.

"It looks good," he called, as he inspected the house. "Let's see what happens when I move it." He inched the truck forward and the house moved with him, away from the foundation. It looked so odd, a house floating in midair. But it didn't collapse or topple over.

We clapped our hands and hooted. We walked along beside it, all except Karina. She ran to the cab. "Pa, don't we need to tie the house down?"

Pa grinned. "Karina, don't worry. Friction will hold it in place." And it was true. Pa kept on driving, and the house swayed as it bumped over the last of the foundation. All of us skipped back to get out of the way. I expected the house to crumble into matchwood, but it stayed there, perfectly together.

Pa kept the truck moving at a steady crawl and turned onto the road. Away from the trees the house looked huge. It straddled the road and ditches on both sides. "It looks okay," Pa called out to us. "Get into the truck. Let's take this beauty home."

But a mile up the road we came to a bridge. It was made of railway ties. "Pa," Mik said, "it doesn't look wide enough."

Pa stopped the truck and smacked his forehead. "I'm such an idiot. I forgot to measure the bridge."

I looked at Pa in dismay. How could he have forgotten? We couldn't back the rig to where we had started. We couldn't sit there forever either. How could we have come all this way, only to get foiled? We had to get across somehow.

Pa sighed. "Get the tape measure, Mik. If it doesn't fit, I don't know what we will do."

We jumped from the truck and measured the bridge. We measured the inside distance of the inside wheels of the rig. Only two inches of each inside wheel would fit on the bridge. Pa nodded. "That's just enough to cross. Toma, Mik, I want you at the front guiding me. Jana, Karina, you keep an eye at the back. Make sure everything is okay."

"Will the bridge be strong enough?" Jana called out to Pa.

"It had better be, or else we're going for a swim."

We nodded, and Mik and I kneeled in the middle of the road. We shouted instructions to Pa. "An inch that way." "Half an inch the other way." "Straight ahead." We had to center the truck exactly, to make sure the rig behind was centered as well. No one had to tell us there was no room for mistakes.

The truck crawled over, and I climbed into the stream. I had to get a better view of the rig. I didn't notice that I stood in water. "Stop," I shouted as the rig touched the bridge.

Pa stopped and jumped out to inspect. "Well done," he called. "Now make sure it stays on."

The first two inside wheels of the rig rolled on. The bridge groaned.

"Stop," I shouted again.

Again, Pa jumped out, joining me under the bridge. "It's okay. It will hold!"

Back in the truck, Pa put it into gear, and Mik and I shouted instructions to him. It hit me how crazy the whole thing looked, the outside wheels hanging in midair, the house creaking above my head, the bridge groaning under its weight. But inch by inch the house edged forward, and the bridge didn't collapse underneath it.

The last wheels rolled off and I whooped with joy. "We're clear," Mik shouted.

Pa stopped the truck and jumped out. He threw his arms around Mik and me. "Well done! I didn't think we could do it. Nothing can hold us back when we work together."

Mik and I grinned as we climbed into the truck. But as I sank down on the seat, the danger hit me with renewed force. What if I had given a wrong instruction? What if I had mixed up my lefts and rights? What if the truck and rig had toppled over? What if we had died? I pushed the questions away one by one. "We did it," I kept assuring myself. "We did it."

A few miles later Pa stopped at a crossroad. He idled for a minute. "There are power lines up ahead," he said, "and I don't want to risk them snagging on the house. I telephoned the electricity company yesterday. They said it would take a week to lift the lines. I can't sit here that long. I will have to take the house down the highway for the last quarter of a mile."

Pa turned left and drove up to the highway, waiting for a space in the traffic. But when he pulled out, the house took up two-thirds of the road. An oncoming truck slowed down and pulled over. Cars pulled over. Pa glanced at Mik and me. "Get me as close to the edge as possible."

Pa didn't stop for us to jump out, and we sprang from the cab to avoid the slow-moving wheels. "Three yards," we shouted. "Two feet. One foot. Straighten the wheel!"

"Keep me steady," Pa shouted. "The traffic can pass us now."

We jogged in the ditch beside the rig, and ten minutes later Pa stopped at our driveway. Mik and I ran onto the highway, holding up our arms like policemen. The traffic stopped, and Pa crossed over, driving the rig onto our land. He only stopped when the back end of the rig was about thirty yards from the road. "We got away with it," he called, as he jumped from the cab to the ground.

At that moment a police car drove up and two police officers got out. They headed toward Pa. "Good afternoon, sir," they called. "Someone rang saying you needed an escort."

Pa shook his head and pointed to the pecan grove. "No thanks. We're just moving the house over there."

The police officers waved. "Sorry to detain you, sir. Hope the move goes well." They climbed back into their car and drove off.

We stood there, watching them, and Pa laughed, a nervous edge in his voice. "That was close."

We moved the house the last 300 yards, and Pa backed it onto the new foundations. We finally set it down that night. I gazed at it in the dark, only a shadow against the trees. I smiled. *"Thank you, God,"* I prayed. *"We can move Ma in soon. I can't wait for her to get better. Maybe then I can go to Bible School."*

The next evening Jana still hadn't filled in her application form. "Please, Jana," I begged, "I need to send the forms out tomorrow."

Karina jumped down from her bunk, her application in her hand. "Here Toma. I did mine." She handed it to me, but Jana made a face and looked away. "Leave me alone."

I wanted to cry. *"God, what's wrong with her? Is she finally coming unglued? Has she lost the will to live? Now we won't get to that Bible School. Why is life so unfair?"*

But two days later Jana did fill in her form. She almost threw it at me. "Here it is, your majesty."

I stared at her, taken aback. She acted as if it was all my fault. Had she forgotten what Pa had said? It was the only place we could go. I sent off the letter, anyway, feeling like the prison door had been slammed shut yet again. *"God, please do a miracle. Please make that letter get there faster than normal. Please, please answer this prayer."*

Three weeks later a letter arrived from the Bible School. I pulled it from the mailbox, and my hands trembled as I opened it right there on the spot. A lump rose in my throat. I had better brace myself for bad news. Good things didn't happen to me.

"Thank you for your application forms," I read. "We are happy to inform you that you have been accepted and can start in September."

A tremor ran through me. I read it again, hunting for where it said, "Application rejected." Surely, they hadn't prayed to God enough, sought his guidance and found out how weird we were. He would have told them we lived in a barn, that we had no money, that we were a laughingstock. But maybe those things didn't matter in that Bible School. They had a different set of values, like loving God and serving him.

I raced to the office and knocked on the door. There was no answer. "Ma," I called, "we've been accepted."

"Come in, Toma."

I tiptoed in and found her on her bed, reading a missionary book. I handed her the letter. "How will we pay for it, Ma? It starts in three weeks."

Ma looked up at me, a faint smile on her lips. "I telephoned your grandmother, and she has offered to pay for the three of you. You can go, and Pa has agreed! He even said that Mik and I can take you. But Pa wants me to check out that school. If I think it's bad, I'm to bring you back."

CHAPTER 23

Jana, Karina and I stood in the Bible School parking lot with Ma. Mik sat in the car, the engine idling. Ma had followed us through registration, seen our dorm rooms, and even had a meal in the school dining room. Now we awaited her verdict.

I searched her face, trying to determine what she was thinking. "I am not sure about this," she finally said. "You will get spoiled here. With having your own bedrooms, and others cooking your meals, you might get into your heads that you are better than us."

The three of us instinctively reached out our hands. "No, Ma!" we beseeched. "That isn't true!"

She shook her head. "Pa has entrusted me with a big responsibility. You are his daughters." She pursed her lips as she studied us, moving from one face to another.

Mik put his head out the car window. "Come on, Ma. For Pete's sake, they'll be okay! I want to get going. It's a long drive home."

Ma didn't turn to look at Mik, instead she rested her eyes on me. "I'm leaving you in charge, Toma. Make sure Jana and Karina toe the line. Is that clear?"

"Yes, Ma'am."

Ma opened the car door and slid inside. The car started moving before she even closed the door. It was as if Mik wasn't going to let her change her mind, and he had to get her away before she did. "Be good," she called back to us.

We waved and stood there watching them disappear. Karina giggled. "Bye, I'm off to explore."

Jana nodded. "I'm glad we're here! I want to meet my roommate." She hurried off as well.

I stood alone, still looking down the street, sadness washing over me. *"Dear Jesus, please help me. I should be feeling happy, but I feel so lost. I don't know what to do. I don't even know what I want."*

I turned a full circle, looking around me, clasping and unclasping my hands. I looked at the students walking by in pairs, chatting, laughing, and knowing where they were going. They looked confident and well-adjusted, with their store-bought clothes, nice shoes and coats. I sighed. I was going to stick out like a sore thumb.

I hurried to the dorm, my long homemade purple dress swishing as I moved, my sandals squeaking, my thin white sweater flapping in the breeze. Back in my room I unpacked my small cardboard box of clothes. A dress. Two blouses. Four pairs of underpants. An extra bra. A nightgown. It took me minutes to arrange everything perfectly. Now I had nothing to do. No family meals to cook. No younger ones to teach. No clothes to sew. No outhouse to clean.

I sighed as I looked out the window, at the clear blue autumn sky. For the last six years I had poured out my life, to make sure my brothers, sisters and mother survived. I would treat Bible School the same way. I would give it my all. I wouldn't waste a moment in frivolous activity. I wouldn't make friends. I didn't need friends. I had come to study.

Supper was announced, and I hurried to the dining room. The place was packed with students, standing in line for their food. The air buzzed with laughter and chatter. I felt as if I had stepped into another world. Where did they find the capacity for happiness? Life was about survival, about staying alive.

I slipped into line and Karina joined me a few minutes later. "This is wonderful!" she whispered, her eyes shining.

Fear suddenly filled my heart. I was already failing at the task entrusted to me by Ma. Karina was enjoying life. I gave her a stern look. "Be careful, Karina! We came here to study."

"Relax, Toma! Classes haven't started. Maybe it's time you

lightened up. Life isn't all about being serious."

I stared at her, taken aback. Where had she learned to talk like that? We hadn't been allowed to entertain thoughts of pleasure or rest. Life was too tough for that. Whether we liked it or not, it was about hard work and suffering. But the words Karina spoke kept coming back like an echo. Others said it as well. "Toma, it's okay. You can lighten up!"

One such person was a teacher who invited some of us students over for an evening meal. I felt I should go, even though it took me away from my studies. I sat at the meal and didn't know what to say. The rest of the students chatted with each other, but I had forgotten how. I had worked in silence for far too long.

The teacher smiled and asked me about my family. I gasped. How could I confess that we still lived in a barn, that I had hoped to move Ma into the house before we had left, but she had refused, that I obeyed my parents in every detail of life?

I felt such shame and looked down at my hands. I could mumble out answers to his questions. "Yes, we live in the country." "No, my father is self-employed." "I come from a big family."

The teacher gazed at me, his face sad. It was as if there was something about me that disturbed him. "Toma, would you like to stay for a game of scrabble?" he asked at the end of the meal.

"I mustn't. I need to study."

"But you need to take a break once in a while."

"I can't."

The teacher nodded, pain on his face. "Toma, you can't push yourself like that. You will break."

I looked up into his face. "Please, may I go?" I asked.

He walked me to the door and opened it. "Toma, if you ever want to rest, you are always welcome here."

I thanked him and fled. I went back to work, and I kept on working every evening until the library closed. I was afraid to go back to the dorm. I was afraid to socialize.

One such evening I hurried back to my room late, grabbed my nightgown and towel. I could just squeeze in a shower before lights out. I ran up the hall to the shower room. No one was there. In a flurry I stepped into the shower and threw off my clothes, hanging them over the shower-curtain rail, along with my towel.

I turned on the water and sighed. It felt so good. After having had to take baths outside for two whole years, a shower was still such a treat. I closed my eyes as the water massaged my back.

Suddenly I heard a noise. My towel and clothes had disappeared. I poked my head out of the shower cubicle, thinking they had fallen to the floor, but they were gone. "Whoever it is, please give my clothes back," I called. But there was no answer.

I didn't know what to do. No one could hear me. No one had left an extra towel in the shower room. I grimaced. Was this because I was such a sourpuss in Bible School, always working, never playing? Did the girls not like me? But then I chuckled. It didn't matter. The pressing problem was to get to my room. I would wrap myself up in the shower curtain instead, even though it was translucent white!

I unhooked it and draped it around my dripping body. I poked my head out the shower room door to check if the hall was clear. But just about every bedroom door was open, and girls stood in doorways grinning at me. "Hey, Toma," one of them called, "did you lose something?"

"No!" I called back and stepped into the hall. I walked to my room as if on a catwalk, my nose in the air, water trailing behind. Cheers and laughter broke out.

I grinned. Those students liked me. I liked them. It was so nice to get teased. So nice to be noticed. So nice to be accepted. And, on my twenty-third birthday, only a week later, I received five homemade birthday cakes. FIVE!!! What had I done to deserve such love?

Two months later Pa telephoned the Bible School, asking if he could speak to me. I ran to the switchboard. Had someone died? Pa hardly ever called, mostly Ma did. "Toma," Pa said. "I have decided to move the family up. I have worked out the numbers and it is cheaper for us all to live up there than for the three of you to live in the dorms. I have already rented a house and will use the rest of Grandma's money. You can move in with us as soon as we get there. The house is only a block from the school."

I couldn't think of what to say. I could barely breathe. "Did you hear me, Toma?"

I gripped the phone with both hands, forgotten pain resurfacing in my chest. I had to stall him, persuade him it was a bad idea. "But, Pa," I reasoned, "we've already paid for everything."

"Toma, it will be fine. I have talked with the Bible School, and they are willing to give the money back. And it gets even better. The children can go to the Christian school. Ma won't have to teach them anymore. Then Ma and I can take some classes. Someone has to keep an eye on you. I hear there are boys who are interested in you."

"Who?" I asked. "I don't know of anyone."

"Never mind," Pa said. "We'll be there in two weeks."

Pa couldn't see my tormented face. It was true, I wanted Ma to be happy, for the younger ones to get an education, but I was just starting to find my own feet. I didn't want him around. He would start telling me what to do. "Okay, Pa. That sounds good," I lied.

After Pa hung up, I wandered back to the dorm, my head down, not feeling the biting winter wind. "*Why, God?*" I howled in my heart.

A verse I had discovered pushed into my mind. "The Lord will fight for you; you need only to be still."q It was as if God himself was saying it, but his voice was gentle and firm. All I had to do was keep quiet. God would do the fighting for me.

I sighed. *"Dear God, it's obvious you're not worried about this. If going to Bible School requires my whole family coming, please help me cope. And, thanks for letting us stay. Pa could very well have told us to go home."*

Two weeks later the family arrived, and Jana, Karina, and I moved back in with them. This time we three shared a bed. We lived out of cardboard boxes again. But God was fighting, as he had promised. A couple of days later Pa announced that he would be going back. He and Ma wouldn't be taking classes. Instead he wanted to sell our house and barn. He wanted to buy another airplane.

Pa returned three months later, just as Bible School ended. The house hadn't sold, so he took us back. But Pa kept trying, and, finally in August, the house did sell. Now Pa had the cash he needed to buy another airplane. He sent us all back to Bible School alone, and he stayed behind.

Two months later he found one and ferried it to a desert airport, far away from civilization. He left it there and came to join us. He even took a couple of classes with Ma. Then, at the end of the academic year we packed up our boxes again. We headed into the unknown. I stared out the pickup window as we drove south. *"Amazing, isn't it, God. We're homeless again, and it doesn't even bother me."*

We travelled for three days, and I watched the landscape change, from green to desert. We rolled down the windows as the temperature increased. Finally, Pa pulled into a campsite with a few scraggly trees. I climbed out and shielded my eyes. Mirages stretched out on every side, disappearing into the horizon. "What an adventure!" Pa called out. "Let's set up camp."

We moved in slow motion as we unrolled our orange tents, and my head ached from the intense heat. Filip and Peter sat quietly in the shade of the pickup truck, their faces pale. I didn't know how to make things easier for them. How did one escape from desert heat?

The next morning Pa woke us at dawn, and already the air was hot. We older ones piled into the back of the pickup and headed out to an airfield. The wind blew in our faces, and we looked around. The scenery was the same in every direction. Sand dunes. Prickly pear cacti. Tumbleweed rolling in between.

Finally, a windsock appeared in the distance, and as it grew bigger an airport came into view. Two Quonset huts and a trailer house. A few airplanes in between. Pa pulled up beside a twin-engine airplane. It towered over our heads. "I bought a Twin Beech again," Pa said. "This one has more seats."

We jumped from the pickup to look around. "Pa?" Karina asked. "Why did you fly it here, to the middle of nowhere?"

Pa grinned. "This airplane was confiscated by the government for drug smuggling. I thought it best to keep it out here, away from the CIA and their prying eyes."

"But, Pa," Karina replied, confusion on her face, "the government sold it to you! Why would they care?"

"They could still send in their sniffer dogs. You see, this Twin Beech is perfect for getting in and out of tight spots. They might think we are drug smugglers as well. If they found even a trace of drugs left over from the last owners, they would confiscate it again."

Pa picked up some cans from under the airplane wing. He handed them to us. I read the label. "Paint remover?"

"This airplane has lots of layers of paint on it. I want it all stripped down, right to the aluminum. It will look beautiful then."

Jana studied her can. "But Pa? What does this have to do with getting to South America?"

"Nothing. It will make it easier to sell later on."

Jana looked over at me and raised her eyebrows. I raised mine back. The mission field wasn't the reason Pa wanted us to fix his airplane. All he wanted was an airplane, and the mission field was his excuse. He was pouring out his life, his money, and the lives of his children. He was sacrificing us for his idol.

I sighed. *"Dear God! Pa has already wasted a quarter of my life. Will there be anything left when he's finished?"*

A familiar verse then popped into my mind. "The Lord will fight for you; you need only to be still." It seemed so impossible, but that verse reassured me. God had everything under control, and I had better be quiet, or I might wreck things up again. It seemed to be an unfortunate talent of mine.

I fell on my knees and opened a can of paint remover, pouring the goop into an old tin can. Jana and Karina did the same. Then we climbed up on the step ladders Pa had borrowed. But the wind blew so hard, our dresses billowed up, and the men who worked there stopped to gaze. Pa called us immediately down. "I want you to wear pants from now on," he said. "I will not have my girls exposed like that." Oh! God was fighting for us.

Every morning we drove in at dawn, and Ma and the younger ones stayed at the campsite. But a week later they killed two rattlesnakes, one just outside a tent. Ma sat down beside Pa at the picnic table that evening. "Linard, please, we need someplace safe, somewhere cool. We're burning up out here. It's too much for us."

Pa put his arm around her shoulder. "I thought you might say that.

I asked about the trailer house at the airfield, and the owner says we can rent it right now. It has air-conditioning and furniture."

Ma closed her eyes, and tears glistened between her eyelashes. "Then we will move in tonight."

"But it only has one bedroom," I said.

Ma's eyes flew open. "It's better than nothing, girl."

I felt like kicking myself, yet again. Why had I opened my mouth? How could God fight for me, if I kept spouting off? *"I'm sorry, God. But, I don't think we will fit in."*

Regardless, Pa started giving us orders. "Girls, no need to pack properly. Throw everything into the back of the pickup and roll up the tents." A half hour later we were on the move, us older ones in the back with all our worldly possessions at our feet, the wind blowing in our sweaty faces.

Pa pulled up in front of the trailer house. He opened the pickup door for Ma and took hold of her hand. He led her up the front stairs. Suddenly he bent down, whisking her off her feet. "This is for you, my bride."

Ma threw her arms around Pa's neck, as he carried her inside. She smiled, as he placed her on a couch and turned on the air conditioning. He adjusted the vents to point directly at her sunburnt face. She smiled again. "Thank you, Linard! You and I will sleep in the bedroom."

Jana sidled up behind me, getting close to my ear. "Toma, I suppose all of us kids will have to sleep right here in the living room, squished in like sardines. Someone should write a book about this."

"No one would dare," I whispered back.

We worked the rest of the summer, on Pa's airplane in the day, on antique cars in the evening. Pa said we could sell those cars and raise the extra cash needed for South America. But by the end of the summer Pa only sold one; his wallet was still empty, and we still lived in that trailer house.

At supper one evening, Pa surveyed us girls. "Toma, Jana, Karina, you three will have to go to Bible School by yourselves this time." A week later at supper he surveyed us again. "Girls, I've changed my mind. I want us to go to South America instead. I have delayed too long."

"Pa," Jana cried out. "You can't do that. This is our last year. We won't be able to graduate."

"I can do what I want. I have been noticing that all you talk about is Bible School now. It's Bible School this. And Bible School that. You think that going there will make you happy. That's a lie."

"Pa, please," I begged. "We're not girls anymore. If we put it off, I won't graduate till I'm twenty-six. That's old, Pa. Please let us go."

"No! You're MY children. If you can't learn to be happy at home, you will never learn to be happy anywhere else. Anyway, I don't have the money to get you there. I need $800."

"Then I shall pray!" I said. I swallowed my tears and that evening I wriggled behind the couch with a flashlight and my Bible in hand. That was the only place I could find to be alone at night. It was too dangerous to walk in the desert in the dark, with rattlesnakes coming out to warm themselves on rocks.

I lay on the carpet, squished in tight against the wall. *"God, what are you doing? Pa already pulled me out of high school. Does he have to pull me out of Bible School as well? Don't let him. Please give us the $800 so we can go."*

Three days later Pa drove off to an auction and came back with an old border patrol van, one used to pick up people who had crossed the US border illegally. Pa called us together. "I want you children to clean this van. I will sell it again for a profit."

We each grabbed a bucket of water and opened all the doors. We scrubbed the walls, ceiling, seats and floor. Peter followed us in, saying he was looking for treasure. He slid his hands down into the cracks of seats and pulled out a pen knife. Suddenly he screeched. He leapt from the van, holding something up high. "Gold! I found gold!" he shouted, jumping around like a grasshopper.

We dropped our wash rags and gathered around him. Pa strode over from a Quonset hut, where he had just been chatting with other pilots. "What's all this commotion?" he called. "I thought I told you to work."

Peter showed him a large gold coin. "Gold! Pa, I found gold. It's mine."

Pa extended his hand. "Give it to me."

Peter handed it over, and we watched Pa wipe it off in his shirt. He held it up toward the sun and chuckled. "If this is gold, I should be able to bite it."

We watched him, as he put it into his mouth, as he sank his teeth into it. We waited as he took it out, and we all leaned forward in unison. A perfect imprint of Pa's teeth lay imbedded in both sides of the coin.

We whooped with joy, and Pa slid the coin into his pocket. "I'm going to the bank right now," he said. "It must be worth a lot."

He drove off straight away, and two hours later we saw billows of dust rising from the road. Pa was driving like a maniac. We dropped our washrags and sprang from the van. Pa skidded to a stop and jumped from the car. "It was solid gold!" he cried. "I got $800 in cash." He pulled a wad of money from his pocket, running his fingers through the bills.

"That's amazing, Pa," I cried, clapping my hands. "Now we can go to Bible School."

"What are you talking about?"

"You said we needed $800 to go, and I told you I would pray. God just answered us."

"No, he didn't! This is for South America. This proves that we will get there this fall."

I stared at Pa, stunned. There was no way I could make him hand over the money. I couldn't even make him let us go to Bible School. *"God, help me. You just gave us $800. How can I follow you when Pa goes against your answers?"*

I hid behind the couch that evening and wept. I propped up the flashlight and opened my Bible. I read, "Don't be afraid; you are worth more than many sparrows."[r] I might be valuable to God, but what good did that do if I wasn't valuable to Pa. *"Do something, God,"* I prayed. *"Don't just sit there and let him get away with it. There are only five more days till registration. Please get us there on time."*

Grandma telephoned the next day, and when she heard that Pa wasn't going to let us go, she offered to send him extra money straight away. She rang the following morning to say that she had sent us $2000 and mailed it special delivery. It would arrive in the next day or so.

I squeezed behind the sofa that evening, squeaking in silent joy. *"You did it, God! You did it. Everything will be alright. And, I didn't even have to say a word."*

Two days ticked by. Then three, and still the letter hadn't arrived. The morning we should have left, Pa telephoned the Bible School. "My children won't be coming back this semester. We're going to South America as missionaries."

My heart spiraled down like a crashing airplane. Where was Grandma's money? I hid in the kitchen after lunch and slumped down onto the floor. I leaned my back against the cupboards. Maybe I could find some comfort in the Bible, but I gasped as I read the next words. "Honor your father and mother."[s] It felt like a punch in the gut.

"That really hurts, God. How could you ever agree with Pa? You know I'm an adult now. Why are you asking me to go along with his wishes? He's wrong to treat us like this."

Later that day the mail truck arrived. It drove up to the trailer, and the mailman climbed out. Pa sauntered over and signed for a letter. He tore it open, pulling out a $2000 check. Instead of telling us, he folded it and put it in his pocket.

I ran into the trailer, but Ma was sitting in the living room. I locked myself in the bathroom instead, sitting on the toilet seat. *"God, why didn't you send that money earlier? It would have been so easy for you to get it here on time. Now we can't go to Bible School."*

I leaned my head against the bathroom wall, tears running down my cheeks. "I hate you, Pa," I choked. But I couldn't tell God how I felt about him, although I'm sure he knew. I had served him faithfully, just like I had served Pa. Now he had let me down as well.

The next day I opened my Bible again, but only out of duty at being a good Christian. I didn't expect God to do any miracles, say anything nice, or even care about me. But who else could I turn to? My eyes fell on, "Whoever wants to be my disciple must deny themselves and take up their cross daily and follow me. For whoever wants to save their life will lose it, but whoever loses their life for me will save it."[t]

I paused and stared at the words in front of me. Something clicked, like a pin dropping in total silence. I read the verses again. This wasn't Pa speaking to me, bawling out instructions. This was GOD speaking, in a gentle and quiet voice. He wanted me to let go of something special in my life, because he had something even better for me. I shook my head, not comprehending. What could be more special than finishing Bible School? But whatever it was, it was secure from Pa's grasp. Pa wouldn't be able to stop what God had planned, no matter how hard he tried.

I bowed my head. *"Dear God, I'm so sorry for my rotten attitude, and not trusting you. I let myself get so messed up by Pa. Please help me stay strong."*

Autumn came, then winter, and we still lived in that one-bedroom trailer house. But Jana and I began getting invitations to speak at afterschool clubs, and after one such session a teacher approached me. "Toma, you're a good teacher. You have a gift." Another teacher said the same.

I had been noticing it as well. Children listened when I taught them. Their eyes sparkled. I couldn't believe it. God had actually given me a gift, a direction in life! Now I saw what I had to do, change from my three-year accelerated Bible course, to another one the Bible School offered, a four-year Bachelor of Religious Education. I would never have known if I hadn't listened to God.

But, wait a minute. Was this what God wanted for me? I hadn't asked him. And, also, was it even his will that I go to Bible School? *"Please, show me,"* I prayed. I opened my Bible to Exodus 6:8. "And I will bring you into the land… and I will give it you as a heritage: I am the LORD."[u]

I hugged the Bible to my chest. Pa would never give me an inheritance, but my Father in heaven was already doing it. Bible School was my heritage. It would be with me all my life. God would make sure it happened.

December came, and I told Pa I wanted to switch to the four-year teaching course. He shrugged his shoulders. "We didn't make it to the Amazon jungle this time. We will try again next summer. You can go to Bible School if you want."

Ma looked up sharply. "Only if we all go!"

CHAPTER 24

We arrived just in time for the winter term, and I felt like a puppy yapping for joy. Teachers, workers, and students hugged me. Some even cried and said they had prayed that I would come back.

A month flew by, and I still couldn't stop smiling. One morning I gazed out the window of the grey clad house where we lived. The dawn sky sparkled in the sub-zero weather. It was as if God had sprinkled glitter into the atmosphere. I laughed. God had given me a wonderful inheritance! *"Thank you,"* I whispered. *"Thank you."*

Ma's brown leather Bible happened to be laying open on the windowsill, its pages worn ragged with use. I glanced down and read an underlined verse, without even thinking. "See, your king comes to you, gentle and riding on a donkey…" ᵛ

I started. It was as if that pin had dropped again, and in the utter silence it sounded like a clang. I read the verse again. That instant a thought came to mind. "Your husband will be like this!"

I pushed it away. There was no way I could think about marriage. Only the week before I had made another vow. A speaker in chapel had urged us to give our twenties to God. He asked if we would be willing to wait and not consider marriage until we turned thirty. He said God desired single-minded young people, available to him.

My heart had stirred as I listened to that speaker. He made sense, and how I wanted to give God my best. So what if Pa had already stolen the first half of my twenties, I could at least give God the remainder, and I would trust God for marriage after that. The speaker asked us to stand if this was what we wanted to do.

Dozens of us stood in the auditorium that morning, and when the speaker prayed for us, a solemn silence filled the place. This was the deepest sacrifice a young person could make. For me it meant no dating, no looking at boys, no daydreaming of being whisked off my feet. It meant concentrating on God alone.

I read that verse in Ma's Bible again, and that same pin dropping click startled me. *"God, I'm confused. Are you saying you want me to get married? Are you revoking the promise I made in chapel? Are you saying this man, my future husband, will be humble and gentle? That he will be different from Pa? I have heard that most girls marry someone like their fathers. I would rather stay single my whole life than have that ever happen to me. Or, maybe, just maybe, I just plain want to get married, and I willed that verse to speak to me."*

I looked up into the sky again, at the floating glitter. *"God, I don't know if I heard you right. But if this is of you, I give you three years. That should be enough time to produce a husband."*

I waited. The first year passed. The second year passed, and Jana, Karina and I graduated. Pa moved us back to Texas, but somehow, his heart had softened at Bible School. He rented us a place, an old-world adobe house, with a grape arbor, French doors leading into the dining room, and a fireplace. It didn't matter that there were bars on the windows, two-foot-thick mud walls that had crumbled in places, or uneven floors, it felt like a palace. We girls even had our own bedroom, and we could shut the door and feel safe.

But Pa still planned to take us to the Amazon jungle that autumn, and every morning we drove to the airport to work on his Twin Beech and antique cars. My job now was to upholster the car seats and make new wall panels for the airplane. All day I sat on a wooden stool in a makeshift lean-to, with a sloping corrugated iron roof. I worked on an old industrial sewing machine Pa had bought off the government, and I cut material on a table made from an old door. I stayed in that lean-to all day, but that didn't stop my eyes wandering. I searched the desert dunes, the mirages, hoping a "Lawrence of Arabia" would appear on his camel, with sticks of dynamite in his canvas bag, and blow up Pa's airplane.

"What are you doing, God?" I whispered. *"If you promised me a husband,*

why are we still in the desert? Still going to the Amazon jungle? How can this future husband ever find me, if I'm stuck in a shed, hidden from view by sand dunes? It doesn't make sense."

Another thing didn't make sense either. My Religious Education degree wasn't valid in the States. I had studied for four years, and it was all in vain. How could I use my gift in teaching if I wasn't even allowed to teach?

A couple of months later, after a long day at the airport, the telephone rang. "Toma," Filip called, "someone wants to talk with you! It's a man."

I ran from my room, down the hall, across the living room, into Pa's study. Who would ever want to talk with me? Breathless, I grabbed the telephone with both hands. "Hello, this is Toma Rose."

"Howdy!" said a voice. "I'm the principal of a Christian school here in town. I just heard you graduated from Bible School and might be looking for a job. I hear you have two sisters as well, and I was wondering if ya'll would like a job. I need a mathematics and science teacher, and a fourth-grade teacher for this September."

I drew in a deep breath. "I'm sure we would love to, but our bachelor's degrees aren't valid here."

"That's okay. You at least have a degree, and that's what counts. How soon can you give me an answer?"

My heart began to soar, but I pulled it back down. Life had thrown me too many disappointments. "Let me talk with my sisters. I'll get back to you as soon as I can."

I told Jana and Karina straight away, and they clapped their hands, laughed, and twirled around in our bedroom. Even Pa nodded his head in approval. "Girls, you can work there until we go." I rang back the next day, and then I too danced for joy.

Life at home grew happy as well. One Saturday morning I headed out the back door, barefooted, to take in the laundry. Suddenly I stepped on something long and round. I instantly knew what it was. A rattlesnake!

I screamed, and jumped, my arms and legs going in every direction. Filip and Peter suddenly appeared, falling to the ground, laughing like they would split. "It's dead," they called, barely able to get the words out. "It's dead!"

The third year ticked by and still I was single. Something must have gone wrong. Three years should have been plenty of time for God to come up with a husband. Had I misunderstood that verse from Ma's Bible?

I sat alone in my bedroom one evening, my own Bible open on my lap. I read the verse again. "See, your king comes to you, gentle and riding on a donkey…" I stopped and waited for that pin-drop feeling. I waited some more. I read the verse again. Still no affirmation in my heart.

A wave of sickness rolled over me. I pushed my Bible onto the bed and jumped up. "Idiot!" I derided myself. "Numbskull! You put words into God's mouth, and then you pretended he spoke. You just wasted three years of your life!" I paced in circles around the room wanting to punch and kick at the walls.

I would just have to take things into my own hands and find that man myself. But nothing ever worked, no matter how hard I tried. The fourth year passed, and most evenings now, Jana and I sat in our bedroom, bemoaning our sorry fate. But one evening Jana stopped me. "I can't go on like this, Toma. I have to leave."

I looked at her stunned. "What do you mean?"

Jana brushed a strand of hair from her face. "I know Pa said we can't leave until we get married, but he's wrong. We're adults now. And you and I know he will never take us to South America. It's just another reason to keep us prisoners at home."

I sighed so deeply, I coughed. "I know."

"How long has it been, Toma? Fifteen years since he first said that God told him to flee? He expects us to obey God, but he isn't doing it himself! And it's our rent money that keeps him alive. He's a grown man, Toma! He can stand on his own two feet."

I looked down at the floor. "Where will you go?"

"I have been saving up a little on the side. Pa doesn't know it. I have enough to go back east. Remember Joan? She said I can stay with her until I find a job."

I nodded. I had liked Joan a lot. She was a friend we had met when we were kids. "Jana, will you tell Pa?"

Jana laughed, but it sounded hollow. "Yah. He would find out anyhow."

The next day Jana did tell Pa, but his only question was, "How much money do you have in the bank?"

Jana shrugged. "Nothing really."

A few days later as Jana packed her car, Pa realized that she did have money. "You lied to me," he shouted.

"No, I didn't," Jana said. "That money is set aside for my trip. I have nothing to give to you."

Pa clenched his fists. "You will never succeed at anything, girl. I won't give you my blessing."

Jana stood up straight, but her face went pale. "I don't need your blessing, Pa. I'm following God, not you."

Jana left us early the next morning, and I watched her drive off. Now it was me, an old maid, Karina, Filip and Peter still at home. How had this happened? *"God, you said you would fight for me. I have been waiting for you to step in. Don't tell me I misunderstood you in this as well. Have I wasted a decade of my life?"*

Again, that same sickness rolled over me. I wanted to pull out my hair. What was wrong with me? Why couldn't I learn from my mistakes? Here I was trusting in delusions again. God had never spoken to me. I had no right to claim promises he never gave. Why was I so slow?

On my twenty-ninth birthday, I drove home from work. I stood by my bedroom window looking out over Pa's junk in the back, rusted cars, machinery and a Cessna with only one wing. I looked up toward the setting sun, shielding my eyes with my hands, and a promise I had made in Bible School came to mind, to remain single until I turned thirty. For better or for worse, I still was single. I had kept that promise, despite my best efforts to break it. God, in his mercy, had held me true. *"Only one more year,"* I whispered.

I thought back over my twenties. I should have been happy doing what God wanted, but all I had done was moan. "Where is my future husband?" "What's taking so long?" "Doesn't God care that I'm getting old?" If one of my students at school had moaned at me like that, whining day in and day out, moment by moment, we would have had a chat.

I slumped on the bed and sat cross legged, resting my arms on my knees. I kept staring out my bedroom window. The sun had already set, and the sky had turned deep purple. *'I'm so sorry, Jesus. I don't know how you put up with me. I'm tired of being negative. I'm tired of moaning, of making myself miserable. I'm tired of complaining to you. I want to draw a line and start all over again. I want adventures with you. I want to have some fun."*

I sat in the growing darkness, and it suddenly made sense. I didn't need a husband to be happy. I didn't need a home to feel secure. I didn't have to fear Pa. I didn't have to worry about Ma. I didn't even have to worry about my siblings. I could follow God wherever he led. It was him, and Jesus, and me, from now on.

A tingling sensation ran through my body. I smiled at the blackness outside. God could take me anywhere. *'I'm all yours,"* I whispered. *'I'm so excited."*

I kept my ears open for adventures after that, and when I heard of a Bible study group for young professionals, led by a Christian organization, my ears pricked up. This might be something worth investigating. This might be God's adventure for me.

Later that week I drove to the house where the study was being held. I knocked on the door, a nervous excitement in my heart. I was invited in a few seconds later, and I looked around me, my eyes growing big. About fifteen people had already arrived. A pleasant chatter filled the room. It felt as if I had stepped back in time, back into my Bible School days. Could this even be possible, that my inheritance could follow me around?

We sat down on couches and everyone pulled out Bibles and notebooks. Suddenly the front door burst open, and a young man rushed in. The woman to my left leaned in close to me. "That's Michael, our resident Englishman. He's leading the study tonight."

The resident Englishman hurried to the last empty seat. "Sorry, I'm late," he said, opening a brown briefcase. "I just got back from a business trip."

I had never seen a real Englishman before, and I studied him as he pulled a Bible out. He wore brown polyester slacks with dozens of snags, some of them over an inch long. He also wore a stained green tie, green socks that barely reached up to his ankles, a freshly ironed blue shirt, and black shoes. Either this guy was color blind, or he simply didn't care how he looked. Did all Englishmen look this shabby?

An hour later the study ended, and Michael strode over to me. "Hello, I'm Michael. I haven't seen you here before."

"I'm Toma. I teach mathematics at a Christian school."

Michael stared at me. "Sorry to be so nosey, but in the study, I could tell you knew what you were talking about. I have never met anyone outside this organization who is real about their faith. You have just blown my perceptions apart."

I grinned. "I studied at a Bible School for four years."

"That still doesn't explain it. Lots of people know their Bibles, but it doesn't mean it's real to them."

I looked up into Michael's face, and I suddenly liked him. "Careful, Toma," I warned myself. "You've come here to have an adventure with Jesus. Leave this guy alone."

I took a step back. "When things get tough, you can't help but grow."

Michael shook his head. "I have noticed that often people turn bitter. I can tell that hasn't happened to you." But at that moment someone interrupted us, and I turned to talk with someone else. Man! That guy was interesting.

A few weeks later Michael told us of a month-long training program that summer. The plan was to help rebuild a children's camp in the morning, have seminars on how to grow in God every afternoon. And, everyone who attended would get individual help. Some of the group had already signed up.

I signed up, too. It might help me nurture my children in school, and that would be an adventure worth having. But then I heard Michael was going as one of the leaders. *This isn't good, dear Jesus. I like him a bit too much, and I don't want to mess up my heart. Maybe I shouldn't go."*

But I had made a promise, and it was wrong to break promises. I got up at four on the morning I was to leave. I tiptoed through the house in the semi- blackness, not wanting to wake anyone up. But as I reached for the front door, Pa loomed out in front of me.

I leapt back, startled. Was he going to physically bar me from leaving? There had to be another way I could get out to my car. I would try the friendly approach. "Hi Pa! I'm just off," I said, my voice bright.

Pa stepped aside as I reached for the handle. But then he put his hand on my shoulder. "Toma, I want to pray for you."

"Here it comes," I prayed inside. *"Will he never stop trying to manipulate me?"*

Pa bowed his head. *"Dear Father in heaven, please find Toma a husband at that camp."* My head jerked up. What had come over him? But I wasn't going to argue, tell him he was going against his principles in life. "Thanks, Pa," I sputtered, just as bright, and then I fled to my car.

Two weeks into the training program, as I sat in the dining room doing homework, someone tapped me on the shoulder. I looked up from my notebook. It was Michael. "Toma, I need to talk with you," he said, his face serious.

I stood up, grabbed my jacket, and followed him out. Was I in trouble? Had someone complained to Michael about me? Had I somehow offended him? But I loved the training program and participated with all my heart. I couldn't think of what I had done wrong.

Michael led me away from the hall, to the center of the camp, by the water pump. I groaned as we stood under a lamp, our faces illuminated with yellow light. This must be serious. He leaned against a split rail fence, pushed his hands deep into his pockets. But I stood up straight, looking him in the face. I waited for his rebuff.

"I like you," Michael whispered, not daring to look in my eyes. "I can't hide it anymore. I have liked you for months, but I have to go back to Britain. My visa expires in a few weeks. I didn't want to tell you, and start a relationship, especially if it didn't work out. I didn't want to hurt you. Do you mind if I write?"

I stared at him. Had I heard him correctly? Then the verse I had read in Ma's Bible, the one I had discarded as wrong, came to mind again. "SEE, your king comes to you, gentle and riding on a donkey…"

Michael had taken the move. He was the one coming to me!

I drew a deep breath. "Sure, we can write."

Three days later Michael tapped me on the shoulder again. "We need to talk, Toma. Let's go into town and find a diner." But as we drove in, Michael made a strange noise. I glanced over at him. He was crying!

I could only imagine that I had caused him some great pain, but I couldn't think of what I had done wrong. "What's the matter, Michael?"

He said nothing, and the tears increased. He had to pull over on to the side of the road, his voice breaking in between words. "I didn't know this would be so hard. I'm leaving! What was I thinking wanting to be friends with you?"

I didn't know what to say, but now it made sense. Michael REALLY liked me, and maybe even more. I watched him reach into his pocket and pull out a crumpled handkerchief. I watched him blow his nose, wipe his tears. I knew I shouldn't stare, but I couldn't help it. No guy had ever wept over me before, ever cared for me like that.

At the diner Michael finally found his voice. "I had wanted to say, let's not write, Toma. But I hadn't realized how much I feel for you. I think it would be best if we didn't talk until the end of this program. I need to concentrate on my work. Let's pray instead and ask God what he wants, and let's meet again at the end of the training program. If God says it is right, oh, that would be wonderful! I don't trust myself anymore."

I could cope with that. I didn't want to mess with my heart, either. Two weeks was long enough to figure out which way to go. I nodded. "That sounds good. I want to concentrate on the training program as well."

For two weeks we prayed; we stayed apart and didn't even make eye contact. But I watched Michael, as he led a team and gave seminars, as he talked with guys and sawed wood with his team. *Dear God? Michael is an amazing guy. But is he the one? Please give me another verse to confirm it.*

I read the Bible, and nothing came. I didn't know what I was going to tell Michael, so I hiked into the woods the day before we agreed to meet. I sat on a log and looked up into the trees. *"Dear God? I want the best for Michael. If it doesn't include me, that's okay. But if it does, he belongs to you, not me."*

Michael took me to the same diner the following evening. We sat opposite each other at the mock-wood laminate table. Michael gazed at me, his hazel eyes big. "This is scary, Toma. What if God told us different things? I don't know if I could cope. You start."

I gasped. "That isn't fair. This was your idea. You go first."

He raised his eyebrows. "Fair enough. One main verse came to me." Michael drew in a deep breath and opened his Bible. He looked up at me tentatively. "It's quite a surprise, really. I wasn't expecting this. It says, 'Enjoy life with your wife, whom you love, all the days of this meaningless life that God has given you under the sun.'"[w]

Michael paused, and fumbled with the pages of his Bible. "Toma, I asked God to confirm it, and this came from a sermon in a church I visited last Sunday. It's just as direct. 'A wife of noble character who can find? She is worth far more than rubies.'"[x]

Michael looked down at the Bible again. "There is one more. 'Two are better than one, because they have a good return for their labor: If either of them falls down, one can help the other up. But pity anyone who falls and has no one to help them up!'"[y]

I stared at Michael, and my mouth fell open. Michael grinned as he gazed at me, as if I was a masterpiece. "That's who you are, Toma! You're worth far more than rubies, and I believe we should get married."

I couldn't find anything intelligent to say. "Really?" I finally stammered.

Michael studied me, and his smile disappeared. "Your turn now." But there was no arrogant bravado in his eyes, that just because God had spoken to him, he was right. If I said "no" he would accept it, and never hold it against me.

I told him of my five-year-old verse. I told him that even though I had doubted God, and given up hope, Michael had fulfilled it anyway. Out of the blue he had come to me. But when I finished, I looked away, not sure what I had said. "Yes?" or "No?" I didn't want to grasp something God had not given. The verse didn't specifically talk about marriage.

Michael was silent for a few long seconds. "Toma, it sounds like a 'yes'."

I lifted my head, blinking, as if waking up. "I suppose so!"

Michael and I traveled back to Pa and Ma's, and I couldn't wait to introduce him to the family. But when Ma met us at the door, her face looked tense. She invited Michael in, and even though my younger siblings gathered around him and shook his hand, Pa sat in the corner, in his usual chair. He didn't even look up.

"Pa," I said, "this is Michael."

Pa got up on his feet, but he walked right past me, out the front door! I stared after him. This wasn't how things were supposed to turn out. But minutes later Pa reappeared and pointed at Michael. "I want to speak with you. Yes, you, young man."

Michael stood up and followed Pa out, but I paced the living room floor, wringing my hands. Pa had been practicing domination for years, and he had developed it into a talent. I didn't think Michael could survive his tactics. I barely did, and that was after a lifetime of practice. Pa would probably drive Michael away.

Michael returned a few minutes later, and I followed him outside, searching his face for clues of rejection. "What happened, Michael?" I could barely whisper.

"Your father got straight to the point. He really doesn't mince his words."

I gave a nervous laugh. "What did he say?"

"He said, 'I want you to do three things, young man. Get off my property. Never see my daughter again. Never come back again. Goodbye.' Then he turned his back on me."

I searched Michael's face again. Was this the point where he turned away from me? Michael smiled and continued speaking. "But I stayed there, and I told him I love you, and I couldn't do what he wanted."

I gasped. "You did? You stood up to my father? You told him that?"

Michael's eyes sparkled. He grinned. "Yes, and I told him I'd be back tomorrow."

I grasped Michael's arm. "Thank you!"

It really was true. Two ARE better than one. I couldn't escape from home without Michael. Not many people can escape on their own. Even Jana had a friend who offered her a room. Didn't it say in the Bible that God sends people to release prisoners from darkness?[z] Someone had to be willing to get involved, to believe in freedom the way God did. Already Michael's verses were proving true.

CHAPTER 25

Michael left for Britain to look for a job, and I went back to teaching at the Christian school. Pa started smiling again. But when I told him Michael was coming back for a visit, to make our engagement official, the harshness in Pa's eyes returned. He burst into my bedroom one evening, only a week before Michael flew in. I looked up from the floor where I sat grading tests, a red pen poised in my hand. "What is it, Pa?"

"Girl," he said, his voice even, "you have two choices. If you want my blessing, you must get married in two weeks. If you don't want to do that, you must go to the Amazon jungle for two years, and during that time you will not communicate with that boyfriend of yours, and you will leave immediately. Do you hear?"

I stared at Pa, my eyes growing big. "What did you say?"

He sneered. "You heard me, girl. Go telephone your boyfriend. Tell him what I said."

"But Pa?"

"Do you want my blessing or not?"

I stumbled to Pa's study and dialed Michael's number. When he answered his voice sounded so far away. "Toma, your father's blessing is important. Let's get married in two weeks. I don't mind. I don't want to have to wait two years."

"I don't want to either, but I can't cope with two weeks. Michael, I know it sounds strange, but I'm not ready in my heart. And what will people, my students think if we get married that quickly. They would think I was pregnant. I can't."

Michael listened without interrupting me. "I don't know what to do, Toma. We need to get some advice. I'll ask some friends here and try to ring back tomorrow."

"I'm sorry, Michael" I sobbed. "I didn't mean for any of this to happen."

Michael's voice caught as he spoke. "Toma, it isn't your fault. How I wish I was there to protect you."

The next day Michael rang. "Toma, I talked with several people about your father's proposal. They say your father is emotionally blackmailing us. He wants to gain control of our lives and that we should not give in to him. They say he will most likely change the goal posts again and that we should pray and do what God wants. Otherwise we will reap bad consequences later in life."

"Let's pray right now," I begged.

I could hear Michael sigh. "That's a good idea... *Father God, I pray that you give us a clear mind. That we wouldn't respond in fear, but would do what's right, even if it brings what we think is a bad result. Help us to respond to Mr. Rose in love. Help us to be firm, but at the same time be a blessing to him. Please give us words that will touch his heart. Please prepare all our hearts for your will. Amen.*"

Michael paused. "Toma? I think we should do what we originally planned. When I come next week, let's get officially engaged, and then get married at Christmas time. If we did the two-week option, we wouldn't be able to get you a visa on time. That would mean that after we got married you wouldn't be able to join me in Britain. We couldn't even go on a honeymoon. Two weeks is not an option."

"Thank you, Michael. I agree with you. But I suppose I will be the one who has to tell my father."

"Don't!" Michael said. "I'll be there in a few days. We can tell him together. I don't want you to have to face him alone. You have suffered enough already."

But as I hung up the telephone, Pa appeared by my side. He loomed over me. "Well? What did your boyfriend say? Have you made a decision?"

243

I leaned back, feeling the weight of his oppression. "Yes, but we want to tell you together."

"You're still my daughter. Tell me now!"

Why hadn't I thought of this? There was no way Michael could protect me or stop me from facing Pa alone. He was in Britain, thousands of miles away. I looked up at Pa, ready to cry. "We want to get married as we planned."

"What? You dare to defy my authority. Get out of this house!"

"Please Pa. Don't."

He stormed from his study, into the living room, slamming the front door behind him. He slammed it so hard the windows rattled. I stared after him, stunned. He had never slammed a door before.

Ma appeared in the living room. "What's going on?"

I stood in the middle ringing my hands. "Pa almost kicked me out of the house."

Ma led me to the couch and sat me down. I stared at my hands, folded together as if in prayer. "Toma, listen to me," Ma said. "I know it is right for you and Michael to get married. I have a special verse from Jesus. But whenever Pa is around, I must support him. I want you to know that it's only on the outside. On the inside I'm with you."

I looked up at her, blinking back tears. "Thank you, Ma. What is the verse?"

She reached for her Bible and read from Zechariah 4, about two olive trees that stood before God, who were "anointed to serve the Lord."[aa] She said, "You and Michael are like those two trees. You will stand together before God and serve him."

My eyes grew big. "That's amazing, Ma! What a promise. I don't have a clue what God wants us to do."

Ma smiled and patted my still-folded hands. "Toma, he will show you."

Michael arrived on Friday afternoon, and Pa cornered me again that evening. "I will not have you gallivanting around with that man. I used to like the British; now I hate them. I forbid you to see him."

I tried to keep calm. "Pa, before you say 'no,' please pray to God.

Please ask him what he thinks."

"I don't have to! I can see that your boyfriend is a wretch. I can tell by his eyes. He will be cruel to you. He will hurt you. I'm ashamed that you even find him attractive. He will be a disgrace to our family."

I steadied myself and looked Pa full in the face. "Pa, how do you know? You have never talked with Michael. Just give him a chance. He loves God and follows him. That is the most important thing anyone can do. You've told me that lots of times."

Pa sneered. "You will not date him, do you hear. I will not tolerate it."

"Pa, please ask God."

"No! And I forbid you to go to all those Bible studies. Is that clear?"

The next morning early, Pa was back. "If you date him, I will disown you. You won't be my daughter anymore."

"Pa, please don't say that. I've been faithful to you, doing everything you wanted all these years. Will you dump me just for this?" But Pa scoffed and walked away.

Michael arrived a couple of days later in a friend's car, and I ran toward him as he drove into our driveway. "What's happened, Toma?" he asked, as he opened the car door.

"Michael, Pa is furious. He's trying to tear us apart. He's saying horrible things." I couldn't keep my tears back anymore. They slid down my cheeks.

Michael reached into his pocket and pulled out his crumpled handkerchief. It looked like it had never been washed. He offered it to me. "I never meant for you to be hurt like this. I'm so sorry."

I stared in dismay at his handkerchief and pulled back. "No thanks!"

Michael looked at it, his eyebrows raised. "What's wrong with it, Toma? It's dry."

I laughed. "It's dirty, Michael. When was the last time you washed it?"

Light dawned on Michael's face, and he pushed it back into his jeans. "Oh, I get it. Girls like clean things. I'm sorry, Toma. I grew up with brothers and went to an all-boys school. I don't know much about girls."

"You will learn."

"I hope so," Michael said, but then he paused. "Toma, I want to do things properly. I don't want us to have any regrets. I would like to give your father a chance to bless us and to ask him for your hand in marriage."

"I agree. Maybe Jesus will do a miracle. Pa's in his workshop now."

Michael pressed his lips together and strode alone down the driveway. I watched him open the door to Pa's workshop and heard the squeak as it closed behind him. I stood there and waited in the shade of a scruffy poplar tree that grew at the edge of the drive. A minute later Michael reappeared, a surprised expression on his face. "Toma, your father didn't get angry. He just shrugged his shoulders when I asked him. He said you can do what you want. You're an adult now."

Pain welled up in my heart. "Michael, can't you see what he's doing? He hasn't changed his heart. He doesn't want to work things out. He's just disposed of me. But at least he admits that I'm an adult. That's a first."

Michael stopped me. "Toma, I know it hurts, but if he said you can do what you want, take it literally. You are free to do what you want."

We drove to a park outside of town, and sat on a stone bench under a tree, sheltered from the desert sun. We talked, prayed and read the Bible until the sun began to set. Stars appeared in the horizon, and Michael suddenly chuckled. "Toma, I had planned to do it tomorrow, in a restaurant after a meal. I wanted to do it properly, but I think this is the right time."

My heart leapt inside me as Michael turned and looked me full in the face. He held my hands in his. "Toma, will you be my wife?"

I threw my arms around his neck. "Yes!" I whispered in his ear.

Michael squeezed me tight and then he pulled away. He reached up and cradled my face in his hands. He drew himself close and rubbed his nose against mine. A thrill ran through my heart. Maybe this was the moment where Michael would kiss me. We had promised each other to wait until we were engaged. Then I felt the light touch of his lips on mine…

We sat arm in arm under the stars, a streetlamp above our heads. Michael closed his eyes. *"Thank you for our engagement, Father God. We don't deserve your mercy. Help us to be strong. Help us to walk with you…"*

That night I didn't tell Pa that Michael and I were officially engaged. I would leave that secret for Michael to tell. But Pa stood at my bedroom door that evening again. "Alright, I will bless you if you finish teaching at Christmas and go to the Amazon jungle for six months. Then I will walk you up the aisle, and the whole family can go to the wedding."

"Pa, I will talk with Michael."

"You make your decision now!"

"I can't Pa. Michael and I are in this together."

Pa's face grew red; his nostrils flared. "HOW DARE YOU!"

I shuddered at his rage, but he couldn't move me to go against Michael. I suppose I was as stubborn as he. I loved Michael. Pa hated him.

On Sunday morning Michael came early. We walked hand in hand into the house. We found Pa in the kitchen with the rest of the family, everyone perched here and there, having cornflakes for breakfast. Michael told everyone our news.

Pa glared at Michael, his eyes like ice. "I take back everything I said, boy. I am against your wedding. I will not bless it, and I want to have nothing to do with you."

Everyone in the kitchen stared at Pa, but after he had stormed from the house and was out of earshot, they clapped their hands. They laughed and threw their arms around me. My brothers shook Michael's hand, congratulating him. Ma hugged us both. "Have you set a date?" Karina asked.

I smiled. "December 31st."

Ma handed Michael a cup of coffee. "Two months. How sensible. That's plenty of time to get ready for a wedding."

Three days later I took Michael to the airport, and it was as if Pa had been waiting for him to leave. Pa turned savage. He physically barred the door when I headed out to a Bible study or prayer meeting.

He refused to let us go to church. "Evil is taking you over. In my house you will obey me."

"This is my house!" I said. "I pay the rent." Pa knew it was true. Many months before he had told me he couldn't keep up with the rent, and the only other alternative was moving back into tents. I couldn't bear my brothers and sisters having to live like that again. I couldn't bear the thought of them suffering even more. And, even though I knew Pa was manipulating me, taking my wages so I couldn't escape, I still agreed to give him my paycheck. But Pa kept coming back month after month. I let him take it for my siblings' sake.

"I don't want your money anymore. Get out."

"No."

"Get out! You're shaming me in front of my family."

"Pa, please!"

"Get out!!"

I fled to my room, sobbing into my hands. A few moments later Ma followed me in, tears running down her cheeks. "Ma, I have to leave," I said. But I stopped mid-sentence. We could hear Pa whistling at the other end of the house.

Ma sighed. She patted my hand. "I know." Then she stood up and left.

I pulled out an old suitcase I had found at the flea market and placed my clothes inside. What was I going to do? I had no money to move out.

Tears dripped from the tip of my nose. Michael would know what to do. I telephoned him, but I could barely steady my voice, and Michael cried out in shock. "I can't believe it! Oh, Toma! I'm so sorry this is happening to you! I will sort it out. Give me fifteen minutes." And true to his word, Michael rang back saying some friends would take me in. They lived on the other side of town and had an extra bedroom where I could stay.

I packed my car with all my possessions, my clothes, Bible School notes, and my guitar. An hour later I drove away, my brothers and sister waving in the driveway. Ma stood beside them, silent and still.

But ten days later Pa telephoned the Christian school where I taught. He left a message asking me to ring him back. I put it off till the end of the day. "Yes, Pa?"

"Toma, please come home. Now that I know you won't change your mind, you can stay here until your wedding."

I didn't know what to think. Michael's friends had been so generous, and I didn't want to keep imposing on them. But if I returned home, Pa might turn on me in anger again. It didn't matter. There was a lesson I still needed to learn – how to walk in trials without fear. "Alright, Pa. I'll come back this evening."

After school that day I packed my things, and Michael's friends came to my car to wave me goodbye. The husband put his hand on my shoulder. "If your father ever gives you any more trouble, let me know."

The wedding day came, and Pa did give me trouble. He disowned me, saying he never wanted to see me again. He took the car, so we couldn't get to the wedding.

I wandered around in a daze. Was this what happened to beautiful things? Did they always have to get smashed to pieces? But Mik found the key to Pa's old work van, and two hours before the wedding we emptied it out. Mik spread a carpet on the oily floor. We all piled in, my siblings, Grandma, Ma and me. Mik drove us the forty-five minutes to the church. But Pa was inside my head yet again, demanding I give him my undivided allegiance.

I looked out the rear van window. *"Help me, Jesus! I can't fight Pa anymore. I'll tell him I'm sorry. I'll do it right now."*

I studied the van door, searching for the rear door handle. I would jump out when Mik stopped at the next red light, run home and find Pa. But the door had no inside handle. *"Help me, Jesus!"* I begged yet again.

I pulled up my knees and grasped my legs. I glanced over at the back door again and a realization hit me. God had already helped me, and he had set in motion the solution a year before. Pa had bought a van with no handle on the inside back door. Without him knowing, Pa's choice of van had kept me from running away.

I looked over at my wedding dress with new eyes. I ran my fingers along its seams, lingering over the white lace and pearls. This was MY dress. This was MY wedding. I had decided to marry Michael. I had made a promise, and I would keep it, no matter how I felt about Pa.

Mik pulled into the church parking lot and hurried around to the back. He opened the door and helped us out. Then he patted me on the shoulder and grinned, his mustache stretching out. "It's a miracle, Toma. You're finally getting married. I almost gave up hope."

I smiled up at my brother with his kindly face. "Mik, I surprise myself as well."

Mik laughed and helped us carry things in. I checked the parking lot to see if our car was there and if Pa had changed his mind. "Pa isn't here," I said.

Mik pulled a face. "Forget about him, Toma. You're doing the right thing."

I nodded and hurried to a back room, to change into my dress. Jana pinned on the veil Michael's friends had given to me. I slipped into white shoes.

By the time I stood outside the church, it was full of students, parents, teachers and friends. I could hear the piano playing, the quiet movement of 250 people inside. I could feel the wind pulling at my veil, and I watched it billow out. All my bridesmaids stood beside me. They fussed over Peter with his little silk pillow, the rings tied on top with ribbon. The scene couldn't have been more beautiful, but tears rose to my eyes. I blinked them back. *"Dear God! Where is Pa?"*

Pastor John limped outside. He rested his hand on my shoulder. "Toma, it's time. The church is packed. This is wonderful. For many this will be the first time they see a true Christian wedding." I nodded, not knowing what to say.

He paused. "Do you want to wait a bit longer for your father?"

I looked at him in surprise. How did he know? But the voice, the one that had told me to run to the gate and back all those years before, spoke in my heart again. "Toma, you can choose to be happy or to be sad today. You choose."

I pondered a moment and then smiled. "We can go."

Pastor John grinned and squeezed my arm, his eyes sparkled with joy. "You're making the right decision. See you at the front in a couple of minutes." He turned and limped away, his shoulders hunched, a bump on his back. He, too, had endured much in life. But that didn't stop him from standing for what was right and encouraging the rest of us as well. When I had told him about Michael, and how Pa wanted me to marry someone from my own people group instead, Pastor John didn't do what I expected and uphold Pa's wishes to sort me out. Instead he tilted back his head and laughed. "Toma, you have chosen a good man. Your father will come around sooner or later. Let's hope it's sooner, for his sake."

I looked around at my wedding party and laughed. "Let's go, everyone!"

I watched my bridesmaids go in. Peter, with the rings. Soon I was the only one left. I stood in the doorway, feeling the desert sun on my back. Only six weeks earlier had I finally turned thirty. God had helped me keep my vow to him, and he had kept his promises to me. He had worked in my life what was best. Why had I ever doubted him?

The music changed, and I stepped inside. Michael stood at the front in a tuxedo, smiling at me. I smiled in return. He was there. I was here. But there was no one to take my arm and steady my gait. I clung to my flowers instead and took the first step.

I could hear my dress swishing on the carpet. I could sense everyone staring at me. What kind of a daughter walked up the aisle without her Pa? But Grandpa had anticipated this a few months earlier. He said that when he lived back in his homeland it was common for a father to refuse to let his daughter go. She would have to get married behind his back and walk up the aisle alone. Grandpa, too, had laughed, his eyes sparkling with joy. "Be brave, my dear granddaughter," he said. "You're doing the right thing. I'm so proud of you."

Comforted, I kept right on walking, my eyes fixed on Michael. I reached the front, and Michael offered his hand. I grasped it. "I love you," he whispered, as he pulled me to his side.

I looked up into his smiling face. God had sent this man to rescue me, and he had dared to get involved. He had dared to fight for me. Now I was free.

I felt the gentle pressure of his hand and smiled. "Michael, I love you."

Epilogue

Early one morning, before Michael rushed off to work, we exchanged wedding anniversary cards with each other. We read them and laughed, and then thanked God. Three years had just flown by.

Later that morning, the telephone rang, and I thought it might be Michael, wishing me a happy anniversary once again. I dashed to the telephone and picked it up. "Hello, sweetheart!" I sang.

There was a pause. "This is your Pa."

My knees went weak, and I could barely breathe. I slid to the floor. In the last three years, he had written several cruel letters, but now his voice sounded kind. He even acknowledged that he was my father. "Hi, Pa," I whispered.

My eighteen-month-old son could sense that something was wrong. He toddled up to me and threw his arms around my neck. He kissed me all over my cheeks. I hugged him back and waited for Pa to speak.

"Toma, happy anniversary."

"Thanks, Pa."

"How is your son?"

"He is fine. A real boy, full of fun and affection."

Pa laughed.

"Pa?"

"Yes?"

"I'm expecting another baby. We haven't told anyone yet. I just found out."

"Wonderful, Toma. Teach your children to love God. That is the most important thing you can do."

"I'll try, Pa." I paused. "There's one more thing. Michael will be leaving his job. We're going to be missionaries."

Pa laughed. "Ma told me. That's wonderful."

We talked a bit more and then hung up. But I stayed on the floor, still too weak to get up. My son still sat on my lap, and I rocked him back and forth. "That was your Grandpa," I finally said.

For decades I had hoped that Pa would treat me with dignity and respect. I don't know what changed him, but I never gave up asking God. Hope is like that, defying the facts.

Then three weeks later the telephone rang again, but at two o'clock at night. It was Karina. "Toma, Pa died two hours ago. He had a massive heart attack."

Again, I slumped to the floor and Michael sat beside me, holding me tight. I covered my face with my hands, but I sat in stunned silence. God had just dished out to Pa what Pa had always dished out to us. Pa had demanded instant and uncompromising obedience, expecting us to do his bidding, "Right now!" God was demanding the same of Pa. His presence was required, "RIGHT NOW", and there was no getting around it.

I had hoped for justice, and God made it happen. But now, many years later, there is yet another hope. Maybe I'll see Pa when I get to heaven, and then I can say, "Pa, I would love to get to know you. Do you mind? We have plenty of time."

Quoted Bible Verses

[a] Psalm 45:10

[b] Hebrews 5:8

[c] Colossians 3:18 NKJV

[d] 1 Chronicles 21:1

[e] 2 Corinthians 6:12 NASB

[f] 1 Samuel 15:23 NKJV

[g] Genesis 19:8

[h] Isaiah 40:1

[i] Isaiah 40:31

[j] Matthew 5:16

[k] Matthew 5:48

[l] Numbers 30:3-4

[m] John 8:29

[n] Hebrews 12:15

[o] Deuteronomy 1:6-7

[p] From Isaiah 53:3

[q] Exodus 14:14

[r] Luke 12:7

[s] Matthew 19:19

[t] Luke 9:23-24

[u] Exodus 6:8 NKJV

[v] Matthew 21:5

[w] Ecclesiastes 9:9

[x] Proverbs 31:10

[y] Ecclesiastes 4:9-10

[z] Isaiah 42:6-7

[aa] Zechariah 4:14

Printed in Poland
by Amazon Fulfillment
Poland Sp. z o.o., Wrocław